**whistle
BLOWER**

Complain

AND *Claim*

Dedication

I dedicate this book to all those people who are trying to help others against the odds.

I would also like to mention one person whom I never met, but whose forthright views on consumer affairs and sense of justice struck a chord with me. Her words and advice inspired me to write this guide. That lady was Dame Sheila McKechnie who was Director of the Consumers' Association, and died in 2004 of cancer, age 55. This book is my tribute to her.

MONEYGUIDES

Peter Robertson

Cartoons by BANX

Complain
AND *Claim*

Published by Whistle-blower Money Guides
an imprint of Whistle-blower Publishing Ltd

Text © Peter Robertson 2006
Cartoons © Jeremy Banx 2006

First published 2006

Original design by Keith Shaw
Illustrations by Jeremy Banx
Cover design by Keith Shaw

Printed and bound in Great Britain by Biddles Ltd
ISBN 0-9552250-0-0

Preface

This is an exciting time to be writing about the financial services industry. For the first time in many decades, things may be about to change for the better. In this book you will encounter stories of my own experiences and of people like you who never had this book to help them, but wished they had.

Whistle-blower Money Guides have two aims:

- To lift the lid off the mis-selling practices of the financial services industry
- To teach consumers how to take care of their money.

I have been motivated to write Complain & Claim for one reason: to help ordinary working people hold on to their money by bringing about much needed change in an industry tainted by convoluted methods that encourage poor practices.

Complain & Claim will show YOU how to navigate your way through the minefield of financial products and services, and will help YOU seek justice through a successful compensation claim. It will also give you the information you need to make your own informed decisions.

And for those who need help, there is a growing band of financial planners who are trying to make the advice process more professional. If you need a good adviser, this guide will also show you how to engage their services.

This guide will give you all the tools you need to reclaim your own money, which will help fund your life goals. It is my sincere hope that it will begin a groundswell of public opinion and reform that will lead to a transfer of the balance of financial power from the city to the people who earned it – YOU.

I am indebted to a number of people for their support, advice and help, and my heart-felt thanks go to George Gooder, my editor Helen Wilkinson and above all, to my family.

The Large Print

None of the information in this guide constitutes a personal recommendation to invest or change your existing contract(s). Whilst every care has been made to compile information accurately, no liability can be accepted by the author or the publisher, for any errors or omissions therein, or consequences arising.

The author and publisher will defend their right to provide the public with information that is in their interest.

The information in this book is provided in good faith using the guiding principles of common sense and integrity. I cannot guarantee every claim will be successful, but the guide will make its readers much wiser about managing money.

The process of continuous development needs your help. To this end I am receptive to innovative ideas and advice which could improve financial services in the UK. If adopted, your ideas will be rewarded.

Please contact me via our web-site www.whistleblowerguides.co.uk

I thank you for your support.

Peter Robertson

Table of Contents

WEALTH WARNING

Do not accept any commission-based advice until you have read this guide.

Part Two Complaints 67

Part Three – Tailor Made Complaint Letters 249

"HE'S HAD HIMSELF CRYOGENICALLY FROZEN TILL THE PENSION SITUATION'S SORTED OUT."

Introduction

How to use this Guide

Every Whistle-blower Money Guide is a simple STEP by STEP handbook to help you achieve a financial result.

The guide is split into three parts.

Part One: Advice

Part One describes the way the Financial Services industry works, and contains all you need to know about advisers, charges (especially commission), and the factors which currently influence the selling of most financial products and services.

Some sections in Chapter 4 are very detailed, and you can skip these, but make sure you read summaries (like the commission summary guide) as these will save you money.

Chapter 5 describes how to spot 'rogue advisers', and explains how to seek out truly objective financial planners who can help. This section is particularly important for anyone who decides to switch advisers after reading this guide.

Part Two: Complaints

This section will help you diagnose whether you have been the victim of product mis-selling, and will show you how to get redress, and claim thousands of pounds in compensation.

For readers who bought this book to help claim compensation regarding an endowment mortgage shortfall, I urge you to hurry. Time could be running out, especially if you have received a warning letter. See Chapter 12.

Part Three: Complaint Letters

Many people know they have been victims of product mis-selling but are unsure how to write a complaint letter. This part converts theory into action and contains 29 ready drafted letters to make an informed complaint and reclaim your money.

Useful Pointers

Throughout the guide common sense advice and practical tips are highlighted using TIP or TOP TIP.

If there is a key learning point that will help you understand how to plan, this will be indicated with a LEARNING POINT.

Occasionally you will be confronted with a WEALTH WARNING. If you ignore this advice, your finances could be seriously damaged!

Lastly, we will examine examples of problems using a CASE STUDY.

Bungles and Botch-ups

Many of you will have suffered from unscrupulous mis-selling. Money will have been taken from you without your prior knowledge or consent. You may have been a victim of poorly advised pension transfers, endowment mortgages, product switching from one poor investment to another, or the winding up of a final salary pension scheme. And the list goes on. Sometimes you'll be completely unaware of the true extent of your loss until much later.

Have you seen undercover TV programmes exposing plumbers who charge £450 for a new waste system when they only changed a washer? How would you describe that? Deception, a con, a swindle, scam, or plain fraud – certainly an act for unlawful gain. So what should we call the action of an adviser towards a customer who asks for advice and is sold an inappropriate high-charging commission product?

Read this book, and then you tell me.

Profit, Profit, Profit

I must begin by explaining that Financial Services (FS) is an industry much like any other owned by shareholders, it exists to make a profit. In terms of earnings it is the largest industry in the world (source S&P 500, 2004). The term financial services is used to refer to the services provided by firms such as banks, insurance companies, investment banks, and brokerages. They all provide money, investment and related services, and in the UK all must be authorised and regulated by the Financial Services Authority (FSA).

These companies are always looking for new opportunities to make money out of customers. In the same way that the processed food industry is allowed to include ingredients that are detrimental to your health, the FS industry may include charges and penalties that are detrimental to your wealth.

It is the norm for such organisations to motivate sales staff by using targets and remuneration schemes that may be seen as irresponsible, because they encourage mis-selling. Consumers experience a process that is commission-driven rather than advice-driven. Regrettably in such a climate, profit is often more important than the best interests of the consumer.

Roll of Dishonour

One company with a particularly poor record is St James's Place UK plc, that sells high commission contracts which earn some of its salesmen over £250,000 per year. The company was co-founded by Sir Mark Weinberg who also founded Abbey Life, Hambro Life and Allied Dunbar (companies whose contracts will pop up in this guide). He was awarded a knighthood despite St James's Place having a very poor record with the regulator. In 2003 the company was fined £250,000, (taken from FSA/PN/122/2003 - 26/11/2003), for serious monitoring and record-keeping inadequacies. The company is an habitual offender with the first similar disciplinary proceedings launched in 1994. Like so many of its competitors, this company presents an up-market image. So the first lesson to be learned by consumers is, *Do not be fooled by appearances*.

The media attempts to expose the worst cases to an unsuspecting public. Here is Kathryn Cooper writing in *The Sunday Times*, January 15, 2006:

'Last week the FSA censured a life insurer for wrongly blocking complaints. Guardian Assurance and a sister company were fined £750,000 for "serious systemic flaws" in their procedures for handling mortgage endowment complaints.

Up to 5,600 customers may have had their complaints wrongly rejected as a result of the flaws, according to the FSA. Guardian will now be forced to review their cases.

Many consumers do not realise that you must lodge your complaint within 3 years of first receiving a "red" letter from the endowment firm. Guardian, along with Friends Provident and Royal & Sun Alliance, have barred customers who passed the 3-year deadline before July 1, even though they may never have been told the limit existed.'

As you read a quote like this, you will understand why I felt driven to write Complain & Claim.

Table 1. FSA Fines

Amount	Company	Date	What for	Compensation
£1,900,000	Lloyds TSB Bank plc	25/09/03	Unsuitable sales of high income bond	Approximately £98 million
£1,000,000	Abbey Life Assurance Company Ltd	04/12/02	Mortgage endowment mis-selling and other failings	Compensation estimated to be between £120 and £160 million
£950,000	Royal & Sun Alliance Group	27/03/03	Mortgage endowments failings	£16.6 million set aside for redress
£650,000	Bradford & Bingley plc	22/12/04	Precipice and with-profit bonds mis-selling	£6 million in compensation to the 6,800 customers affected
£750,000	Guardian Assurance plc and Guardian Linked Life Assurance Limited (Guardian)	12/01/06	Serious systemic flaws in its mortgage endowment complaints handling procedures.	
£485,000	Lincoln Assurance Ltd	16/04/03	Mis-selling savings plans	£8.8 million set aside for compensation
£750,000	Scottish Amicable	06/03/03	Mortgage endowment failings	£11 million set aside for redress
£ 250,000	St James's Place UK plc – three companies	26/11/03	Inadequate monitoring and record keeping	

To date the FSA has fined companies over 60 million pounds. Table 1 is just a sample of the numerous fines levied against those who were caught providing inadequate advice to consumers. It proves that mis-selling is rife, but YOU HAVE TO PROVE wrongdoing and claim your compensation.

There is not enough room in this one volume to include everything you should know about the complex world of financial services, but I hope to whet your appetite, and make you ask questions that could change your financial present, and protect your future for yourself and your family.

FINANCIAL ADVISER

BANX

1 Advice

The Advice Rollercoaster

a) Introduction

The aim of Part One is to explain all you need to know about seeking advice and how you are charged for that advice.

Whenever I'm waiting at a supermarket checkout I inspect other shoppers' trolleys and try to guess the kind of life they lead, asking myself why they didn't buy the 2 for the price of 1 butter? And why they're buying so much processed food when fresh ingredients would be a fraction of the cost? I often conclude that most people have such hectic lives that they haven't got time to search out value for money, or perhaps don't understand how money works. If you recognise yourself as this type of shopper, you may be especially vulnerable to financial mis-selling, because no one has ever explained how the advice system really works.

Knowledge about financial services will protect your money. So if you have been a victim of mis-selling, you need to understand how commission influenced the advice you received, and how to play the system to your advantage. To avoid being misled again you'll need to know where to go and what to ask. The next 5 chapters will show you how to apply your new knowledge, use it to your advantage and avoid being a victim in future.

Table 1 shows you the effect of an extra annual charge of just 1% on an investment and loan of £100,000. It could have been avoided, but was included because the adviser wanted his commission.

Table 1. **Effect of 1% Extra Charge**		
Years	**Investment £100,000 Lost Growth**	**Loan £100,000 Extra Interest Paid**
5	£6,194	£3,583
10	£16,195	£7,165
15	£31,763	£10,748
20	£55,384	£14,331
25	£90,552	£17,913

Notes: Growth is reduced from 6% to 5%, and Interest Rate is increased from 5% to 6%

How long would it take you to earn or recoup these amounts after tax? The sums involved may be so large that it is worth checking your records. Could your financial adviser have placed their interests ahead of yours? Read on and find out.

b) The Need for Advice

Glance Back

Before we go any further, we need a short history lesson in how the system works today, and how we got into the current mess.

The industry is regulated by the Financial Services Authority (FSA – See glossary) which has the dual responsibility of regulating the industry and protecting the consumer. The objectives of the FSA are:

- To maintain confidence in the UK financial system
- To promote public understanding of the financial system
- To secure the right level of protection for consumers
- To reduce the potential for financial services firms to be used for financial crime.

The dual responsibility of the FSA can give rise to a conflict of interests. In trying to balance the needs of both parties, decisive action is likely to be exchanged for compromise. Small investors may incur losses, as demonstrated by the handling of the Equitable Life's demise.

The FSA is also closely involved with the government and industry chiefs, and if push came to shove, in a real financial crisis it is hard to see how the consumer's needs would come first.

The FSA and the Consumer

The FSA's method of protecting consumers is to regulate the sales process by creating an audit trail that will track and uncover mis-selling. But the system is very inefficient and the regulator's costs are indirectly transferred to the consumer. So the FSA alone is not the answer to your problems.

Instead this guide will show you how to avoid high-charging advisers and to employ financial planners on a fee basis, saving YOU thousands in unnecessary commission costs.

Regulation & Disgruntled Advisers

Formal regulation of the industry began in 1988. After 18 years you would think the financial environment had improved, but many of the changes and reviews (especially new legislation in 2005) have left old-school advisers disgruntled and looking for the exit. So beware! Some may try to boost their retirement fund at the expense of yours.

Your First experience as a Financial Victim

After a meeting with an adviser are you:

- Confident your problems are solved and that you can trust the organisation to get it right, OR
- Worried about costs, and the adviser's knowledge, but persevere as this is the standard you've come to expect, and it's simpler to sign on the dotted line?

In reality, when the deal is done and commission paid, some advisers take on eel-like characteristics, becoming slippery and hard to catch, disappearing for many years before reappearing to seek out another sale. You're left with documents, policies and plans from various providers who send an occasional statement, and numerous mail-shots for new loans and credit cards.

So you lose track and lose control.

Your Second experience as a Financial Victim

Does this scenario sound familiar? You hope that somewhere in the paperwork you'll discover a gold nugget and accept the 'free service' offered by the adviser at your local bank or building society to tidy up your affairs. After all it's the easiest option.

But like gold prospectors, advisers will sell you dreams of future riches if you buy the right product. Then they identify scary shortfalls and offer solutions to problems you didn't know you had. In ten years time you'll probably have spent a lot of money on their free advice, paid for by the high (and invisible) commission costs.

The Con Goes On

In any industry where you pay people many times their real worth, service and advice will become distorted. In financial services, salesmen are paid a low basic salary and given ambitious sales targets which generate commission that can boost their annual earnings to six figure sums. The big earners have sold a lot of high commission contracts, which are unlikely to be the most appropriate for their customers. They may be good salesmen but are not holistic financial planners.

More Commission = More Sales

The FS industry has traditionally sold commission-based products to the public. Providers design products that earn commission for salesmen, encouraging them to sell a product in preference to any superior alternatives that are commission free.

Numerous studies have shown that if you increase sales commission you will sell more products. And providers know it. If you want to shift a product, increase commission. This is clearly shown by the prevalence of high-charging Life Office products, even though lower charging investments are available.

New adviser and product disclosure requirements came into effect in 2005 and over time these should help change the quality and delivery of advice in the UK. But to put right the past, we need to examine commission in a little more detail and find out what you were not told.

2 Salesman's Commission

Commission is a charge built into a financial product or service, payable to the salesman to encourage them to make a sale. (The different charges are listed in Chapter 4.) It you have been a victim of mis-selling, it will be helpful to understand commissions and fees in more detail. But if you wish, you can skip the next section, and move straight to the commission summary guide at the end of this chapter.

Some salesmen still make incorrect claims about the origin of commission, saying that it is funded from the Life Office's marketing budget and does not affect the contract. This is nonsense. Your money pays the commission, and therefore affects the terms of the contract. Occasionally Life Offices do make extra payments from their marketing budgets to top-up commission, usually to boost their market share temporarily.

How are levels set?

Most commission payments are still calculated with reference to the LAUTRO 'maximum commission agreement' (MCA) that ended in December 1989.

This voluntary agreement sought to limit the maximum commission and soon after it ended, many companies who wanted to build market share quoted percentages of 120% of LAUTRO scale. Today it is not unusual to find companies paying 150%.

This is an admission by the industry that one of the best ways to sell more products is to pay more commission to salesmen – regardless of the quality of the underlying investment/contract.

Business & Commission

There is nothing wrong with commission in principle – it is part of many commercial transactions, from selling cars to computers, and works as a powerful incentive. But while it is built into the price of a tangible product, in financial services it's difficult to assess whether you're receiving fair value. FS companies know this, and have found imaginative ways of disguising high charges within their products.

Advisers often tell us that surveys suggest we don't want to pay fees and therefore assume we prefer commission. For when consumers are asked, 'Do you want to pay fees for financial advice?'

They reply, 'No'.

This leading question actively solicits a negative response. Some respondents may think advice is currently free and don't want to pay anything. Others who know a little about commission may think the fee is an extra charge. The question that should be asked is:

'If you needed a protection policy and you had two choices, which option would you choose?

- A flat arrangement fee of £300 which will result in lower ongoing annual premiums, OR
- Commission charges of £2,500 which will be recovered from you by charging higher annual premiums.'

If you were asked THAT question, what would your answer be?

Some salesmen benefit from extortionate incentives, which bear no relation to the amount of work involved. This is how mis-selling can happen.

a) Commission on Regular Contributions

If you pay regular contributions into a life assurance protection or savings plan, the salesman can choose one of two options:

Option 1. Level Commission

The salesman receives commission of 25% to 50% of every premium paid for an 'initial earnings period' of up to 48 months, AND at the end of the initial earnings period, they will receive renewal commission of 2.5% of the premiums paid each year for the life of the contract.

If you cease premiums, the commission stops. For example if you agreed to pay £100 per month into an endowment savings plan for 20 years the adviser could receive the following commission payments.

Table 1. 'Level' Commission on £100 monthly Premium

Year	Contributions	Type %	Commission
1	£1,200	Level 37.5%	£450
2	£1,200	Level 37.5%	£450
3	£1,200	Level 37.5%	£450
4	£1,200	Level 37.5%	£450
5 to 20	£19,200	Renewal 2.5%	£480
TOTAL	£24,000		£2,280

Option 2. Indemnity Commission

This is the most popular form of commission. The salesman usually receives 100%+ of the first years premium up-front AND at the end of the initial earnings period, renewal commission of 2.5% of the premiums paid each year for the life of the contract.

If the contract ceases within the earnings period (usually in the first 4 years), the salesman is contractually required (indemnified) to pay back the unearned commission to the Life Office.

Using the same example quoted above, the adviser could receive the following commission payments.

Table 2. 'Indemnity' Commission on £100 monthly Premium

Year	Contributions	Type / %	Commission
1	£1,200 p.a.	Indemnity 125%	£1,500
5 to 20	"	Renewal 2.5%	£480
TOTAL	£24,000		£1,980

The salesman receives slightly less commission, but the Life Office policy charges remain the same and therefore the performance of your contract will be the same under both commission options.

b) Commission on Lump Sum Investments – Life Offices

If you pay a lump sum into a life assurance policy such as a pension or bond, the salesman has two options:

Option 1. Initial Commission & Trail Commission

The salesman will receive initial commission of 4% to 5% of the initial investment which is taken from your contract AND trail commission of 0.25% to 0.5% of the value of the investment on the first and subsequent anniversaries.

For example the commission on an investment of £50,000 for 10 years would be:

Table 3. **Initial Commission & Trail Commission on £50,000 for 10 years**			
Years	**Contributions**	**Type / %**	**Commission**
1	£50,000	Initial 5%	£2,500
1 to 10		Trail 0.5%	£2,500
TOTAL	£50,000		£5,000

Option 2. Higher Initial Commission

Here the salesman receives a higher initial commission in lieu of not taking trail commission. This amounts to 6% to 7% of the initial investment and is taken directly from your money.

Here for a £50,000 investment over 10 years the commission could be:

Table 4. **Initial Commission on £50,000 for 10 years**			
Year	**Contributions**	**Type / %**	**Commission**
1	£50,000	Initial 7%	£3,500
TOTAL	£50,000		£3,500

CASE STUDY

Rob Bell worked for General Springs Ltd for 38 years until retirement. His company pension benefits included a tax-free lump sum of £33,000, which was the largest single payment he and his wife had ever received.

Shortly after leaving work, he was contacted by the company pensions adviser who offered advice to retirees. The Bells took advantage of the free advice and were directed towards an investment of £30,000 in a low-risk, managed insurance bond. But as Rob was unwilling to part with this sum, the adviser prepared a new illustration for £28,000.

Three days later, the Bells bank manager suggested a meeting to discuss moving their money to a high interest account. At that meeting Rob agreed to place £5,000 in a high interest account to use as an emergency fund, with the remaining £28,000 invested into a safe with-profits insurance bond. This bond would provide 5% income each year.

The Bells had to make a decision between the two products. Although they didn't know it, the commission payable was as follows:

Table 5. **What the Bell's lose via Commission Costs**				
Adviser	**Initial Commission**		**Ongoing Commission p.a. (trail)**	
	%	£	%	£
Bank Manager	7%	£1,960	Nil	Nil
Company Adviser	5%	£1,400	0.5%	£140

(Note: The bank take higher initial commission in lieu of receiving annual trail commission.)

Rob Bell actually opted to invest through the bank that took the higher initial commission. Did he get a good deal? Unfortunately not – both recommendations were inadequate. Rob was a victim of bond mis-selling which we will cover in more detail in Part Two Chapter 14.

c) Commission on Lump Sum Investments – Fund Managers

If you pay a lump sum into an investment fund such as a unit trust or OEIC, (see Glossary), the salesman will receive initial commission of 3% of the investment which is taken from your contract, AND trail commission (usually 0.5%) of the value of the investment on the first and subsequent anniversaries.

Table 6. **Commission on the investment of £50,000 for 10 years.**			
Year	Contributions	Type / %	Commission
1	£50,000	Initial 3%	£1,500
1 to 10		Trail 0.5%	£2,500
TOTAL	£50,000		£4,000

Initial Commission Ready Reckoner

You can estimate the initial commission taken from your contracts by using our ready reckoner. When I did this exercise with Geoff and Elaine Bishop they were astounded to discover that they had lost around £21,000 in commission charges across their portfolio. If this money had remained invested and grown at 5%, it would have provided them with an estimated extra £60,000 to spend in their retirement! How much have you lost in commission?

Initial Commission Ready Reckoner		
Regular Premium Contract Commission = 100% of first years premium	Premiums Paid £9,260	Commission £9,260
Lump Sum Investments Commission = 5% of investment	Investment £232,000	Commission £11,600
TOTAL		**£20,860**

Unfortunately this is only the cost of the initial commission. Commission is also paid on **all** increases in premiums and **annually** on the value of your investments.

d) Trail Commission – 'THE GREAT TRAIL ROBBERY'

Trail commission is paid to the salesman by the investment company annually as a thank you for introducing and maintaining the business. It is based on a percentage of the value of your investment (usually 0.5%) which is taken from your fund.

What has the adviser done to deserve it?

It is supposed to cover servicing of the contract, but has become a receipt that many financial advisers take for granted. How can they justify taking money out of your investment as a service charge when the client has no guarantee that they will receive any service?

Why trail commission is wrong

There is no link to work involved – As with the initial commission, the salesman gets trail commission linked to the size and type of the investment and not to the amount of work done. An adviser who recommends you invest £10,000 into a life insurance bond will receive £50 a year from YOU, in many cases for doing no extra work. But why should an investment of £100,000 generate £500, ten times as much for doing the same amount of nothing?

Poor Fund Choice – Salesmen defend their trail commission stating that they need it to keep an eye on your investment and perhaps switch funds. This is nonsense as much of the money is invested in default managed funds where the Life Office is left to get on with managing the money. By using such funds, the adviser effectively opts out of making decisions about where the money is invested and is free to move on to the next sales 'hit'. For the past 20 years 'with-profits' funds have been very popular. These are mixed asset funds which hold shares, property and bonds. They use an opaque bonus system to try and smooth and average returns, but many have failed investors, and will continue to do so.

Charging for NO Service – If the adviser was actively keeping an eye on your investment with a view to moving the money, why recommend bonds with high punitive exit charges for the first 5 years, often starting at 9% in year one? Or with-profits funds where the client is exposed to potential market value adjustment (MVA) penalties applied on surrender, sometimes amounting to 20% or more? Both costs make switching prohibitive and help lock your money into the provider. This is proof that servicing is ignored and investors are being charged for service that is not provided.

Life Offices encourage poor servicing standards – Advisers are given the option of forfeiting their trail commission by increasing commission from 5% to 7%. But what happens to the servicing if the adviser retires, goes bust or the client moves to another adviser? There is no ongoing strategy to maintain any sort of service, even though you have paid for it in advance via this higher commission. As Life Offices do not have a policy of clawing back initial commission on lump sum investments, they are in effect admitting that this is not a servicing charge but a disguise for taking higher initial commission to attract more business.

Firms admit to NO ongoing Servicing – To avoid being accused of failing to undertake routine servicing tasks that you would expect from a trusted adviser (e.g. addressing under-performance), many commission firms protect themselves by including a clause in their terms and conditions such as: 'We will not undertake any periodic reviews of your investment but will be glad to advise you any time you ask us to do so.'

How can they justify claiming 0.5% of your money EVERY year for doing nothing and admitting to doing nothing?

You should pay for what you want – There is only one person that should be paying an adviser to look after their investments and that is YOU direct. This is the only way to guarantee objective advice. If it comes from the provider it can be construed as a carrot to maintain a poor investment.

e) Commission Summary Guide

You have now seen that there is plenty of scope for an adviser to take commission for doing very little work. To help you compare different commission structures, refer to this guide:

Table 7. Commission Summary Guide

Salesman's Commission on Regular Contributions

Life Office Contracts	Term	Commission Type	Annualised Contribution			
			£500	£1,000	£5,000	£10,000
Term Assurance, Critical Illness,	10 Years	Initial	£400	£800	£4,000	£8,000
Income Protection,		Annual	£12.50	£25	£125	£250
Whole-of-life Cover,		Initial	£500	£1,000	£5,000	£10,000
Flexible Protection,	15 Years					
Endowments,		Annual	£12.50	£25	£125	£250
Regular savings		Initial	£625	£1,250	£6,250	£12,500
Plans, etc	20+ Years					
		Annual	£12.50	£25	£125	£250
Personal Pensions	10 + Years	Initial	£150	£300	£1,500	£3,000
		Annual 0.25%	£1+	£2+	£12+	£25+
Stakeholder Pension Plans	10 + Years	Initial	£80	£160	£830	£1,660
		Annual 0.25%	£1+	£2+	£12+	£25+
Private Medical Insurance	1 Year	Annual	£75	£150	£750	£1,500

Salesman's Commission on Lump Sum Investments

Life Office Contracts	Term	Commission Type	Initial Investment			
			£10,000	£25,000	£100,000	£250,000
Bonds, Pensions,	Usually none	Initial	£500	£1,250	£5,000	£12,500
Draw-down, etc		Annual	£50	£125	£500	£1,250
Annuities	NA	Initial	£150	£375	£1,500	£3,750
Investment Managers	Term	Commission Type	£10,000	£25,000	£100,000	£250,000
Unit Trusts, OEICs, etc	Usually none	Initial	£500	£1,250	£5,000	£12,500
		Annual	£50	£125	£500	£1,250

Table 7 Observations

Commission variations – These figures do NOT represent the highest or lowest rates available, but are a general guide. Some contracts tend to pay more commission, such as term assurance. This is why salesmen are always keen to re-broker your life cover as it pays well compared to some traditional contracts such as personal pensions which have been affected by the introduction of lower-charging stakeholder products.

Size does matter – Table 7 shows how salesmen's remuneration is linked to the size and type of investment and not to the amount of work done – the work involved in setting up similar contracts is the same.

For example, if you visit a commission-based IFA and have a lump sum to invest, 9 times out of 10 you will be recommended a life insurance bond. If they can encourage you to invest more, then they earn more. A £20,000 investment earns twice as much commission as a £10,000 investment for no extra work. There may be more appropriate investments that suit your circumstances, but the adviser will provide a 'Suitability Report' that tells you why you need one. In my experience 9 out 10 people definitely do NOT need an insurance bond.

NOT commensurate with the work undertaken – The same happens when seeking life cover. A young person buying £100,000 of term assurance to cover their family for 20 years may generate £300 in commission for the adviser. An older couple buying £500,000 of whole-of-life cover to meet an inheritance tax bill may generate £12,000 commission for the adviser. Has the adviser done forty times as much work? What do you think?

Commission Disadvantages

Let's summarise some of the points covered in this section:

Poor Returns – If your money is used to pay commission, less is invested so your fund will be worth less at maturity.

Commission Dependency – Commission stifles independent advice because advisers rely on certain providers for their income.

Old Contracts – The Devil's in the detail. Many old savings and pension contracts are riddled with penalties and charges, and all subsequent increases are also subject to commission. Topping up your investments tops up the commission. You should NOT increase contributions to these unless they benefit from contractual benefits that are no longer available in the market place. See Chapter 10 - Pension Complaints & Commission Manipulation.

Overcharging – Commission payments are too high and bear little relationship to the level of work undertaken. For large transactions you are always overcharged, and may in fact be paying £500 an hour for advice (cross-subsidising those who may be paying £30 an hour).

Insurance Premiums Increase – Your premiums have to take into account high commission costs. Strip these out and your monthly premiums fall.

Unethical – High commission encourages greed and is a major cause of mis-selling.

Poor ongoing service – As commission is paid up-front there is no incentive to keep servicing the client. This is definitely the case if you have no new money to invest. Commission from regular premium contracts acts as a disincentive to recommend changes within the earnings period, usually the first 4 years as the salesman will have to pay back some of his commission. Miraculously after 4 years your broker is able to find a better contract, and can now benefit from more commission.

Differential Product Commission rates lead to Distorted Advice – It is unlikely that a commission-based adviser will give objective advice when a good investment trust pays him 0% commission, a unit trust 3% and a poor Life Office bond delivers 7%. Which would you prefer to sell?

Commission Advantages

There are no advantages in dealing with advisers who charge 100% commission. However if commission is used to offset fees, and excess commission returned to the policyholder, then savings can be made.

VAT Savings – You will save VAT of 17.5%, as commissions are not liable to VAT while fees are liable.

Tax man helps with costs – The tax man can help pay for pensions advice as all pension contributions benefit from tax relief of at least 22%, and up to 40% for higher rate tax-payers. For every £78 net you contribute, the tax man contributes £22 making a total of £100 gross. As commission is based on a percentage of the gross contributions the tax man could pay up to either 22% or 40% of the advice bill!

Adviser Fees

Why Fees?

Fee-based professional financial planners have been offering clients a fee payment option for years.

Fees are transparent and should be correlated to the work involved and therefore provide fair value for the consumer.

Some will balk at the prospect of getting out the chequebook to pay fees to an adviser. Hopefully I have quashed the myth that commission is 'free'. Consider this scenario: If you wouldn't hesitate to pay an emergency plumber several hundred pounds to sort out a burst pipe, why not call on the services of a professional planner to do some emergency work on your finances?

Fee Structures

You are likely to encounter the following fee structures:

One-off Advice

Hourly Rate – Most professional, well-qualified advisers will have a charge rate of £100 to £150 an hour, with secretarial support at £25 per hour and technical support at around £50 per hour. They will provide a fee menu of the likely cost of advice.

Fixed Fee – Advisers provide a table of fixed fees which equate to the average time taken to undertake a project.

Task	Fee
Basic Report 5 to 10 hours	£500 to 1,000
Complex Report 20 hours, such as; Pension Transfer, Retirement Income Analysis, Inheritance Tax planning, etc.	£1,500 to £2,500
Implementation of Recommendations. Variable 3 to 10 hours	£300 to £1,500

Note: In reality most fee-based advisers will use a combination of the above depending on the degree of complexity.

Ongoing Advice

Most investment advice will require ongoing advice to monitor returns and take into account changing legislation. This will be covered in a Client/Adviser 'Service Agreement'. Advisers cannot monitor your investments on a daily basis, but will do so monthly or quarterly depending on the fee paid.

Fixed fee – To cover research and regular review meetings charged at about £250 - £500 per meeting dependent on complexity. Investors with large portfolios will pay more.

Retainer Fees – If you and your adviser are in regular contact by phone and meet more than once a year then you may prefer an inclusive charge that takes into account all routine servicing and advice. This could take the form of a monthly or quarterly direct debit. Note: Beware of being charged twice. Make sure any annual commissions are rebated / offset and renew annually.

Fund Based Fees – Currently most investment managers pay annual trail commission of 0.5% of the fund value to the adviser. Most good financial planners will use this to contribute to, or cover the costs of investment reviews. If the renewal commission is greater than £500 per annum, negotiate a rebate / offset against other services.

Performance Fees – The case for these is harder to assess. What benchmark should you measure the performance against, and how much risk do you take to beat this benchmark? If you have an excellent adviser whose methods consistently result in your portfolio outperforming an agreed benchmark then they may deserve extra recognition. But if someone wants more of your money for performing well, they deserve less for under-performing. A fair compromise would be to increase and decrease fees by a fixed %. We recommend 0.1% for every 1% of out/under-performance, capped at 0.5%. A loss in adviser income will help concentrate their efforts in your favour. Proceed with caution.

Fees – Methods to Avoid

Be sceptical of advisers who use:

Arbitrary Charging – The total billed hours result in fees that are similar to the commission they would have received before the fee menu. Steer clear.

Notional Accounts – The adviser opens up a notional account into which all commission is paid and offset against future advice services. There is no guarantee that you will receive advice or services, and rebating terms are usually ambiguous.

The FSA does not stipulate how fees are charged, as long as the consumer knows how much they are being charged. Do not expect the big commission-based IFAs to win any awards for use of plain English! Steer clear.

Fees & VAT

One of the anomalies of the current system is that pure advice that results in a product sale is subject to VAT of 17.5%, whereas advice that generates commission can offset that commission against the fee and is not subject to VAT.

Fee Advantages

- Fees are professional and more in line with other professions.
- Provide you with a transparent charging structure and better value while considerably reducing the chances of you being over-charged.
- Increase the likelihood of a long-term relationship with your adviser based on trust and integrity.
- Put the unscrupulous salesman out of business.

Fee Disadvantages

The only disadvantage is the VAT anomaly as described above.

a) Fees Vs Commission

It's a fact that not everyone would be able to afford up-front fees, but most people would be better off over the lifetime of the contract if fees were chosen. These 3 examples prove the point.

CASE STUDY

Family Protection Cover

I was asked to advise Mr and Mrs Armitage, a young couple aged 35 with two young children, who had £100,000 of debts needing protection cover and a monthly budget of £140.

Table 1. FAMILY PROTECTION COVER

NEEDS	A. Commission			B. Fees	
	Premium	Initial	Annual	Premium	Fee
MR £350,000 Life cover, 25 years	£33.0/m	£600	£10	£29.0	£250
MRS £250,000 Life cover, 25 years	£20.0/m	£330	£6	£17.0	£250
MR Income Protection, 25 yrs	£37.0/m	£600	£11	£34.0	£250
MRS Income Protection, 25 yrs	£45.0/m	£700	£13	£40.0	£250
TOTALS	£135.0/m	£2,230	£40	£118.0/m	£1,000
Total Annual Premiums	£1,620			£1,416	
Costs over 25 years	£40,500	£3,070		£35,400	£1,000
FEE Advice savings over Commission	£3,100				

By choosing the fee-based option the family will save £204, around 14% each year, although it will take about 5 years to recover the £1,000 fee. Over the 25 years the family will save £3,100.

CASE STUDY

Retirement Drawdown

Neil Watkins is a retiring director aged 65, with a pension fund of £500,000 invested in a Drawdown pension plan, where £25,000 income is drawn each year.

Table 2. RETIREMENT INCOME – Drawdown Plan

Investment	A. Commission		B. Fees	
	Initial	(1.) Annual	(2.) Initial	(3.) Annual
£500,000	£25,000	£2,500	£2,500	£1,000
After 10 years	£25,000	£29,154	£2,500	£11,464
TOTALS	£54,154		£13,964	
Net savings after 10 years using Fees over Commission			£40,190	
Reduction in Growth: The reduction in the investment return after applying all charges, assuming 7% per annum compound investment growth over 10 years.				
Assume no Charges	£614,000		£614,000	
Annual Management Charge	1.5%		0.7% + Fee	
After Charges	£471,000		£543,000	
Reduction in Growth	£143,000		£71,000	
Extra growth provided by Fees £72,000				

Explanation notes:

1. I calculated annual commission as 0.5% of the fund value.
2. The initial fee of £2,500 is taken from the investment. Neil is a basic-rate tax-payer and there would be a one-off income withdrawal of £3,205 gross to cover the 22% income tax bill of £705, leaving £2,500 net.
3. The annual fee starts at £1,000 and increases at 3% per annum. This is taken annually from the investment. This requires an initial annual withdrawal of £1,282 gross to cover the income tax bill of £282, leaving £1,000.

My Observations

Effect of Charges – While the immediate savings in paying fees was obvious, I emphasised to Neil the effect of extortionate commission charges on his future returns.
Savings – If Neil chooses fees, after 10 years he will have saved a massive £40,190 in adviser charges and have an extra £71,455 to buy an annuity.

CASE STUDY

Lump Sum Investment

Bill and Eileen are both 60, and received an inheritance of £250,000 which they wanted to invest wisely.

Table 3. LUMP SUM INVESTMENT

Investment	A. Commission		B. Fees	
	Initial	Annual	Initial	Annual
£250,000	£12,500	£1,250	£2,500	£1,000
After 10 years	£12,500	£14,577	£2,500	£11,464
TOTALS	£27,077		£13,964	
Net savings after 10 years using Fees over commission			£13,133	
Reduction in Growth: The reduction in the investment return after applying all charges, assuming 5% per annum compound growth over 10 years.				
Annual Management Charge	1.5%	0.5% + Fee		
Lost Growth	£74,627	£37,704		
Extra growth provided by Fees	£36,923			

Charges – After 10 years the fee option will save Bill and Eileen £13,133 in adviser charges.

Effect of Charges on Growth – While the immediate savings in paying fees was obvious, I showed Bill and Eileen that by choosing fees, after 10 years they would have an extra £36,923 to spend, or gift to their grandchildren. (For those lucky enough to have larger funds to invest, the pro rata commission costs can be extortionate. A £750,000 fund over 20 years would result in the fee option providing an extra £356,434, to distribute to the family!)

Like many other people I have met, Bill and Eileen were stunned when they saw the long-term benefit of choosing the fee option instead of commission.

Conclusion

Simply ask yourself the question, 'Who is the adviser working for: me, his company, or himself?' If you want the adviser to work for you then you must engage the services of a genuine fee-based adviser and avoid commission.

TOPTIP

i recommend you reduce your debts before you consider long-term savings plans. The arguments around long-term savings are largely irrelevant to the majority of people who cannot afford such commitments, especially after rises in national insurance and council tax, which has increased over 80% since 1998.

b) Low Charging Contracts

The way to protect the majority

Whistle-blower believes one of the simplest ways of protecting most ordinary consumers is by providing access to a suite of low charging, penalty free investment and protection products that can be bought off the shelf with confidence.

Underlying investments may still fall, but at least you know you're getting a fair contract.

This would release the FSA from spending so much time regulating the sales process, far fewer products would be mis-sold, and the FSA could spend time improving the quality and design of products.

Stakeholder ('Sandler') Products

These are simplified low-cost products which set minimum contract standards, and were introduced to help consumers buy products with more confidence. There are no initial charges, and annual charges are restricted to 1.5% for the first 10 years and 1% thereafter.

In July 2002 Ron Sandler's report concluded that 80% of consumers could be recommended simplified products through the use of an advice filtering system. This would reduce the costs to both provider and consumer. These rules were outlined in an FSA Policy Statement PS04/22 and were immediately rubbished by advisers, the very people who had mis-sold 100,000s of endowment mortgages and pension transfers and investment bonds!

More low-cost simplified products are needed

Whistle-blower believes that if the government wants to encourage people to save, they must increase access to low-cost, penalty-free products. 2005 saw the launch of two new Sandler / stakeholder based products, a savings plan and the new Child Trust Fund. You can check out the latest information on stakeholder products on www.stakeholdersavings.gov.uk

Those with vested interests disagree

The industry is not receptive to the idea. No-one wants to be the first to cut commission in case they lose market share, and most are reticent to play ball.

Another car industry scenario

A few foreign providers may give the campaign some impetus. Institutions like the Dutch Bank ING (that offers extremely good instant-access savings accounts) could steal a march on UK companies. American fund managers such as Vanguard, Fidelity and Dimension Data that manage funds for 0.5% or less could also, should they wish to do so, change the scenery in the UK.

IFAs and dyed in the wool fund managers should take note: antiquated commission-based business models are the equivalent to the restrictive and complacent work practices that lead to the demise of the UK car industry.

Low-cost contracts, the future

To take control of the debate about 'cure' or 'prevention', the FSA needs to move from its current reactive position to proactively policing the industry and educating the public.

Low-charging tax-efficient products, combined with a simplified tax and benefits system are what ordinary consumers need and want.

c) Commission Rebates

To avoid commission you can take the following action:

Use fee-based advisers – Choosing an adviser is covered in Part One Chapter 5.

Do it yourself – Use execution-only brokers to transact business. Throughout this series of guides we recommend various distributors to save you money. As an initial one-stop-shop, consider the distributor Hargreaves Lansdown, contact details below.

Use a Trail Rebating Service – Millions of investors are sitting on investments and policies they started years ago, for which they receive no ongoing service, but which pay the original salesman ongoing commission. Many have lost contact with the original salesman. New advisers are keen to become your adviser, which gives them the right to claim the trail commission on your contracts. On lump sum investments this is 0.5% of the fund value and on insurance contracts 2.5% of the annual regular premiums. Every year hundreds of millions are taken from ordinary people's investments and paid to advisers many of whom are doing nothing. Some companies are building their businesses by taking this charge. You can STOP this debacle now by transferring the agency of all your contracts to a company that rebates 100% of your commission. For an annual fee of £35, Intelligent Money Ltd will give you back your money. This is the first company to specialise in this area, others will follow. There are other companies that do not charge a fee but limit the percentage they rebate on some investments.

Table 4. Commission Rebating Service

Company	Service	Remarks
Intelligent Money Ltd 20 Fletchergate Nottingham, NG1 2FZ Tel: 0870 1166117 or 0115 9477570 www.intelligentmoney.com	Collect and rebate 100% commission on all investment, savings and protection policies for an annual fee £35. They do not provide ongoing advice or service.	Do not leave business accruing commissions with organisations that are providing nil service. Do not use unless commission exceeds £35.
CommShare Marlowe House, 109 Station Road Sidcup, Kent, DA15 7ET Tel: 020 8308 1308 www.commshare.com	They are a low-cost distributor providing execution-only services at a discount. You can buy at nil / low commission. They rebate between 30% and 50% of your trail commission.	Trail commission only available on unit trusts and OEIC Funds. Excludes insurance funds and contracts.
Hargreaves Lansdown Kendal House 4 Brighton Mews Clifton, Bristol BS8 2NX Tel: 0800 138 2121 www.hargreaveslansdown.co.uk	They are a low-cost distributor providing execution-only services at a discount and a fund supermarket where you can buy at nil / low commission. They rebate around 30% of your trail commission.	Access by phone, post or internet Excellent web-site and support staff. Trail commission only available on unit trusts and OEIC Funds. Excludes insurance funds and contracts.

d) Commission Recommendations

Does the current commission-dominated system best serve the consumer?

Quite simply NO.

Often the discovery that unfathomable charges have had a detrimental effect is made too late to take corrective action. That is why the talking must stop and the incentive for change must begin.

Action Required by the FSA

Simple products cannot exist without a simplified charging structure and tax system. With immediate effect the FSA and government should make illegal all incentive schemes that have resulted in decades of mis-selling, for example:

- A ban on up-front commission schemes.
- A ban on automatic trail/renewal commission schemes.
- The introduction of a comprehensive suite of investment and protection products with a fixed front-end charge, and capped annual charges.

The Positive Effect

These three measures would end the 'money for nothing' culture which is anti-competitive and distorts the advice process. It prevents consumers buying direct at nil commission rates. It would also stop the promotion of inferior products at the expense of superior consumer-friendly products and force the industry to concentrate on charging for the two things it should be doing:

Providing holistic financial planning and ongoing service

A ban on commission would oblige advisers and service providers to charge fees commensurate with the work involved, taking into account their qualifications, knowledge and level of service.

Our Recommendation

In the meantime our recommendation to you is:

ALWAYS seek fee-based advice.

DO NOT accept an offer of free advice - it does not exist. All businesses must make money and have to charge.

DO NOT accept a commission split. If your adviser's recommendation generates £30,000 in commission which is quite common with very large cases, do not fall for the line, 'I'll split this with you 50/50'. Agree a much smaller fee and save yourself thousands of pounds.

AVOID extortionate commissions by using Whistle-blower Money Guides and doing it yourself.

USE the services of a commission rebating company.

Charges

a) Disclosure

The government are trying to make the sale of FS products more transparent and from 1st June 2005, new 'Depolarisation' legislation came into effect which introduced two big changes. First it reclassified existing advisers and introduced new multi-tied advisers, (see Chapter 5). Most importantly it introduced new disclosure requirements and gave consumers the chance to consider different charging methods.

Now when you sign up to a new policy or product, you will be shown how your adviser operates, and how they charge for their service. This is an improvement on the past, but will only work if you understand the small print. This next section tells you exactly what to look out for before you sign on the dotted line.

You will be provided with these important guides to the product or service you are buying:

The Initial Disclosure Document (IDD) is the Keyfacts Guide to a firm's services. It describes what they do and what they're authorised to do. An example of an IDD is available on the FSA web-site at: http://www.fsa.gov.uk/Pages/Doing/small_firms/general/templates/index.shtml

A firm that offers several services can either issue separate documents for each service, or combine them into a Combined Initial Disclosure Document, (CIDD). The entries you need to check are:

Scope of Advice (Entry 2.) Advisers may deal with all providers in the market place (whole market), OR a limited number of product providers, OR a single product provider.

Type of Advice (Entry 3.) Advisers may offer 'Full advice' and make recommendations after assessing client needs, OR information but not advice, you make your own choice (known as a 'non advised sale,' or 'execution-only' business), OR basic advice on a range of stakeholder products. This would not include a full assessment of your needs and would only cover limited advice.

How you will pay for those services? (Entry 4.) If you buy a packaged product (such as personal or stakeholder pension, life policy, unit trust or OEIC – see glossary), the firm will provide you with a 'fees and commission statement', or 'menu of charges'. If the firm is advising on non-packaged products, they will provide a list of their charges.

The Fees & Commission statement – is the Keyfacts Guide to the cost of services and the form will depend on whether the adviser takes commission, a fee or a combination of both.

a) Any firms using the title 'independent financial advisers' should offer contracts from the 'whole market,' and must now offer a fee-paying option to clients.
b) If a firm charges fees only, they must provide details of charge rates and provide an estimate before any work is undertaken.
c) If an advisory firm is commission-based, it must also include the FSA Commission Menu which compares their product commissions to the market average, as shown in Table 5. It is in your interests to COMPARE costs, but in most cases commission based advice is not the answer, as we saw in Chapter 2.

Table 1. Example – Part of a Commission Menu

Lump Sum Products	Commission % (Market Average)	Adviser Charges
Collective Investments (e.g. unit trusts)	3.78%	4.0%
Investment Bonds	4.99%	6.0%
Annuities	1.4%	1.5%
Income Drawdown	5.04%	7.0%

Terms of Business / Client Agreement You will also be provided with a Terms of Business / Client Agreement, which sets out the terms and conditions by which a firm will conduct its business. It tells you what you can expect from a firm, and could be accompanied by a servicing agreement.

Summary

When you seek advice or buy a FS product you should be given the following:

Table 2. Summary of Consumer Information Documents

Document	Which Products	When	Information
KEY FACTS Initial Disclosure Document (IDD)	All Packaged Products such as all life policies, stakeholder pensions, unit trusts, ISAs	First contact	Firm's adviser status, products & services recommended
KEY FACTS Fees & commission statement	Packaged Products	First contact	Payment / charges options
Terms of Business	Most Products	First contact / First meeting	Predecessor to (IDD). Details the terms of engagement
Product Key Features / Simplified Prospectus	Packaged Products	Before sale	Description covering charges, tax etc
Product Illustration	Packaged Products	Before sale with key features	Based on projections using expected charges

The net effect of these changes is that you will receive more information to help identify providers who offer poor value. This is good news for all your FUTURE transactions but ignores the effect of poor PAST advice on your current finances. To protect your money you need to understand how the charging system works and how it may have been used against you, which will help you identify whether you have been a victim of mis-selling.

b) Effect of Charges

Everyone agrees there has to be a charge for investing. If you seek investment advice, the adviser must be paid, and so must the investment manager. But lifetime contract charges vary considerably, and make a huge difference to the amount you receive to fund your lifetime goals. A simple example will demonstrate the point.

Table 3. **Effect of charges on £10,000 growing at 5% compound per annum**				
	Option 1. Salesman's Recommendation HIGH Charges		Option 2. Whistle-blower Recommendation LOW Charges	
Initial Investment	£10,000		£10,000	
Initial Charge	7%	£700	1%	£100
Amount Invested	93%	£9,300	99%	£9,900
Annual Charge	1.5%	£150+	0.5%	£50+
10 Years	£13,024		£15,338	
20 Years	£18,239		£23,762	
30 Years	£25,542		£36,813	
YOUR EXTRA CASH				
10 Years	-		£2,314 (+18%)	
20 Years	-		£5,523 (+30%)	
30 Years	-		£11,271 (+44%)	

Look how much you are losing!

A quick glance at Table 3 shows the power of compound interest working against you. Even though the underlying investments in options 1 and 2 grow at exactly the same rate, the second fund has paid lower charges and can grow much faster. Imagine a situation where over 30 years you and your neighbour invested exactly the same but, because your adviser took 6% commission and recommended a high charging fund, at 65 you receive a retirement income 44% lower! Reason enough to take up Whistle-blower recommendations.

Charging the consumer

As a consumer I strive to be reasonable, but it's becoming harder and harder to be patient. When it comes to charging, I can handle honesty – even if it means digging deeper into my wallet. But I object to the half-truths which are exposed in every industry.

While I was writing this chapter, I took a break to collect my car after repair at a dealer. I was charged £364 for the work, drove off the forecourt and noticed that the problem warning light was still lit. So I went back to the mechanic who said, 'The light must have come on since you left, it was OK when we road tested it. It'll take us 15 minutes to check it out.' An hour later, he told me the sensor he fitted yesterday was faulty, 'It has to be re-ordered, but it'll arrive tomorrow and can be fitted in 10 minutes while you wait'.

At this point I asked why he'd charged me £65 for an hour's labour to fit the sensor yesterday, when tomorrow it would take only 10 minutes? The mechanic looked sheepish and replied, 'Ah, testing the new sensor could take a further 45 minutes'.

So tomorrow morning, they will do the job in 10 minutes and make me wait a further 45 minutes to justify their original invoice!

I can't remember when I first heard the expression 'If it ain't simple then something's wrong,' but no saying could be more apt for the charging structure of the Financial Services industry. In the next few pages I will attempt to explain some of that complexity, because buried within it are the wily ways in which YOUR MONEY VANISHES every time you invest.

These complex charging methods are all detrimental to your wealth and apply to all forms of investment products and services. For readers who love the detail, fuller definitions of charges are provided in the Glossary.

c) Types of charges

Initial Charges

Commission has to be extracted as a deduction from your investment. Salesmen are like magicians, and can make charges 'disappear.' It's time to start asking, 'How did they do that?' Over the years many elaborate schemes have been devised to disguise charges. Here are six of them:

Initial / Capital Units – high-charging units that disguised up-front costs and devalued plans. Now ceased for new contracts. A detailed explanation is found in Part Two, Chapter 10 a) Pension Complaints, Commission Manipulation. Used by: Life Office Funds

Allocation Rates – a charging system that allocates a percentage of your invested money to your plan. Used by: Life Office Funds

Establishment Charge – a percentage charge made every month or quarter over a period of 60 months. Used by: Life Office Funds

Bid / Offer Spread – the spread between the cost of buying units in a fund at the higher 'Offer' price and selling them at the lower 'Bid' price. Used by: Life Office Funds, Unit Trust Managers

Initial Charge – an initial charge of around 5%, similar to the bid offer spread, and relatively transparent. Used by: Life Office Funds, OEIC / Unit Trust Managers

Reinvestment Charge – an unscrupulous charge for re-investment of income in your fund. Used by: A few Unit Trust Managers.

Annual Management Charge (AMC)

This is the explicit annual charge quoted by the fund manager to manage the fund and pay ongoing commission to the salesman.

For many years consumers have been led to believe it covers all annual charges, when it does not. It fails to take into account auditor's fees, custodian / trustee's fees, legal fees and dealing charges, which the salesman rarely discloses.

Quantifying Charges

These are complex charges that try and take into account the effect of several charges lumped together.

Recent European directives are trying to standardise comparisons of charges across Europe. This information will be provided before the point of sale in either the 'key features' document or a 'simplified prospectus'.

Types of Quantifying Charges are:

Total Expense Ratio TER (%) This is the drag on performance of a fund caused by annual operating costs and includes fund mangers charges, administration, audit and legal fees, but excludes initial charges and dealing charges. This is always more than the Annual Management Charge (AMC) quoted by salesmen. Information on TERs is freely available from investment association web-sites listed at the end of this section. Do take the time to check them.

Reduction in Yield (RIY) %. This is a percentage by which the total explicit charges (initial and annual) are expected to reduce the return on the policy contract compared to a contract with no charges. All packaged products such as personal pensions, ISAs and unit trusts must include this figure. Standard growth rates are used by all companies so direct comparisons can be made, which will help you assess value for money.

The RIY is helpful but rarely disclosed by salesmen who prefer to talk about the lower Annual Management Charge.

Portfolio Turnover Rate (PTR)% This is the percentage change of a fund's assets following purchases and sales over the last calendar year. The greater the change the greater the transaction costs. An active portfolio may expect to turn over at least 50% of the fund each year. Used by: Funds with a UCITS certificate, appropriate unit trusts and OEICs.

If you want to check a fund's Total Expense Ratios the following web-sites are useful:

Table 4. **TER Information**		
Funds	**Web-site**	**How**
Unit Trusts and OEICs	Investment Management Association www.investmentfunds.org.uk	Home > Investors > Find a Fund > Sort by TERs Will then list c. 1400 TERs. You can find lowest TER by > 'sort' at top of column.
Investment Trusts	Association of Investment Trust Companies www.aitc.co.uk	Home > Search for an investment trust (six choices) > choose fund > Financial Profile OR Home > statistics > TERs

5 Advisers

Most people seem to believe it's easy to get independent financial advice. After all, it's something everybody wants at some point in their lives. But in reality it is a very rare commodity. In Chapter 2 we've already examined how commission-based earnings prevent traditional financial advisers from being truly independent.

Types of Adviser

If you seek advice in the mass market you have four choices:

- **Independent Financial Advisers (IFAs) Commission-based**
- **Independent Financial Planners (IFPs) Fee-based**
- **Tied Advisers**
- **Multi-tied Advisers.**

a) Commission-based IFAs

Although called independent and able to offer products from the whole market, many IFAs push products from a limited range of providers with whom they have arranged lucrative commission deals. They tend to skew advice towards high commission products, which leads to overcharging.

Because they are 'product pushers,' their businesses usually suffer from the following inadequacies:

They ignore the whole Market – As they are dependent on commission from product providers, they ignore commission-free alternatives.

Poor Service – As the products they sell tend to pay commission up-front, there is little incentive to provide ongoing service. The claim made by many to offer financial services is a misnomer as there may be no service at all.

Limited financial experience – Their reliance on Life Office products has resulted in the majority having little experience of using better alternatives.

Poorly qualified – Many advisers only hold basic qualifications which do not give them the depth and breadth of knowledge to advise competently across the investment spectrum.

It has always amazed me how IFAs have escaped notice by the Office of Fair Trading based on a breach of the Trades Description Act for the use of the title Independent. I believe that label should be used only by the truly impartial, which commission-based IFAs cannot be.

Steer clear of Commission-based IFAs.

Since 1st June 2005 all IFAs who want to retain the title IFA must offer clients a fee-based option and a menu of charges. But for many, this may mean little more than a different way of keeping records. Those that do not offer a fee option must call themselves 'Whole of Market Advisers'.

b) Independent Financial Planners (IFPs) Fee-based

While not officially recognised as a separate category, Whistle-blower believes it is important to distinguish IFPs (who offer fee-based holistic financial planning) from commission-based salesmen. These IFPs are the truly independent advisers. A small but growing band have realised there must be a better way to look after clients by placing their needs first. You will recognise IFPs because they won't push products and they usually have the following credentials.

Professional Status – An adviser who works in an ethical manner and who puts your interests first at all times. This is the main difference between fee-based financial planners and commission-driven salesmen.

Methodology – A professional planner will help you achieve your life goals by objectively managing your finances, considering cash flow, assets and liabilities. Their advice may or may not involve the recommendation to purchase a financial product.

Seek out IFPs by contacting the Institute of Financial Planning, contact details in Table 4, page 58.

Qualifications – Most have qualifications achieved through continuous professional development that gives accreditation to professional bodies.

c) Tied Advisers

These advisers sell products and services from just one company, usually those provided by the high street banks and some building societies. They rely on your inertia not to look for better advice. Beware:

They are not independent – They offer you no choice. Why buy life cover from one provider when there are another 50 to choose from, 30 of which may offer lower premiums?

Their advice may be poor – The salesman will try to achieve a sale, regardless of your real need. Targets drive them, and some have been known to sell to colleagues (and cancel within 14 days) in order to achieve quarterly sales targets.

Poor Product Range – Most life companies have gaps in their product range and therefore cannot offer comprehensive solutions. So an adviser may try to push inappropriate products as a second best solution. In reality if a tied adviser does not have an appropriate product, they should refer the client to an IFA. Try telling this to a salesman who is 30% below their annual target with a month to go!

Variable Charging Structure – While some companies offer competitive charges, they do not offer the best products. You may end up paying above market price for below average products.

Variable Investment Track Record – While there are exceptions, most money ends up in large managed funds that charge as highly as the best actively managed funds yet deliver poor performance.

d) Multi-Tied Advisers

These advisers sell the products and services of several providers, usually from 5 or 6 companies. This type of adviser was introduced as part of 'Depolarisation' (see Part One, Chapter 4, 'Disclosure') to provide greater choice between tied and independent advice.

Many large banks are conscious of the shortfalls of being tied to one Life Office and multi tie, and while this type of advice is better than tied, it is not independent and therefore suffers, albeit to a lesser degree, from the same inadequacies listed under tied advisers.

e) Other Advisers

There are other advisers who do not operate in the main market but are worth a mention.

Specialist Advisers (Stockbrokers/Private Bankers)

These advisers offer wealth management services by creating share-based portfolios. The market provides for the wealthiest clients, but moderately wealthy clients may be lured into believing that private banking and client stock-broking offers an exclusive service that's not available to the masses. The major players include Lloyds Private Banking and Barclays (who own Gerrards Stockbrokers).

Investors are also misled into believing that their private banker or stockbroker will be keeping an eye on their portfolio on a daily basis. This is not the case. Their services fail to deliver results and value for money for the following reasons:

High Charges – Annual management charges are 1% to 2%, plus bid offer spread on share dealing, dealing charges and stamp duty. So annual charges are often 3% to 3.5% – a big drag on performance in a low inflationary economy.

TOPTIP

Advice from tied advisers may be dangerous. Although no adviser should knowingly withhold information relating to better alternatives, in reality it does happen. The adviser can hide behind the fact that they sold the most appropriate product from their 'stable'. You need to prove that the advice you received was negligent rather than inappropriate.

NO GO ZONE – Steer Clear At All Costs

TOPTIP

Steer clear of Multi-Tied Advisers

Portfolio Management is Poor – Your portfolio is probably reviewed only once every 6 months. At the review date, 'weak' or 'sell' shares are replaced with the 'buys'. So what happens if a share in your portfolio is declared 'weak' a day after your review? You'll be stuck with it for another 6 months until your next review. These large firms don't sell a share holding en masse in case they move the market. The dotcom demise proved the inefficiency of their systems, with many portfolios bought-in too late and sold-out too late, leaving clients with big losses.

Research and Analytical systems are Poor – The best analysts do not work for private advisory firms, so their information is often second or third hand. By the time your adviser suggests changes, the city has already moved on.

Destined to Under-perform – These investment services are difficult to assess. They claim that as their portfolios are bespoke, it is difficult to provide meaningful historical performance figures. But believe me – if they had done well they would be wheeling out the testimonials to prove it!

Financial Mentors / Life Coaches

A new breed of adviser may be about to emerge, borne out of the meltdown created by so many financial scandals. These advisers are common in the USA, and aim to mentor consumers personally through the vagaries of the investment world while also offering life coaching.

I believe there are already a few advisers in the UK who are operating in this manner. They may or may not be authorised by the FSA.

Experienced advisers who hold professional qualifications may want to follow such a path. Many of them are disillusioned with mainstream advisory firms that don't offer fair value, and with the FSA that deals ineffectively with the industry miscreants. For example they cite the problems associated with mis-selling, and the need for good honest advisers to pay an ever increasing levy into a compensation scheme to cover the damage caused by many who walk away with impunity.

If these advisors are not authorised you would only be able to claim compensation if the company they recommended defaults, not for the advice received.

Their aim is to offer a personal, fee-based holistic financial planning service. Their fees are likely to be lower than an authorised adviser, ranging from £40 to £100 per hour.

f) Adviser Qualifications

Too many exam bodies

For decades many competing governing bodies have maintained their own qualifications. Over the last decade, The Chartered Insurance Institute (CII) has gained universal recognition for setting the standards by which most financial advisers can be measured. A wing of the CII called the Personal Finance Society (PFS) oversees the activities of most financial advisers.

Low Standards

For years the regulator and the industry has allowed salesmen/advisers to operate with a lack of basic knowledge, more interested in volume advice (sales) than its quality. This attitude continues today.

In the past all a salesman needed to be let loose on the unsuspecting public was the Financial Planning Certificate (FPC). This involved three passes equivalent to NVQ levels 1 to 3. It was replaced in 2005 by the Certificate in Financial Planning (Cert PFS), now the minimum level of competence required by The FSA. This qualification is sufficient for a supporting role but not sufficient for a fee-based adviser.

To its credit the FSA is working with both the Financial Services Skills Council and CII to complete a review and determine which examinations are appropriate for certain regulated advice.

The birth of a Profession?

In 2005 the Privy Council gave the CII the authority to grant advisers chartered status as a 'Chartered Financial Planner'. The Institute believes this will put the very best advisers on the same professional footing as the legal and accountancy professions. Existing advisers will be eligible to use the title providing they have accrued 290 points through a process of examination. It is believed that around 500 to 1,000 of the 100,000 or so advisers that work in financial services will initially qualify to use the title.

The status will depend on maintaining stringent standards. Whistle-blower believes it should not be awarded through examination alone, but take into account the adviser's track record of ethical advice. Those with a history of mis-selling claims should not be given the title or the status, but unfortunately this could happen.

Remember you can test for knowledge but you cannot test for integrity.

You will come across business cards with many different designations which are summarised below in tables 1 and 2.

Table 1. The Chartered Insurance Institute (CII)

Basic Exams & Qualifications

Qualification	NEW Designation	Remarks	OLD Designations
Certificate in Financial Planning	Cert PFS	Basic adviser qualification	FPC, MLIA Dip
Certificate in Mortgage Advice	Cert CII (MP)	Required to give mortgage advice.	MAQ

Notes: Advisers should hold further qualifications if they wish to advise on 'Equity Release Schemes' and 'Long Term Care Insurance.

Advanced Exams & Qualifications

The Advanced Financial Planning Certificate (AFPC) is awarded to those advisers who pass more specialist exams.

LEVEL	Qualification	NEW Designation	OLD Designations
Advanced level 1	Diploma in Financial Planning	Dip PFS	MSFA, ALIA(dip)
Advanced level 2	Associate of the Personal Finance Society	APFS FLIA(dip)	ASFA,
Advanced level 3	Fellow of the Personal Finance Society	FPFS	FSFA, FLIA(dip)

Chartered Status

In 2005 The Chartered Insurance Institute was awarded the right to grant financial planners the status of 'Chartered Financial Planner' for those who have completed their Fellowship exams.

You will also come across business cards with the following designations:

Exam Body	Qualification	Designation	Remarks
Table 2. Other Qualifications			
Chartered Insurance Institute	Associate & Fellow of the Chartered Insurance Institute	ACII, FCII	Old exams with an insurance bias, equal to DipPFS, APFS
Institute of Financial Services	Certificate in Mortgage Advice	CeMAP	Bankers equivalent to the old MAQ and new Cert CII (MP)
Institute of Financial Services	Professional Investment Certificate	PIC	Bankers equivalent to the CII Dip PFS
Securities Institute (Professional Body primarily for Stockbrokers)	Member of the Securities Institute	MSI FSI	A diploma based on Private Client Advice. Fellowship is automatically conferred after 3 years
UK Society of Investment Professionals	Investment Management Certificate	IMC	A single exam based on investment management, equivalent to the CII G70
UK Society of Investment Professionals	Investment Management Asset Management qualification	IMAAQ	Out of date exam based on creation of broker funds, no longer sold. Equivalent to the CII G70

g) Institute of Financial Planning (IFP)

What is it?

This examination body deserves a special mention as it has pioneered the development of financial planning as a profession, only granting licenses to those who (through a process of examination and continuous professional development – CPD), have the experience and knowledge to advise in an ethical, professional manner. They are bound to work to a code of ethics.

Financial Planning is Different

Pure financial planning is different to traditional financial advice as the adviser uses different tools (such as cash flow analysis) to manage your finances holistically and achieve your life goals. All planners are encouraged to improve their skills, with CPD a pre-requisite to maintaining their licences.

Many accountants and solicitors also hold an IFP license as they consider holistic financial planning as fundamental to their clients needs.

Table 3. **The Institute of Financial Planning IFP**		
Accreditation	**Letters**	**Qualification**
Level 1: Associate of the Institute of Financial Planning	AIFP	Advanced Financial Planning Certificate (AFPC) or equivalent professional qualifications. Not licensed.
Level 2: Certified Financial Planner Licence	CFP Licence	By examination / 60 hour case study. Must hold AFPC and have 3 years relevant experience and complete a minimum of 30 hrs training p.a. (Other professions such as accountants and solicitors can use their own professional qualifications to gain accreditation).
Level 3: Fellow of The Institute of Financial Planning	FIFP Licence	By examination. Must hold AFPC and have 5 years relevant experience and complete a minimum of 30 hrs training p.a.

h) Finding & Selecting an Adviser

If you need the assistance of an adviser to sort out your financial affairs, this guide will lead you towards the top 10% of advisers in the UK. To reduce the chance of disappointment you will be steered clear of salesmen.

Why Salesmen fail to Deliver

Lack of Integrity – The FSA *Code of Practice for Approved Persons* states that, 'An adviser should act with Integrity.' But in reality, this principle is flouted every day.

First Impressions can be Deceptive – There are many sales people who look and sound like professional advisers. As first impressions influence up to 80% of our decision-making we sign on the dotted line and realise our mistake when things go wrong.

Long-term relationships are rare – Remember commission-based advisers are likely to desert you if you have no new money to invest.

Long-term servicing is rare – Many FS companies tuck a statement away in their 'Terms of Business' similar to this; *'We will not undertake any periodic reviews of your investment but will be glad to advise you any time you ask us to do so'*.

So they are admitting there will be no servicing – They may as well say, *'If your circumstances change, the investment is inappropriate, or the fund takes a dive, don't blame us for anything that's happened after we have banked our commission'*.

TOPTIP

The combination of technical competence, a code of ethics and financial planning methods geared to fees make make members of the Institute of Financial Planning stand out from the crowd. SEEK OUT.

A Better Way

You must do your homework – Look beyond the outward appearance and use a more rigorous selection process. Question the adviser about their level of experience, qualifications, knowledge and levels of servicing next year and every year thereafter.

Avoid future problems by managing expectations – The key to avoiding problems is for you to understand the service you will receive. The adviser must manage your expectations based on a clear fee-based Servicing Agreement that tells you:

- What you can expect,
- When you can expect it,
- How it will be delivered,
- Who will deliver it,
- What it will cost.

Adviser blind date – 'Good adviser wants to meet good clients.' There are some excellent, dedicated professional advisers in the UK. Your difficulty may be finding one who lives close to you. Do not compromise on the fundamental issues of fees and competency.

Let's look at the steps you must take to find one.

How to Find an Adviser

{Step 1}

Consult Table 4 and obtain names of local fee-based advisory firms from the IFP or the PFS. You can phone the organisations direct or use the web-site to see a brief resume, detailing the adviser's competences and services.

Table 4. Find a Financial Planner – Industry Directories

Organisation & Contact	Remarks & Recommendation
Institute of Financial Planning Whitefriars Lewins Mead Bristol BS1 2NT t: 0117 945 2470 e: enquiries@ financialplanning.org.uk w: www.financialplanning.org.uk	The Institute of Financial Planning is dedicated to the development of the financial planning profession. Web-site: Useful source of information and search facility provides details of financial planners who are AFPC qualified and who are committed to competent and ethical behaviour. Majority are fee based. Recommendation: MAKE CONTACT.
The Personal Finance Society 20 Aldermanbury London EC2V 7HY t: 020 7600 0766 e: info@thepfs.org w: www.thepfs.org	The Personal Finance Society is the largest UK professional body for financial advisers and provides technical support. Its parent the Chartered Insurance Institute is the largest of its type in the world. Web-site: Consumers > 'find an Adviser' > Use 'Fees Only' search facility to find an adviser. All advisers listed are AFPC qualified. Recommendation: MAKE CONTACT.
Financial Services Authority FSA 25 The North Colonade Canary Wharf London E14 5HS t: Consumer Helpline 0845 606 1234 w: www.fsa.gov.uk	Via its web-site (homepage) the FSA provides a register where you can search for details of Firms and individuals, and check their authorisation and history, including disciplinary actions. Order 'FSA guide to financial advice' from the helpline or via internet. Plenty of generic information about seeking advice. Recommendation: CONTACT as a double check.

{STEP 2}

Make direct contact with the adviser and arrange an introductory meeting. Just in case their status has changed, confirm with the adviser that:

✓ they are fee-based
✓ they operate independently
✓ they offer the type of advice/service that you are seeking
✓ there is no charge for the introductory meeting if you do not proceed.

Be prepared to take details of your investments and policies to the meeting so the adviser can assess the depth of planning you will require.

{STEP 3}

An introductory meeting should normally last half an hour. This is a two-way process and gives you the chance to assess the adviser and the adviser to decide whether they can help you as a client. Most importantly you need to trust each other. Remember, a good adviser will be in demand and may have limited scope to take on new clients. I have compiled a list of suitable questions.

Table 5. Adviser Suitability - General

Question	Ideal Answer
1. Are you both independent and fee-based?	Yes. The adviser should show you their 'Initial Disclosure Document', detailing how they operate, range of advice, and how they are regulated etc.
2. How long have you been predominately fee-based?	Several years. Will indicate whether legislation forced them to change in 2005 or they moved early of their own accord for ethical reasons.
3. What experience do you have?	A potted history/C.V. covering their time with this company and previous companies.
4. What experience do you have in the area in which you need assistance such as inheritance tax planning?	One of our core competences, we regularly advise clients with estates in excess of a million, etc. We work with other professionals, etc. (May offer testimonials/references.)
5. What qualifications do you hold?	Minimum AFPC. Discloses membership of professional bodies.
6. What other services do you offer?	Tax & Estate Planning, Investment Portfolio Service, etc. If the adviser has established links with other professions introductory fees should be disclosed.
7. What is your approach to financial planning?	Looking for a strategy based on assessing the relationship between your assets and liabilities, income and expenditure, current and future cash flow, and determining what is required to achieve your life goals within certain defined parameters of risk.
8. How do you charge for services?	Should provide you with a menu stating the hourly fee rate and list the type of services offered, providing indicative costs. Should state clearly how commission is refunded /offset.
9. How much do you think my planning will cost?	An estimate will be provided based on a typical case.

10. How will I be charged for ongoing service and what service can I expect?	Can show you a Service Agreement detailing what you can expect from your planner. There may be different levels of service and costs dependent on your needs. Charges based on hourly rate / trail commission/Fund based %.
11. Having briefed the adviser on your current position ask, ' Are you aware of any conflicts of interest that may affect your advice to me?	No.
12. Have you ever been disciplined for unethical or unlawful advice/ behaviour?	No.
13. Can I have it in writing?	If the adviser takes you on as a client they will give/send you the Initial Disclosure Documents, Terms of Business, specimen Client Servicing Agreement.

Those with large lump sums to invest may wish to ask a few extra questions.

Table 6. Adviser Suitability – Wealth Management

Question	Ideal Answer
1. What particular investment experience do you have of managing portfolios?	Varied – able to objectively consider all options from across the whole investment spectrum.
2. What qualifications do you have?	Looking for minimum AFPC, in particular the G70 Exam in Investment and Portfolio Management or the Investment Management Certificate (IMC).
3. How do you construct and balance a portfolio?	You are looking for a methodical approach, consideration of all asset classes. Ask to see examples.
4. How do you measure risk?	This causes more general complaints than any other issue. The adviser should have a clear method of defining your tolerance to risk and matching your risk profile to a suitable portfolio of investments that will achieve your objectives.
5. What types of investment do you use and why?	Looking for balance of – OIECS, Unit Trusts, Investment Trusts, Exchange Traded Funds, Gilts, National Savings and Deposit Funds.
6. Are there any investments you can't use and why?	Some companies restrict their choice to a very narrow panel of providers and one type of investment which restricts your choice.
7. What investment research do you undertake?	Their preferred funds need to be constantly monitored to take into account change in fund personnel, charges and performance.
8. What performance have you achieved?	Hopefully above average. Examples, testimonials?
9. What are your total charges for setting up my portfolio and the annual management?	SET UP – Scrutinise anything in excess of 2% of fund invested, and capped for large portfolios over £250,000. ANNUAL – Depends on service. Adviser charges no greater than 0.5% of the value of the fund, and capped for large portfolios.
10. What would you expect the annual Total Expense Ratio to be?	The Total Expense Ratio (TER) takes into account all charges, both adviser and fund manager and administration. Do not pay above 2% per year for the whole portfolio. Aim for 1% to 1.5% per annum.

11. How often will my portfolio be reviewed and rebalanced?	This refers to routine servicing whereby agreed %'s into different asset classes are reviewed depending on your new attitude to risk, income needs etc. Depends on complexity and servicing agreement. Suggest at least twice a year.
12. How do you monitor my portfolio?	This is the second most common complaint that the adviser did not move early enough when things appeared to be going wrong. The adviser should be keeping an eye on all the recommended funds and tax legislation with a view to suggesting changes prior to the review dates.
13. What communication will I receive, by which methods and how often?	Looking for clear reports and valuations sent as often as you require.
14. Can I monitor my investments and obtain valuations from the internet?	Yes. It's your money so keep an eye on it. Offers you reassurance by knowing you can check and make changes yourself at any time. Stops all this nonsense of waiting once a year for a statement.
15. Are there any other services you offer?	May offer associated tax and trust services.
16. How quickly could you exit the market if I asked you to sell everything?	One day this may be important – gauge response.
17. If things went wrong, other than statutory compensation, is there any restriction on the amount of compensation I could receive?	Refers mainly to very large portfolios managed by private client stockbrokers. Make sure their professional indemnity insurance adequately covers all their investors.

{STEP 4}

If you are satisfied with the answers you can now agree terms. Your objective is to deal with someone who is both competent and trustworthy, and with whom you can strike up a long-term relationship. The adviser wants exactly the same as you – it's in both parties' interests to be discerning but not over demanding.

i) What to expect from your adviser

As an absolute minimum, a truly independent fee-based financial planner will always act with integrity and place your interests first, by pragmatically evaluating all your options.

In practical terms they need to be a good listener, and a good communicator – responding promptly to your phone calls and messages. They will be good at coaching you about money, and will operate with strict rules of client confidentiality.

Points to look out for

- They will provide a report recommending action appropriate to your circumstances and to move towards your life goals. A good planner can develop into a 'life coach' as many personal goals rely on achieving financial independence. The recommendation will compare your current position and shortfalls with the proposed position, examining costs and potential benefits.
- The planner will ask for feedback, seeking your opinion and never taking action without your authority. At no time should you feel pressurised to act.
- A good planner will always signpost the way ahead, outlining time-scales and potential pitfalls.

- On your instruction the planner will implement the plan which may not involve the purchase of a financial product. If the process is complex, involving Life Offices who are slow administrators, you will receive regular updates.
- A good planner will outsource specialist legal, tax and investment advice and manage the relationships on your behalf.
- On completion of the agreed action, an ongoing servicing agreement will start.
- Your planner should proactively inform you (personally or by newsletter) of changes in the following key areas which could be detrimental to your finances and achievement of life goals:
  - Tax legislation
  - Abnormal market conditions
  - Provider structure/solvency
  - Interest rates
  - Introduction of better products
  - Fund changes
  - Geo-political changes
  - New opportunities.

Note. Even if you have a long established relationship with an adviser you must not compromise on the fundamentals: receiving fee-based advice from a competent adviser. If you lower your standards you expose yourself to the risk of a future disappointment.

j) Changing Adviser – Immediate Action

When you have read this chapter you may want to take immediate action, especially if you feel angry that your current adviser never fully disclosed the true nature of the commissions taken (and will continue to take if you don't act). This will be all the more pressing if a transaction is pending.

{STEP 1}

The first step is to contact your adviser and establish the facts. If they are commission-based, ask how much commission they will receive immediately and every year throughout the life of the contract.

{STEP 2}

If excessive you must renegotiate the terms. If the adviser fails to compromise, then do not proceed. If you have handed over the cheque – cancel the transaction.

For lump sum investments

It is imperative that you inform the product provider that you do not wish to proceed:

- within 30 days of receiving the cooling off notice for insurance contracts
- within 14 days for investment contracts.

You will get your money back to reinvest on more preferential terms.

Market movements may or may not work in your favour. In the unlikely event that the investment has increased 7% over 14 days, this may be sufficient to cover the commission costs. But if markets go down and you cancel you will get less than you invested and you will have to claim the difference through a mis-selling claim.

For protection policies

For policies which are required to cover a specific need, cancellation may not be an option. Find a fee-based planner or execution broker and re-propose for cover on nil commission or much smaller commission terms. Wait for the new policy to be underwritten and in place before cancelling the old policy. This will mean paying double premiums for 1 to 2 months, which will be handsomely offset by a lifetime of lower premiums. The original adviser will lose most of their commission as it will be clawed back by the Life Office.

{STEP 3}

For long established business where the adviser is providing little or no ongoing service, there is still scope for change.

For lump sums

The adviser's firm will be receiving trail commission of 0.25% to 0.5% of the value of your fund every year. Some firms will aim to use as little as possible on client servicing, to boost their profits.

Do not let them get away with it. Ask for a statement detailing all the commission that your broker receives each year from investments in your name. If they cannot, or will not supply, and you feel your custom is being taken for granted then switch, either by finding a fee-based financial planner or an execution-only broker who will collect and rebate some of your trail commission. Alternatively you can switch the agency to a commission rebating company. See Part One, Chapter 3.

For protection policies

Within 4 years of their start date the adviser is still liable to commission claw-back. After 4 years they will receive renewal commission of 2.5% of the annual premium. At these points you should have some leverage in renegotiating your position. For very large policies taken out by company directors and couples involved in inheritance tax planning, the savings can be huge. I strongly advise that you make contact with a genuine fee-based planner. Again if you feel your custom is being taken for granted then switch.

{STEP 4}

For all new business you must use our STEP by STEP guide to choosing an adviser. Check the credentials of your current adviser, and evaluate their worth in accordance with the guidance given in this chapter.

WEALTH WARNING

Many independent financial advisory firms belong to networks which provide the members with business services. They make money by withholding commission (usually around 15%) from their member firms. As the networks are responsible for negotiating levels of commission with the Life Offices, it is in their interests to keep commissions high to maximise their own profits. Be careful of dealing with such firms.

{STEP 5}

If you are unable to reach an amicable agreement with your existing adviser and cannot find a suitable replacement, switch your investments to a commission rebating company, as described in Part One, Chapter 3.

It is not possible for this guide to give a resumé of all advisers in the UK. Suffice to say there is only one IFA in the Top 20 that is 100% fee-based, and that is Grant Thornton UK LLP. Yet its percentage of the UK financial advisory market is probably less than 1%.

Firms are reluctant to change. But change can be forced upon them by a better-informed public who will not deal with them on such poor terms.

k) Top Tips – Summary

1 DO NOT accept commission-based advice, ALWAYS seek fee-based advice.
2 If a pension product is required it may be feasible to offset the commission against the fee, while re-investing or rebating the excess.
3 BEWARE of fees that by coincidence always match the commission.
4 If you have an adviser, negotiate a servicing agreement. Make sure all trail commission on existing investments is accounted for and used to cover reviews and further advice. Any excess should be rebated to you.
5 If your adviser is not willing to be reasonable OR proves to be under-qualified, contact the IFP or PFS for details of fee-based advisers in your area. (See 'Finding an Adviser' Part One, Chapter 5.)
6 If you do not use an adviser for NEW BUSINESS, always use a discount broker who:
   • Rebates all or most of the initial commission AND
   • Rebates some of the renewal commission on regular premium plans, and some of the trail commission on lump sum investments.
7 If you do not have an adviser and have EXISTING BUSINESS, transfer the agency to a rebating broker. This will give them the contractual right to collect the commission and rebate the bulk to you. Full details see Part One, Chapter 3 – Commission Rebates.
8 If you feel you do not need an adviser, use the other Whistle-blower guides and do it yourself.

Conclusion

No transparency – There is no transparency in the current system. The uninitiated consumer who seeks advice is most likely to stumble on commission-based, product-pushing salesmen who masquerade as IFAs.

Complacency – Some in the pro-commission camp believe the government cannot afford to tamper with the current system while there is a need to raise the levels of pensions and savings. Whistle-blower believes that reform is vital before the public will begin to trust the industry with their money again.

We need a forest fire – The FSA has launched an initiative 'Treating Customers Fairly' to encourage advisers to do what's right for customers. It's a tacit omission that they currently don't! This initiative will struggle to work because of the influence of commission. A forest fire appears to destroy everything in its path, but is actually nature's way of clearing out the old and bringing in the new. This industry needs its own forest fire. The complete removal of all commission would light the touch-paper. You can help light the fire. If the government doesn't start the fire, you can. You can hasten the demise of commission-based sales by moving your business elsewhere. Today.

The green shoots of hope – For consumers who seek advice, professional fee-based planners who offer truly impartial advice and use transparent charges, can help you achieve your life goals. Their service is focused on your needs, placing you at the heart of the business. Make every effort to seek one out and build a relationship on mutual trust.

WEALTH WARNING

Beware of advisers who may suddenly reincarnate themselves as fully fledged fee-based financial planners. A drastic culture change cannot be achieved by the same advisers putting on a new shirt.

Any decision to switch roles must be based on a change of attitude and ethos, not just a fear of commercial extinction.

As the profession develops, it will attract people with professionalism and integrity. This should squeeze out the commission-based advisers to be replaced by a new generation of advisers who want to build a worthy profession.

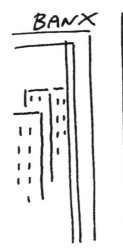

6 Mis-selling

a) Introduction

The aim of this section is to help you understand whether you have been the victim of a mis-selling practice and show you how to get redress and claim thousands in compensation. Don't be like the man in my local pub who tells me he can't be bothered to fight for what is rightfully his. He wrongly assumes he'll never win, and that the fight isn't worth the winning. This money is rightfully **YOURS** and it will help you achieve your life goals. You and your family should be enjoying your own hard-earned money.

Thousands Deceived? The potential number of valid complaints for incorrect advice received by consumers probably runs to hundreds of thousands, and may be millions.

Get to the front of the queue. *If everybody makes a claim, the system will implode and many companies will go into voluntary liquidation to avoid paying out compensation. Therefore it's imperative that you get to the front of the queue and register your complaint as soon as possible. You should send your letter now, tomorrow may be too late.*

The 'Mother' of all Complaints – The first complaint that millions of consumers who have sought advice from IFAs should make to the financial ombudsman is:

'I did not receive independent advice from my independent financial adviser who proclaimed to be independent, but is not. They made false claims about impartiality and evaluating the market-place when in reality they arranged all my transactions from a restricted list of providers whom they were dependent on for commission.'

Proving the 'Mother' of all Complaints – In theory this can be proved by examining the Terms of Business which you should have received from your adviser before you transacted the business. This details the rules of engagement, how they would advise you, and usually explains the benefits of their independent status. This document has now been complemented by the Initial Disclosure Document (IDD), and provides details of how your IFA operates.

The Proof

If an IFA has claimed to be independent but has acted in breach of their own Terms of Business, with a bias towards commission-based products at the expense of more appropriate, lower or nil-commission transactions, then you have a valid reason to make a complaint. The adviser has provided you with misleading information and you should be able to claim compensation for financial loss.

The FSA has laid out 11 principles that advisory firms must follow when dealing with clients. ('Firm' refers to all FS companies, partnerships and sole traders. Within this chapter, 'firm' and 'company' are interchangeable and mean the same.)

If an advisor has failed to comply with one of these principles, a complaint for mis-selling should be proved valid.

The principles most often breached by advisers are:

Principle 1. Integrity. A firm must conduct its business with integrity.

Principle 2. Skill, Care & Diligence. A firm must conduct its business with due skill, care and diligence.

Principle 6. Customers Interests. A firm must pay due regard to the interests of its customers and treat them fairly.

Principle 7. Communications with Clients. A firm must pay due regard to the information needs of its clients, and communicate information to them in a way which is clear, fair and not mis-leading.

Principle 9. Customers: Relationship of Trust. A firm must take reasonable care to ensure the suitability of its advice and discretionary decisions for any customer who is entitled to rely upon its judgement.

We can hear but we are not listening

If you made a general complaint about 'misrepresentation and independence' you would be unlikely to win because the authorities are fearful of opening the floodgates against IFAs as a whole. The industry is still dependent on commission and will defend itself rigorously to resist reform.

The unholy alliance

Our sources within the industry have confirmed that many IFAs know they are far from independent. Many product providers also know they have been designing and supplying products for salesmen to push. The commission-orientated industry trade bodies know the score and the industry regulator (FSA) is aware of the true situation but is regularly lobbied by some parts of the industry who fear a crisis of confidence that will lead to a collapse.

And finally, our sources say politicians understand the industry shortfalls, but have an agenda to reduce public spending and reduce our reliance on the welfare state. They need a healthy FS industry and are fearful of a reform which may destabilise the industry.

WEALTH WARNING

DO NOT use the services of complaint handling firms who will make the complaint on your behalf in exchange for 20% to 25% of your compensation on a 'No win, No fee basis'. Once your complaint goes to the ombudsman with facts identified in this guide your complaint will be investigated in the same way as any other, regardless of where it originated.

This guide will show you what to do **STEP by STEP** to get redress. You do not need their services. For example if you use these firms and you have an endowment mortgage shortfall, after the compensation is paid and they have taken their cut, you will still have a shortfall. **Steer Clear**.

We have lost our Trust

What all parties fail to recognise is that the public has lost confidence and trust in the industry. To restore confidence, top to bottom reform will be required.

All Whistle-blower Money Guides make suggestions to correct the inadequacies of the current system which are unlikely to be led from the top, as this would be tantamount to an admission of failure. But whichever way you look at it, the current way is the wrong one for most consumers.

You must be Strong

If you have been wronged you must battle against the system. The fight will test your resolve, but it is vital the mis-sellers are brought to book and you get redress. Don't let them carry on getting away with your money.

b) The Cause of Mis-selling

Background

The Latin saying *caveat emptor*, meaning 'buyer beware' applies as much to purchasing financial services as to any other products. In principle the FSA would like us to take responsibility for all our financial decisions, but most of us simply don't have sufficient background knowledge to make informed decisions. Until we have that knowledge and until there is a radical shake up of our complicated financial system, the FSA will be needed to protect the consumer.

This principle can only apply if the consumer is protected from questionable selling practices that are inevitably linked to high commission, and which take advantage of their trust.

Consumers struggle in an 'Imperfect Market'

Perfect Market – An example of a perfect market is your local market. There you'll probably find several fruit & veg stalls, each with similarly priced potatoes. From the buyer's perspective it's a perfect market because there is knowledge equality. You and the seller understand potatoes. You can see and feel them and the quality can be evaluated. There is healthy competition and you can recognise value.

Imperfect Market – Financial services operate in an imperfect market. There is inequality of knowledge. The consumer does not understand the product and is asked to buy an intangible promise that at some point in the future there may or may not be an expected return. Understanding is handicapped by an over-complex tax system and reams of small print and sub-clauses.

Competition exists but is limited – Most consumers find it difficult to know what to ask for and assess what they are getting, and it's difficult to recognise value.

The fundamental problem with Commission

The fundamental problem with the commission system is that there will always be a conflict of interests between the client who wants to maximise their returns, and the salesman who wants to maximise their earnings. This means placing your money into products that generate high commission which is taken from your fund and ultimately leads to you receiving lower returns. Within this environment mis-selling is inevitable.

The good news

The failings of the industry can be used to support millions of mis-selling claims. By allowing salesman to masquerade as true independent financial advisers, we have the opportunity to retrospectively measure the quality of the advice we received against the standards we would expect from professional advisers. Now let's look at how to expose this mis-selling.

c) Defining Mis-selling

A Layman's Definition

'You sold me something when you knew, or should have known, there was something better, which was more suited to my needs and circumstances.'

Whistle-blower Definition

Mis-selling can be defined as the failure of an adviser to provide a client with suitable advice, taking into account all their needs and circumstances, or a failure to provide all the information a competent adviser should provide to enable a client to make an informed choice.

The Financial Services Authority (FSA) Definition

The FSA does not provide a concise definition, although their Adviser Handbook implies that mis-selling has occurred if a recommendation does not meet the suitability rules, under the 'Know your customer' requirements.

> In order for you to assess whether you have been a victim of mis-selling we need to examine the process the adviser followed starting with basic questions about you and your finances, called 'Know your customer'.

Know your Customer

During the discussion process the adviser should have obtained details about your personal and financial circumstances. In the industry this is often referred to as the 'Fact Find', and contains hard and soft facts.

Hard facts – Relate to known financial facts, such as the amount borrowed, for how long and at what interest rate.

Soft facts – Relate to your lifestyle, the motivators behind those historical financial decisions and how they will affect future financial decisions. An example entry could read, 'Mr Porter has decided he cannot afford to fund a pension as he wants to help his daughter through medical school, and does not want her to be burdened with a student loan while she's concentrating on her studies'.

> Did the adviser use the knowledge about your personal needs to make recommendations that were suitable for someone in your circumstances? This is the key to proving mis-selling.

Suitability of the Advice

To provide advice that is suitable for your circumstances an adviser should have taken into account the following key areas:

Needs & Objectives – Did the adviser correctly identify and prioritise all your needs and objectives? For example did they ignore paying down a debt or addressing an important protection need, opting instead to go straight for a high commission investment?

Optimum Solution – Did the adviser fully examine all the options to meet your needs, comparing the relative advantages and disadvantages, including non-commission investments, gifting money and paying off debt?

Personal Tax Position – Did the adviser examine your current and likely future tax position? Did the advice you received complement your tax position? If not, would a different course of action have lead to a more favourable outcome?

Timings – Within what time-scales did you want to achieve your objectives? Was the plan set up to achieve your objectives within your time-scales? Did the adviser encourage you to extend them, (usually done to earn more commission), e.g. suggesting a personal pension retirement age greater than the state retirement age?

Access – What access did you want and when? Does the recommendation achieve this or have you been placed in a contract that allows access under restrictive conditions, such as the market valuation adjustments applied to with-profit contracts? Does the recommendation include unexplained exit and redemption penalties?

Charges – Were these fully disclosed and their affects discussed prior to the sale? Were these communicated in a clear and fair way? Have you subsequently found out the charges are higher than disclosed? For example quoted annual management charges fail to reflect the true cost of investing.

- Total lifetime charge – To ascertain the impact of the charges over the life of the contract, the adviser should have explained the 'Reduction In Yield' (See glossary). This figure can be found on your illustration.
- Total annual charge – This is the 'Total Expense Ratio' (See glossary). Sometimes salesmen only quote the fund manager's annual charge which may be 1.5%. Add in all the other costs and it can reach 3% a year. What were you told?
- What did your recommendation letter say? - It may have referred only to annual management charges which are misleading. If you had been told that the total annual charge was actually 2% to 3.5%, would you have thought this was reasonable? Would you have invested in such a contract?
- Regular Premiums – For regular premium Life Office contracts, were you aware most of your first year's contribution would disappear in commission and that this could have been **avoided** to reduce the overall charges?

Attitude to Risk – This is by far the greatest source of mis-understanding, as there is a mismatch between the consumer's and the adviser's understanding of risk.

> Risk is relative to your circumstances, so one size cannot fit all. The interpretation of 'Low-risk' can mean different things to different people. It is your capacity for risk – your ability to absorb and tolerate losses – that matters. The industry often fails to adopt working practices that evaluate the consequences of losses and how they may affect a client's lifestyle.

1. **Consumers Attitude to risk** – Table 1 reflects the average consumer's simple attitude to risk. Most consumers consider investments where losses could be greater than 50% as off the top of the risk scale.

Table 1. **Consumer Attitude to Risk**		
Risk Scale	**Description**	
0	No Risk	Will not lose my money, will have instant access, and receive a little interest each year
1	Risky	Could lose some (1% to 10%) of my money.
2	Very Risky	Could lose a lot of my money, (10% to 50%)

2. **Industry attitude to risk** – Instead of delving a little deeper and trying to understand your personal capacity for risk under different investment conditions, you may be shoe-horned into a 'Product Risk Box'. The industry risk box will define the investments they believe match your risk. Problems arise because most advisory firms interpretation of low-risk is different to that of the consumers and of the ombudsman.

Many use a risk scale like this:

Table 2. **Risk Profiler**		
Risk Scale		**Investment Categorisation**
0	NO Risk	Money Funds
1	Low-risk	Life Office With-profit Bonds
2	Low / Med Risk	Life Office Distribution Bonds
3	Med Risk	Life Office Equity Bonds
4	Med / High-risk	Life Office Smaller Companies and International Bonds
5	High-risk	Life Office Emerging Markets Bonds

As far as the consumer is concerned, 1 and 2 are 'risky' and everything above 2 is 'very risky'.

But salesmen often have a premeditated idea of what they will sell, based on the highest commission earner (usually a Life Office bond), so you will be steered in a certain direction.

Problems could be avoided by using individual risk-rated investments instead of generic products. Capacity for risk should be measured against the probability of achieving a financial objective.

How did the salesman evaluate risk? – If a risk assessment took place, were the following covered?

- Did the recommendation reflect your attitude to risk?
- Was the level of risk appropriate for someone in your circumstances?
- Do you have an aversion to risk and if so was this taken into account?
- What losses could you afford to sustain?
- What effect would those losses have on your lifestyle?
- Was the probability of loss examined taking into account historical data? Were you misled by the selective use of data? Was the data accurate and FSA compliant?
- Was a NO risk option evaluated (taking into account affordability and time-scales)?
- What would have been the consequences of choosing a risk-free option?
- Were different risk levels set for different objectives and did the recommendations take this into account?
- Were the contract risks fully explained?
- Were potential changes in the financial markets fully explained (such as interest rates and inflation), and their effect on your contract considered?
- Were the real risks played down / ignored?

Affordability – Could you afford to maintain the contract now and in the future, taking into account your current levels of income and expenditure and lifestyle changes that may affect affordability, such as illness, unemployment and retirement? Were the consequences of failing to maintain the contract fully explained?

Health – If you have a health condition was this taken into account?

Product Selection – Where a product was recommended, was it clearly the best or close to the best in its class? If not why not?

d) Proving Mis-selling

The Financial Ombudsman is likely to support your claim for mis-selling where an investigation rules that the advice was unsuitable because the adviser failed to follow the FSA *Conduct of Business Rules* as listed here:

Acted without fulfilling the 'Know Your Client Requirement' – This resulted in recommendations which did not fully take into account the financial implications of such advice for somebody in your circumstances.

Acted without Integrity – The adviser deliberately withheld or provided misleading information, such as recommending a high-commission product when a more suitable lower cost solution would have been preferable.

Acted Incompetently – The adviser did not possess the required level of expertise, lacking the knowledge and skills needed to provide you with the level of advice required. This leads to losses. Some work can only be undertaken by holders of certain qualifications. All pension transfer advisers must hold a G60 qualification or the equivalent.

Acted Negligently – The adviser failed to use their expertise and did not exercise due care and diligence when carrying out your instructions, which led to losses.

Acted without Authorisation – The firm / adviser acted without having the proper FSA authorisation to advise in a particular area.

Failed to Evaluate Risks – Most advisers talk about generic risks and the differences between various investment strategies. However they may have fallen short on several accounts:

- The adviser failed to explain fully and evaluate the specific risks associated with the recommendation, and relate them to the probability of achieving the objective. (This will catch most advisers out.)
- They failed to evaluate and apply differing risk assessments to different objectives over differing time-scales.
- They failed to talk about losses and the probability of loss.
- They failed to gauge your mental capacity to handle risk to identify the critical point at which your quality of life would suffer.
- They failed to gauge your capacity to absorb losses taking into account your other assets and whether this was tolerable.
- They failed to explain fully the underlying **Contract Risk**, such as the workings of with-profits funds, hedge funds or precipice bonds etc. (This will catch out many advisers.)
- They failed to explain fully market risks, such as how interest rates and inflation rates would affect their recommendation.
- They failed to explain risks in a manner that you could have been expected to understand. (This will catch out many advisers.)

The failure to address any combination of the above may have resulted in you receiving a recommendation which led to your money being exposed to unnecessary risks and losses. **The adviser must be able to produce evidence that you were able to understand and were prepared to accept the risks associated with the advice / product.** Financial loss caused by an under-performing fund is NOT an acceptable reason to make a complaint, but how and why you were recommended that fund could be.

TOPTIP

The key to making a successful complaint is to concentrate on:

Suitability – Did you receive the right advice for someone in your circumstances, with your needs and your risk profile?

Compliance – Did the adviser follow the rules and provide you with all the relevant mandatory information disclosing all the risks and charges AND can the adviser provide documentary evidence that this was the case?

The Adviser recommended inappropriate products/investments – This can usually be attributed to the decision to choose the highest commission product and takes two forms:

- Wrong Type of Product – e.g. the adviser recommended a taxable bond instead of a tax free ISA
- Wrong Product in its Class – e.g. the adviser recommended the highest charging bond, which paid the highest commission.

The adviser failed to provide you with all supporting documentation – In order to justify the sale, you should have been provided with certain documents. Any failure to do so invalidates the sale. You should have received a comprehensive 'Reasons Why' / suitability letter, the provider's current Terms of Business, an accurate product illustration and a 'Key Features' document, providing details of the product recommended.

Since 1st June 2005 the Initial Disclosure Document (IDD) must also be provided, (see Glossary) and a KEY FACTS 'Fees and commission' statement, providing details of charging methods.

The adviser failed to keep adequate compliant records of their advice – Some financial sales were poorly administered, because all parties involved were under pressure to pull in the business. Sometimes internal spot checks reveal shortfalls which are corrected by an addendum (which in some cases is a post-sale work of fiction). If the adviser has moved on, the company is left holding the baby, hoping the client does not complain and the FSA does not pick up on the lack of valid evidence needed to prove suitability.

Making a Complaint

a) Why You Must Complain

Many years ago I was given a tip by a director on how to manage bad debtors. He personally spoke to the proprietor of the company whose credit had reached its limit and said, 'I don't want any of your money; I just want my own.' He was successful at pulling in bad debts, and believed we should never be embarrassed about asking for what is rightfully ours. Complaints about financial services are no different. You must complain and claim back your own money for you and your family.

The onus is on you to find fault

Initially the onus is on you to prove that you were mis-sold by providing proof of negligent actions or omissions. Before the publication of this guide, making a successful complaint would have been very difficult as the power of knowledge was held by the salesman.

The salesman's failures shift power back to YOU

A salesman's poor record keeping will assist your claim. During compliance visits to advisory firms, the FSA continue to discover far-reaching breaches of compliance concerning the suitability of advice, with firms struggling to prove their case because of poor record keeping.

By taking your complaint to the FOS (see below) which mediates disputes, the salesman's company now has to prove they were compliant to a higher authority, so power shifts back to you. You MUST complain and be prepared to use this free service, as they will be able to uncover wrong-doing and pin a salesman down on your behalf. The next section explains how the ombudsman works, and then we move on to the crucial STEP by STEP guide to making a complaint.

The Financial Ombudsman Service (FOS)

Frequently Asked Questions

1 What is the Financial Ombudsman Service (FOS)?
2 What type of complaints does the FOS investigate?
3 Did I receive advice that I can complain about?
4 Are there any exclusions?
5 What else do I need to know about the service?
6 What are complaint time limits?
7 What time limits apply to endowment complaints?
8 How do I complain about advice received before 29 April 1988?

1. What is the Financial Ombudsman Service (FOS)?

The independent complaints handling service of the FS industry. It considers complaints impartially and makes a fair and balanced decision based on the facts. If it concludes that a firm acted wrongly and you lost out, the FOS will direct the firm to put things right, and restore you to the position you would have been in if things had not gone wrong.

2. What type of complaints does the FOS investigate?

The ombudsman will investigate complaints originating from the activities of firms authorised and regulated by the FSA. This includes complaints about the initial advice and ongoing service and covers:

Administration and Management – The provision of all services and products provided by financial institutions such as banks, building societies, insurance companies, Life Offices, investment companies, stockbrokers etc, where you may have been disadvantaged because of bad administration.

Investments – The sale of all investments from 29 April 1988.

Protection Policies WITH investment links – All contracts that result in some of your money being invested, as well as providing protection (such as whole-of-life plans, reviewable premium critical illness plans, endowments and flexile protection plans) from 29 April 1988.

Protection policies NO investment link – All pure protection contracts such as term assurances, income protection policies and critical illness purchased after 14 January 2005. Policies sold prior to this date are covered - providing the firm was covered by the General Insurance Standards Council (GISC).

Pensions – The sale of all pensions sold to the individual (not group company schemes) from 29 April 1988.

Mortgages – The sale of all mortgages sold from 31 October 2004. This includes equity release lifetime mortgages but not home reversion plans. Mortgages sold prior to this date are covered providing the firm was covered by the Mortgage Code Arbitration Scheme.

General Insurance – These are insurance contracts where there was no investment (such as car, household and travel insurance), but also include pure life insurance and loan protection insurance. All contracts purchased after 14 January 2005 are covered. Policies sold prior to this date are included providing the firm was covered by the GISC.

Note: It should be possible to complain to the FOS about advice received before 29 April 1988 if the firm that gave the advice was a bank, building society or Life Office, but not an independent financial adviser.

3. Did I receive advice that I can complain about?

There are three different types of advice which determine how your complaint is dealt with:

Full Advice – advice received either face to face, by phone or email that involves a recommendation to take action, which should be suitable to your needs and circumstances. If you subsequently discover that the advice was negligent or unsuitable you can complain about that advice.

Basic Advice Regime – This regime (introduced in April 2005) uses prescribed questions to identify your financial priorities and decide whether low-cost stakeholder (Sandler) products are suitable to meet your needs. It is possible to complain about unsuitable advice.

Non-advised (Execution-only) – You receive no advice and sign a declaration to say so. You cannot complain about the advice as none took place. Many 'non-advised' investments are completed after clients receive a personalised mailshot or newsletter. Some companies are rejecting complaint claims on these investments, saying they did not give direct advice - even though their personalised newsletters provided tacit recommendations to invest in low-risk products which would suit cautious investors, but which have subsequently proved false.

But it is the firm's responsibility to provide information included in a direct offer advertisement that is both 'adequate and fair'. *If a product carries a higher level of risk than that suggested in the literature, you still have grounds for complaint, even if you signed an execution-only declaration.*

4. Are there any exclusions?

Complaints about the administration of occupational pension schemes must go to the Pensions Regulator.

Complaints about some loans & credit may have to go to the Finance & Leasing Association Conciliation & Arbitration Scheme, but most high street lenders come under the FOS.

5. What else do I need to know about the service?

You must first try to resolve the problem directly with the firm before using the service. **The scheme is free to consumers.** You do not need the help of solicitors or complaint handling companies. Anyone can complain on your behalf, such as family and friends, provided you give them authority to do so. The service can also be used by small companies with a turnover of less than £1 million, charities with income of less £1 million, or trusts with net assets under £1 million.

The maximum award is **£100,000**.

Be prepared to wait 3 to 6 months for a decision. Some complicated pension transfer cases can take a year or more. But after a decision, compensation awards should be paid within 28 days.

If the FOS finds in your favour and you accept the decision within the specified time limit, then its award is binding on the firm. Their award will aim to put you back in the position you would have been if things had not gone wrong. The decision does not affect your legal rights (See below).

6. What are the complaint time limits?

There are two time limits within which you must work if the FOS is to investigate your complaint.

The time elapsing between receiving the advice and making the complaint.

These are covered by the FSA Dispute Resolution rules. If your complaint falls outside the time limits, then the firm is likely to ignore or reject your claim.

The original advice must have been received on or after 29 April 1988, when financial sales regulations were introduced. (See below for advice received before this date.)

The complaint must be made within 6 years from the date you were sold the product or service, OR the complaint must be made within 3 years from the date on which you became aware (or ought reasonably to have become aware) that you had cause for complaint. Slightly different time-scales and terms apply to endowment complaints.

The time elapsing between the firm's final response and referring the complaint to the FOS.

This must not exceed 6 months.

7. What time limits apply to Endowment Complaints?

From 1 June 2004 you must make a complaint within 3 years of receiving your first 'red' letter. You must also receive a letter from the endowment provider giving you 6 months notice that you will be time barred. A 'red' letter is one that tells you there is a high-risk that the policy will not pay the target sum. See endowment complaints Part Two, Chapter 12.

8. How do I Complain about Advice Received before 29 April 1988?

It is possible to complain to the FOS about advice received before 29 April 1988, providing the company is still authorised and if the firm has signed up to a voluntary agreement allowing investigations prior to this date. The FOS has ongoing jurisdiction over companies inherited as a consequence of its own formation (when other complaint handling bodies were amalgamated within the FOS). These include the large financial companies that gave direct advice:

* All building societies
* Most of the banks
* Most of the providers, e.g. Life Offices.

This excludes most IFAs. If not categorised above, a firm can simply ignore or reject your claim. At this stage you have NOT given up your legal rights, and providing the firm is still trading, you can seek legal advice and go to court. This pressure may result in the adviser volunteering to have the ombudsman investigate, or to settle out of court.

b) STEP by STEP Guide on How to Complain

{STEP 1} Make a 'Formal Complaint'

This can be done by phone or in writing.

We recommend you write so you can outline your complaint in greater detail. Use the example letters in Part 3.

Who do I address the complaint letter to? – You need to write to the firm's compliance officer. Phone to ask for their name and to check the company is still in business and operating from the same address.
Alternatively you can phone the FSA Helpline 0845 606 1234, for the name and address of the individual, or check on the their web-site www.fsa.gov.uk/register/

What if the firm that advised me has gone or changed name? Contact the FSA helpline above, who will complete a search of authorised firms and advisers to check whether they have changed name or been taken over, and which firm is responsible for the advice given.

What if the firm that advised me has gone bust? You need to contact the Financial Services Compensation Scheme (FSCS). Details are to be found in Chapter 8 Compensation.

Use recorded delivery to post your complaint – in case you need to prove when the correspondence was sent. Most good companies will acknowledge receipt within 3 to 5 working days.

Request a copy of your personal file – This is your right under the Data Protection Act 1998 to access the personal data held by the firm on computer or in manual files. It will help you assess the legitimacy of information that the firm may provide to the ombudsman in defence of their position. They have the right to charge a fee of £10 and must provide the information within 40 days of your request. If you have any problems obtaining this information contact the Information Commissions Office Helpline 01625 545 740, or their web-site www.informationcommissioner.gov.uk

These actions prove that you are organised and mean business. Making a complaint by phone does not have the same impact. If you do make a formal complaint by phone, make sure you take all the details of the individual who logs your complaint.

{STEP 2} Prepare for Possible Outcomes

Firm's Response

The adviser's firm must get back to you with an answer within 8 weeks of receiving your complaint. Possible outcomes are:

- They accept liability and agree to pay out compensation.
- They reject your complaint.
- They fail to respond within the 8 week time frame.

If the company agrees to pay compensation, do not drop your guard. Some do not always follow the accepted compensation guidelines. If the final offer does not state that it conforms to FSA guidelines, or if the figures look unreasonable then you can still contact the FOS.

Beware of Firms that use these tactics

Ask for more time – Sometimes firms acknowledge your complaint and ask for more time. In my experience there is nothing to be gained by giving them more time to reject your complaint. I have known firms keep consumers hanging on for months, which raises expectations only to have their hopes dashed.

Play the pressure game – This is part of a psychological battle to test your resolve. You must understand that a compliance department exists to protect the profits of the firm, and not to mediate on your behalf. Compliance departments are well schooled in the art of rejection, and armed with a set of standard paragraphs (sometimes written by lawyers) to put pressure on you to capitulate.

Intimidation works – Complaint statistics show that if you delay and fob someone off for long enough – they tend to give up. Firms know this and try to intimidate consumers by sending out automatic rejection letters to most complainants, knowing some will give up at the first hurdle. Some consumers write again and receive another rejection letter two months later. Before you know it, 6 months have passed and you have NOTHING to show for your efforts. There's no doubt the firms' tactics work as people just give up which can save the firm thousands in compensation. Consider the fact that for those who have had their complaints rejected and go on to have their case adjudicated by the ombudsman, 50% are upheld. If we apply this percentage to all the rejected complainants that do NOT use the Ombudsman Service, then thousands of people are losing out. If firms played fair and objectively assessed complaints this figure would be much lower, probably less than 10%.

Take Control

Decide today that you will NOT be bullied, and that you are going to dictate how the complaint is handled. All our sample letters in Part 3 end with a clear instruction that if you have not received a positive response within 8 weeks you will take your complaint to the FOS. This is NON-negotiable and proves you mean business.

For every complaint that goes to the FOS, the adviser's firm must pay a £360 case-handling fee. (The first two complaints in any financial year are free.) You can see why they make it difficult for you to succeed. **It has been rumoured that some companies pay their compliance employees bonuses based on how many complaint letters they successfully reject. Our aim is to reduce their bonuses to zero.**

{STEP 3} Complain to the Financial Ombudsman Service (FOS)

The firm's final response will set out its decision and will include details about your rights of referral to the FOS.

If you are unhappy with the outcome, OR the firm has not responded within 8 weeks, you must take your complaint to the FOS who will mediate and carry out an impartial investigation to resolve the dispute, examining what is reasonable and fair from both points of view.

You have **6 months** from the date of the final rejection letter to contact the FOS, but they have discretion to waive time limits because of extraneous circumstances such as ill health or a bereavement.

Obtain Complaint Form

Obtain a complaint form by phoning the FOS helpline 0845 080 1800 or download from www.financialombudsmanservice.co.uk and click on 'How to complain'. This can be completed on-screen, but you will have to print and post as the FOS requires your hand-written signature.

If your complaint relates to an endowment mortgage, you must complete a further form, the Endowment Mortgage Questionnaire. Its completion is covered in Chapter 12 Endowment Mortgage Complaints.

Complete the FOS Complaint Form

The form is four pages long but fairly straightforward. A simple case should not take longer than 30 minutes to complete. However if you do need assistance you can phone the helpline on 0845 080 1800 and speak to an adviser.

Page 1 – Requires basic facts, names and addresses

Page 2 – In answer to the question 'When did you realise there might be a problem?' you must enter a date within the 3 years before making the complaint.

Page 3 – Question 1 asks for a brief summary of your complaint. Keep your answer simple and let the FOS do a thorough job working through the problems as detailed in the complaint letters, for example:

'*I am making a formal complaint about the advice I received to (invest/purchase/buy) a (product/service) which I believe was unsuitable because the adviser failed to evaluate fully all the options and make a recommendation best suited to my needs and circumstances'. These are detailed in the letter sent to the firm dated ...., a copy of which is attached.*

Question 2 asks you to list in date order the events which are relevant to your complaint, including all contacts from your initial meetings with the adviser right up to their response to your complaint.

Page 4 – Requires your permission to proceed and your signature.

Return to the FOS

Attach copies of your original complaint and the firm's response. As this guide may trigger an avalanche of complaints, I recommend you use recorded post to ensure your complaint is received and logged. They will acknowledge receipt, but expect to wait at least 3 to 6 months for a full response.

{STEP 4} Receive Response – Ask for a Review

If you are not happy about any aspects of the FOS reply you should contact the adjudicator assigned to your case and ask for clarification. If matters still remain unresolved, you can ask for a review conducted by the FOS. Their final decision is the end of the complaints-handling process, and happens in only 1 in 10 cases.

{STEP 5} Go to Court

If the FOS rejects your claim, or you believe the final compensation award is insufficient, then your only choice is to go to court. Time bars do apply, depending on the nature of the complaint. You usually have up to 15 years from the date you received advice about a product or service to go to court.

You have two options:

Use the Small Claims Court

If you decide to go to court this is the preferred route for small investors as firms are usually shocked into a response and put under immediate pressure. Larger companies will feel obliged to dispatch a senior manager and solicitor to your part of Britain, which will begin to cost them time and money. All of a sudden you may find they will try and settle the case out of court. Contact your local court and obtain a claims information pack. Details on the Small Claims Court are to be found at the end of the Chapter.

You pay a fixed court fee up to £120 and your compensation is limited to £5,000 in England & Wales, £2,000 in Northern Ireland and £750 in Scotland, per claim. (See TOP TIP.) When the court meets it is informal, all parties sit around a table and you present your case, and do not need a solicitor. If you win you can claim back all your costs, but if you lose the judge may require you to pay the other side's costs. However you can make it clear when you submit your claim that you would like to proceed on the basis of not having to pay costs. This will not be binding on the judge but will be taken into account.

Use the County Court (Sheriff Court in Scotland)

This would be the option of last resort and should only be considered if your claim is substantial, far greater than the £100,000 awarded by the FOS. Although you can still represent yourself, you may want to employ a solicitor, and if you lose, you will need the means to cover the defendant's legal costs.

{STEP 6} Apply to the Financial Service Compensation Scheme (FSCS)

If the firm that gave you advice has gone out of business and cannot address your complaint, you can seek compensation from the FSCS. (See next chapter.)

TOPTIP

With mis-selling claims involving Life Office contracts (which make up the majority of complaints), it is theoretically possible to make numerous claims about the advice received on the same contract. This is possible because many life contracts are a cluster of 10 to 100 small policies. This is the case with most Life Office pensions, bonds and whole-of-life protection plans.

For example, you could make a claim for the maximum £5,000 based on contracts 1 to 5 and then repeat the process until your compensation is paid in full. Yes this could be a laborious process, but the bad PR and rising costs should encourage the firm to come to its senses early and offer a full settlement.

Compensation

Compensation should restore you to the position you would have had if things had not gone wrong. If the firm admits liability within 8 weeks of making a complaint and pays out within 28 days of admitting liability, then you can consider yourself lucky. Unfortunately complaints are rarely this simple. You will probably have to take your claim to the Financial Ombudsman Service (FOS).

The FOS award for mis-selling also includes compensation for damage to reputation, distress and inconvenience.

The firm fails to make compensation payment – If the advisory firm fails to pay compensation within the 28 days specified by the FOS, then you will have to go to the County Court to enforce the award. If the award is small, they will use the small claims track. If larger it will go to the county court.

Some firms will go bust – An escalation in compensation claims could result in some smaller firms being forced into liquidation. This is because Professional Indemnity Insurers who insure financial services businesses insist that firms pay an excess equivalent to the first £500, £1,000, £5,000 (or even the first £10,000) of a claim. Pension transfer mis-selling claims carry high excesses which will test the solvency of most small IFAs responsible for this advice.

Lodge your complaint early – Complain as soon as possible and get to the front of the compensation queue while a firm is still solvent. If declared bankrupt, your compensation payment could be restricted.

Devious deeds – Unfortunately a trend is developing whereby firms may be engineering insolvency or business break-ups that leave all liabilities with one part of the business. As they are unlikely to be able to honour future claims, consumers will be forced to look for compensation from the FSCS.

Taxation of Compensation – If compensation is paid in excess of the return of premiums paid or capital invested, the excess is classed as interest and is liable to income tax. Pension compensation is excluded from taxation.

Financial Services Compensation Scheme

This is the statutory scheme of last resort for customers to claim losses against authorised financial services firms. Before you can lodge a complaint with the FSCS you must go through the following steps:

{STEP 1}

You must first make every effort to contact the firm that advised you. If they have moved, contact the FSA and check whether they are still trading – phone 0845 606 1234, or log on to www.fsa.gov.uk/register/ and enter the firm's details.

{STEP 2}

If they are un-traceable or no longer trading, you must contact the FSCS who will decide whether the firm in question is 'in default'. In most cases this is because the firm is insolvent, and it could take several months to establish.

Financial Services Compensation Scheme (FSCS)
7th Floor, Lloyds Chambers
1 Portsoken Street
London, E1 8BN
Tel: 020 7892 7300
www.fscs.org.uk

{STEP 3}

It is possible to find out whether the firm that advised you is already in default, because they failed to meet a previous claim, by phoning the FSCS or at www.fscs.org.uk/consumer/Default_information/. Here you will find a pdf file listing all companies that are in default. The published list dated March 2005 was 44 pages long.

The FSCS provides a very helpful free pamphlet 'A Guide to the work of the FSCS', which describes exactly what is covered.

In summary, the scheme can be used under the following scenarios:

The Adviser is insolvent – If you received wrongful advice from a firm of advisers that became insolvent, you can claim compensation. If the business was arranged on an execution-only basis (you did not receive advice), you cannot usually make a claim.

Product Provider is insolvent – If you bought a product from a provider that cannot pay its claims or honour its investment promises, you can make a claim for compensation whether you bought direct, or through an adviser, with or without advice.

Key Points

The FSCS will pay compensation if:

- the firm is unable to pay claims against it, usually because of insolvency - 'being in default'
- advice on investment was received after 28 April 1988
- a mortgage was arranged on or after 31 October 2004
- a general insurance policy was arranged on or after 14 January 2005.

Compensation is limited (See table 1), and claims are currently taking around 9 months to process. You must phone the FSCS on 020 7892 7300 to explain your position. They will send you the forms and questionnaire relevant to your complaint.

Table 1. Maximum Compensation Payable

Type of Claim	Compensation	Maximum Amount
Deposit (Bank, Building Society, Credit Union)	100% of first £2,000 90% of the next £33,000	£31,700
Investment Business (Advice about Unit Trusts, OEICs, shares etc)	100% of first £30,000 90% of the next £20,000	£48,000
Mortgages	100% of first £30,000 90% of the next £20,000	£48,000
Long-term Insurance (Policies provided by Life Offices)	100% of first £2,000 90% of the remainder of the claim	Unlimited
Compulsory General Insurance (Car, employer's liability insurance, etc)	100% of Claim	Unlimited
Non-Compulsory General Insurance (House, holiday etc)	100% of first £2,000 90% of the remainder of the claim & unused premiums	Unlimited

Claims are covered by a levy payable by all financial services firms. The good firms are becoming increasingly frustrated by the need to pay increasing amounts to cover rogue traders who can walk away from the industry with impunity. This is having the effect of driving up industry costs.

List of Complaints

Summary of Main Complaints

This is a summary of the main complaints and is not exhaustive. With the help of the public our web-site will add further suggestions to the list.

Administration & General

A firm may have done one or more of the following:

- Failed to carry out your instructions which led to losses
- Took so long to process your request that your investment suffered a loss of interest / investment growth
- Applied excessive or unexpected charges
- Failed to bring to your attention a strict condition in the contract
- Failed to give you adequate notice about changes to the contract
- Provided inaccurate point-of-sale information describing investments as low-risk which subsequently proved to be false, so their literature was neither 'adequate nor fair'
- Broke confidentiality rules which led to an upheaval in your personal life
- Failed to carry out regular reviews even though there was a client specific agreement to do so, especially when the adviser was still receiving ongoing trail commission to cover ongoing advice.

Endowment Mortgages

These are Life Office savings plans used to repay interest-only mortgages.

- The adviser failed to evaluate fully (or did not mention) other options such as repayment mortgages. Best advice dictates you should repay your debts as soon as possible.
- The adviser did not explain that this was predominantly a stock market investment and you could end up with a shortfall. This was far too risky for someone with little or no previous experience of investing.
- The adviser failed to discuss options if the plan failed to provide a fund sufficient to pay off the mortgage. The adviser advised there may be a surplus at maturity sufficient to go on holiday or buy a car.
- The maturity date was set at many years after retirement age, when you could not afford to continue paying premiums.
- The endowment was due to mature after the mortgage ceases, the consequences of which were not made clear at the time.
- You were advised to cease and surrender an old plan and start one larger policy.

- You received undertakings or guarantees in writing that the fund would be sufficient to pay off your mortgage.
- The adviser failed to point out the strict condition of the contract that the plan could not guarantee to pay off the mortgage.
- You were advised that endowment mortgages were cheaper than repayment mortgages.
- <u>Customers with some investment experience</u> should have been advised to opt for a low-cost Personal Equity Plan (PEP) or Individual Savings Plan (ISA) and low-cost term assurance life cover, if required.
- <u>Customers who wanted an interest-only mortgage</u> should have been advised to opt for a low-cost Personal Equity Plan (PEP) or Individual Savings Plan (ISA) and low-cost term assurance life cover, if required.

Equity Release Plans (Lifetime Mortgages)

This is a mortgage against your home where there are no loan repayments, and compound interest accumulates each year, increasing your debt.

- There was insufficient analysis comparing the charges and tax advantages, and the risks of all other income options. Trading down could have been an option if the true impact of a spiralling debt on your wealth had been disclosed.
- You were advised to release a single lump sum as opposed to the lower-risk, lower-cost monthly income option. For this reason alone nearly all lump sum equity release plans are mis-sold.
- Extra funds were released over and above those required to meet immediate income needs. That money was invested in investments with little or no chance of providing the net returns needed to cover the interest payments.
- The equity could have been released in tranches to save interest charges.
- The adviser did not take into account how a lump sum would affect your state benefits which have since reduced.
- The adviser did not take into account your health and lifestyle needs, and the possible problems surrounding moves to sheltered accommodation and long-term care.
- The product was recommended as a way of mitigating inheritance tax by using the money to feed other investments. These are often high-risk strategies with a high probability of failure and are unsuitable for most ordinary investors. They generate high commission.
- You were advised to take out a plan to fund home improvements without being informed of the numerous charity and public organisations that may have been able to help.

Investments – General

Corporate Bond Funds – You were advised this was low-risk, but now find that both the capital and income are at risk. (These funds buy debts that offer a fixed interest. As the interest is fixed, the value of the bond will rise and fall so the actual yield moves in line with the market rates set by the Bank of England.) If the possibility and risks of capital loss were not made clear, you have a case for mis-selling.

High Income Corporate Bond Funds – You were not informed that a 'high income fund' invests in junk bonds which are high-risk investments with a greater possibility of default, which could lead or have led to capital losses. If the risks associated with junk bonds were not explained, you have grounds for complaint.

Corporate Bond Funds – General – You were misled into believing the yield (income) quoted was just the interest and your capital would remain intact. This is incorrect as the headline yield quoted is often the 'running yield' (which does not take into account capital depreciation). The salesman omitted to give any prominence to the more accurate redemption yield, which takes into account capital depreciation. This lower yield may, after charges, be no better than a cash deposit account.

Precipice Bonds – You were misled into purchasing what you thought was a low-risk product to provide above average income, but now find your money has been exposed to unacceptable capital losses that were not fully explained. The investment was wrongly categorised as low-risk.

Venture Capital Trusts (VCTs) – You were recommended a VCT on the back of income tax relief. The risks associated with share discounts were not fully disclosed. You discover that having reached the first exit point, the shares trade at such a low value compared to their quoted net asset value that all tax relief is wiped out and leaves you with losses. The adviser failed to draw the importance of this valuation to your attention.

Life Insurance Bonds

These are lump sum investments offered by Life Offices.

- You were advised to invest in a high-charging bond when lower-charging, tax-efficient investment options were available. For smaller funds this is easy to prove if your £7,000 annual ISA allowance had not been used. For larger funds the adviser ignored lower charging and lower taxed unit trust / investment trust portfolios and national savings.
- You were advised that you could take 5% per year tax-free. This is false – You can actually make capital withdrawals of 5% of your original investment and defer the higher rate income tax liability.
- You were advised to take a bond to produce income. It is often implied that the income is an amount over and above the capital growth. This is misleading and incorrect, as you are making capital withdrawals. During periods of poor investment returns this will lead to capital erosion. This is not made clear to investors.
- The adviser recommended a switch from one bond to another bond with a different provider. This is 'Product Churning' and is still widely used as a method of generating commission. Advisers ignored the option of free internal switches. Spurious reasons for switching include:
  - To reset the tax clock by securing higher 5% income withdrawals (false, see above).
  - To place in trust – Most Life Offices provide in-house trusts, which probably includes your current provider.
  - To switch to another individual – this can be achieved by maintaining your existing bond and completing an assignment form.
  - Better performance – difficult to prove.
- You were advised to invest and then strip out 5% each year to feed another policy, effectively doubling the salesman's commission, by using one commission-generating bond to start another commission-generating plan.
- You were advised to invest the money instead of repaying debts or loans, where there was no realistic prospect that the net investment returns from the bond, after charges, would be sufficient to cover the interest payments of the loan.
- You were advised to switch the money from no or low-risk investments into bond funds which the salesman classed as low-risk, but were not.

Life & Protection Policies

General

The policy was not written in trust and resulted in an unnecessary inheritance tax bill.

Whole-of-life Plans

- You were sold a high-cost whole-of-life plan when a low-cost term assurance plan was more suitable.
- You were not made aware that the contract had reviewable premiums or the effect of those premium increases on your finances. Future affordability was not discussed, nor were the consequences of not being able to afford the increases. This is particularly important to those close to retirement, or pensioners who would never be able to afford huge increases in premiums (sometimes doubling or tripling) while living on a fixed income.
- You were not made aware that the contract had reviewable premiums and the extent to which the life cover would decrease if you could not afford those premiums. If your life cover has been reduced, this may have caused an upheaval in your planning which on death will leave your next of kin exposed to costs or tax. The possibility of the life cover reducing was not disclosed. If this had been known, an alternative strategy would have been adopted.
- You were aware of the reviewable premiums but the salesman gave you no indication of the likely escalation levels. The information was given no particular prominence and the significance of the reviews was not explained in detail.
- You were advised to switch from a policy with guaranteed premiums to a lower charging policy with reviewable premiums, without the consequences of the loss of guarantees being taken into account.

Critical Illness Plans

- You were advised to switch to a lower charging plan and now find the cover is inferior, as the contract contains reviewable premiums, while applying far stricter definitions as to what constitutes a critical illness, especially the definition of a heart attack, cancer and 'total and permanent disability'.
- You were not made aware that the contract had reviewable premiums.
- The salesman failed to evaluate the whole market and consider guaranteed rates.

Loans

- You were advised to take out a loan which you could not afford and which you had no realistic chance of repaying.
- The loan repayments automatically included repayment protection insurance which was not fully disclosed, and which greatly increased the total loan repayments.
- You were misled into taking the loan as the quoted loan interest rate was too low and excluded additional costs such as repayment insurance and other administration charges which would have resulted in a higher overall interest rate (known as the Annual Percentage Rate).

Mortgages

- An interest-only mortgage was recommended to be repaid using an investment plan that was far too risky for someone in your circumstances.
- The redemption fees were not fully disclosed, or have been increased disproportionately to the work involved in transferring deeds. (They are being used by lenders as client retention tools which are unreasonable and in Whistle-blower's opinion break the FSA's 'Treating Your Customers Fairly' initiative.)
- The adviser ignored long-term deals that result in tracking the Bank of England base-rate, only recommending short deals to enable the adviser to have another go at re-mortgaging in 2 or 3 years time.

Pensions

- As a basic-rate tax-payer you were wrongly advised to fund a personal pension which was unsuitable, as there were no tax advantages to funding a pension instead of a PEP / ISA. Disadvantages were caused by the loss of access to the money and the potential loss of state benefits.
- You were advised to contract out of the State Second Pension Scheme (which is effectively a guaranteed final salary pension related to your earnings), and transfer your rebates to a money purchase pension scheme where there are no guarantees and your income is at the mercy of the markets.
- You were wrongly advised to fund a Free Standing Additional Voluntary Contribution Scheme without a completing a comprehensive evaluation of the company-sponsored AVC scheme.
- You were wrongly advised to transfer your pension from a final salary pension scheme to a personal pension scheme.

Retirement – Annuity Purchase

Many of these complaints emanate from advice received from tied advisers who want you to buy from the one company they represent.

- You were not informed of your right to use the open market and seek an annuity quote from the whole marketplace.
- You were advised to exercise your right to an open market option at the expense of using a guaranteed annuity rate / mortality rate offered by your pension provider.
- The adviser failed to recommend an annuity that adequately catered for the surviving spouse.
- The adviser failed to complete and evaluate a health questionnaire and uncover aspects of lifestyle that may have resulted in enhanced annuity providing a lifetime income of 10% to 20% more.

Retirement – Income Drawdown Schemes

- You were recommended a Drawdown scheme without a full and thorough examination of current annuity rates and future trends, especially on improving mortality.
- You were recommended a Drawdown scheme without a full and thorough examination of phased retirement schemes where your pension fund is drawn in tranches and your required annual income comprises tax-free cash and an annuity / small Drawdown scheme.

- You were recommended a Drawdown plan which was not regularly reviewed in a comprehensive way and resulted in you following a strategy that is too risky for someone in your circumstances.

Savings Plans

- If you were advised to fund a savings plans before having fully used your annual ISA / PEP allowance (currently £7,000 each year), then you have been the victim of mis-selling. PEPs (the forerunner to ISAs) were introduced in January 1987 so everyone who started a non-ISA / PEP savings scheme since 29 April 1988 can complain. This especially applies to those with 10-year savings plans. You can still complain even if the plan has matured.
- The adviser failed to take into account the company sponsored Save as You Earn Plans (SAYE) offered by your employer.
- You were advised to take out 10-year a plan because it provided extra life cover, even though you had no need or no dependants.

Stockbroking

Complaints against stockbrokers will not be upheld on the grounds of poor performance. Performance cannot be regulated, but administration can. If the stockbroker failed to follow your instructions or failed to manage the portfolio in line with your risk profile, as measured at the outset, you should make a claim.

With Profits Investments

- The with-profits proposition is built on the flawed premise, 'you can have your cake and eat it.' Investors are promised (or it is implied) that they will receive higher returns than a cash deposit account, from a fund that contains shares but without market risks – a contradiction in terms.
- The salesman failed to explain how with-profits funds actually work, instead skipped through a generic explanation of smoothing and averaging. He failed to draw attention to the strict policy conditions that could affect the returns and the conditions under which withdrawals could be made without penalty.
- The salesman did not explain how 'Market Value Adjustments' (MVA) (also called 'Market Value Reductions' (MVR)) can affect the surrender value of the policy, if the policy did not run its full term. There was no explanation of the MVA free exit points. While there was a technical explanation attached to an appendix its importance to your circumstances was not made clear at the time. The MVA should have been given more prominence.
- The salesman did not explain the inherent risks of with-profits such as the level of equity content and how this changes regardless of attitude to risk, the embedded liabilities within the fund, the need to pay out to policies with contractual guarantees, or the opaque nature of the system which leaves it open to manipulation and abuse. It is totally unsuited to inexperienced investors.
- The salesman did not fully explain the with-profits bonus system and how Life Offices can arbitrarily cancel, reduce or withhold bonuses.
- The adviser was aware that you would need access to your money and failed to explain fully the early surrender penalties, especially the Market Value Adjustment (MVA).
- With-profits investments are often sold as low-risk. They are not low-risk.

10 Pensions Complaints

a) Commission Manipulation

Who is Affected – Anyone who bought a pension plan from 1970 to 2000.

Pension contracts set up between 1970 and April 2000 often had very high charges which are extremely hard to decipher. If you trawl through your pension statements and find either 'initial' or 'capital' unit values, then you are the owner of such a policy. You were probably sold this without the full details being disclosed.

Your contract may have been set up in such a way as to deliberately hike up commission, with your lump sum contributions classed as regular premiums which pay much higher commission. (The problem extends to all those who were not aware of the charges, whether paid regularly or by lump sums.)

How manipulation worked.

If you invest a lump sum, commission payable to the salesman will be 3% to 5% of your premium paid. But if the salesman can persuade you to split the lump sum and invest it over a period of two years to 'take advantage of market conditions,' then it can be classed as a regular contribution. Then 100% + of your first year's premium will be taken from your policy as commission.

In some cases salesmen did not even inform clients there was a difference, and just pushed everything through as a regular contribution.

The salesman and the Life Office probably disguised how the charges were taken out, or you would never have agreed to it. The whole process is built on covering up the truth, with the salesman misleading you about front-end charges, and the Life Office producing statements that are not a true reflection of the amount of money you have invested.

Basically two charges are taken from regular premium contracts.

Initial Charge – All contributions are subject to an initial investment charge of 5% known as the bid/offer spread. So for every £1,000 invested 5% is deducted, leaving £950.

Capital / Initial Units Charge – With regular contribution contracts the first two years' premiums are invested in capital / initial units subject to an annual management charge of 6%. The contract small print states that the Life Office can take this annual charge regardless of whether contributions continue or not.

Note: Single premium investments are only liable to the initial charge.

LEARNING POINT

It is vital to understand the severity of this charge.

CASE STUDY

I was asked to advise Alison Fielder who had paid two £1,000 premiums into a regular premium contract. The provider, a Life Office, had the right to take an annual management charge of 6% per year for the whole term of her 25-year contract. This large amount of commission had resulted in the low transfer values in Table 1.

Table 1. Effect of Capital/Initial unit charges on an investment of £1,000 per year after 2 years

Years to Retirement	Invested	Transfer Value	Commission / Charges	% of your money taken
20	£2,000	£450	£1,550	77.5%
25	£2,000	£290	£1,710	85.5%
30	£2,000	£180	£1,820	91%

As Alison said to me, 'In any other scenario, if someone took 85.5% of my money, I'd call it robbery.'

The Cover-up

The Life Office must do its best to cover up the true size of the commission and send you statements that show £1,900 invested. This is just a notional value.

Number-crunchers at the Life Office have worked out a plan to hide the true facts from you for the next 25 years. By assuming the fund will grow at 7% a year they know that (after charges) your investment of £1,900 will only grow at 1% year (7% growth – 6% annual charge = 1% growth). They calculate the value of £1,900 growing at 1% over 25 years will be £2,500. With this knowledge they discount back from the value after 25 years (£2,500) and calculate roughly what they need to set aside today to cover this liability. Using a 7% growth rate, they calculate a need to set aside £460.

The figures are explained in Table 2 which compares the 'facts' on your statement 'A', to the actual amount invested 'B', to what should have been 'C' – if the salesman had truly invested all your money as a lump sum.

Table 2. The Commission Con

Investment & Growth Rate	10 Years	15 Years	20 Years	25 Years
A. YOUR STATEMENT SAYS Shows £1,900 invested Effective growth only 1% per year	£2,154	£2,253	£2,380	£2,500
B. THE ACTUAL AMOUNT Only £460 is invested Growth @ 7% per year	£904	£1,269	£1,780	£2,500
C. WHAT SHOULD HAVE BEEN £1,900 invested Growth @ 7% per year	£3,616	£5,071	£7,112	£9,975

Over 25 years they need only invest £460 growing at 7% per year to match the £1,900 growing at 1% per year. If you retire at any time other than the 25-year term you will receive a lower figure. After 10 years you examine your statement and find it is still hovering around the same level.

The reason why your money is not growing, is because most of it does not exist. The statements are a ruse to disguise the costs.

If your money had been invested as a lump sum, at the end of 25 years you would have nearly 300% more! This Life Office has made an unlawful gain by removing your money from your investment without your knowledge, using deceitful methods to cover its tracks.

The commission just keeps on growing

To compound the problem, every increase in your premiums is also invested in these units and subject to the same high charges.

CASE STUDY

A victim of this was Gary Hinton who came to me after investing £5,000 in 1982 in what he believed was a single premium contract, but which the salesman had classed as a regular premium contract. A couple of years later Gary invested a further £10,000 as a single contribution, again classed as a regular premium by the salesman and subject to the same high commission costs which were taken from the increase. When I looked at the facts I discovered that Gary's fund could have been almost 300% bigger if he had not been misled by the salesman.

The huge differences in fund returns are revealed in Table 3, which compares the returns after charges between the high-commission regular premium contract A and the lower-charging lump-sum contract B. Don't wait 25 years like Gary. Complain now. If you have retired and taken benefits you can still complain.

Table 3. Growth comparison Between a Regular Premium Contract and a Lump Sum Contract after 25 YEARS

PLAN	Year	Contribution	Amount invested after Deductions	Return 7% annual growth
Option A. Regular Premiums	Year 1	£5,000	£1,000	£5,427
	Year 3	£10,000	£2,500	£11,851
	TOTAL	£15,000	£3,500	£17,278
Option B. Lump Sums	Year 1	£5,000	£4,750	£25,780
	Year 3	£10,000	£9,500	£45,035
	TOTAL	£15,000	£14,250	£70,815
THE DIFFERENCE Between A. & B.	A. Regular	B. Lump Sum	Difference (£)	Difference (%)
Total Invested	£3,500	£14,250	£10,750	307%
Return	£17,278	£70,815	£53,537	£310%

Automatic Commission Increases

Many contracts were set up with the premiums automatically increasing every anniversary by 5%, allowing the salesman to collect the extra commission automatically, without having to get out of bed.

These discredited charging methods were widely used by unit-linked Life Offices in the 1970's, '80's and '90's as a means of hiding from consumers the true nature of their costs. They went to extreme lengths to disguise these costs. Salesmen went to any length, fair or foul, to extract money out of people's bank accounts. If you hold or held policies issued by Allied Dunbar, now Zurich Financial Services, Abbey Life and numerous other Life Offices, it would be in your interest to dig out the policy documents and consider a complaint.

A lot of the blame for unethical methods must fall to the salesmen, but ultimate responsibility should be apportioned to the line managers for condoning such practices, and to senior management and board directors for creating and marketing contracts that led to these practices. Everyone knew what was going on.

Even the FSA and its predecessors knew what was going on, their 'persistency records' detailed the contracts that ceased early, and as you would expect, high-commission Life Offices were consistently the worst offenders.

Call a spade a spade!

In any other walk of life, if a consumer buys a service for £10,000 expecting to have £500 taken out in charges, but unbeknown to them the contract is set up in a way that deducts more than £7,000 in commission and charges, it would be classed as fraud. In the Financial Services industry it's just good salesmanship. Do you want to let them get away with it?

Consumers Need Justice

The FSA and its predecessors should have resolved this mess years ago. The deceit happened on such a vast scale that every possible means of pressure should have been brought to bear on firms to compensate consumers. But much of the advice was given prior to August 1988 when the 1986 Financial Services Act became fully functional, and IFAs are not liable to pay compensation for advice given before that date. But if you dealt with the Life Office or bank direct you should still be able to claim.

Even now it is not too late to help the victims. Unfortunately the FSA has so many complaints outstanding from so many mis-selling scandals that it doesn't want to add to its woes. Whistle-blower believes that the level of damage done to ordinary citizens is so great that the Office of Fair Trading (OFT) and even the Crown Prosecution Service (CPS) should be involved.

To date the industry has got away with it. Is that right?

Compensation Claim

If you feel you may have been one of these victims, you need to write a complaint letter based on Letter 1 in Part 3.

Don't be put off from complaining because you feel the sums are small. Over 20 years they would compound to considerable sums, as shown in Table 3 above. And don't worry about remembering all the facts. Life Office record-keeping was poor during the boom years, and they're unlikely to be able to produce compliant evidence to defend their position. When your complaint is resolved, your pension fund should be increased to the value it would have reached if you had invested as a series of lump sums.

b) Basic-rate Tax-payers & Personal Pensions

Who is Affected – Most basic-rate tax-payers who have bought personal pensions and stakeholder pensions.

The majority of people plan for their retirement by funding pension plans. For those lucky enough to work for the government or a generous employer, you may be a member of a final salary pension scheme. However as more employers close their schemes, there has been an increase in the number of people who have to make their own provision using personal pension plans (PPP).

A PPP is portable and is for one person. Contributions are eligible for tax relief and grow in a tax efficient fund. When you draw the benefits, 25% of your fund can be taken as a tax-free lump sum with the remainder of your money used to provide a taxable income, usually through the purchase of an annuity. An annuity is an investment which exchanges your pension fund for an income for life, at a rate fixed on the date of purchase.

There are many different types, all categorised as personal pensions. Initially the self-employed used plans called retirement annuities, which were replaced by personal pensions in 1988 and complemented by stakeholder pensions in 2001. Millions have signed up, but have they been well advised?

Unfortunately the nation is currently being misled by a government and life assurance industry who jointly spin the great pensions myth that the income tax relief on their pension contributions is the best way for the majority to fund retirement income. **This is not necessarily the case and here are the reasons why:**

1. Pensions & Tax Relief

Do you recognise this scenario? A salesman tells you he can instantly increase the value of your money by 28%, by investing your contributions into a plan that benefits from tax relief. For every £78 invested in a pension plan the tax-man adds £22, equivalent to the basic-rate tax. (22/78 x 100 = 28%). 'Great', you say, 'I'll have one.' You sign and the salesman disappears.

The perceived tax advantages of pensions can be illusory. The tax relief available on pension contributions at the front end is eroded when you come to draw income benefits at retirement, which are **taxable** (see Table 1). If you want to save for retirement, there is NO advantage for a basic-rate tax-payer to fund a pension plan. (The only exception is the entitlement to certain 'tax credits' which is covered in point 3.)

As an alternative, the salesman could have recommended that you invest your money into a tax-efficient ISA (or before 6th April 1999 a PEP or TESSA). In an ISA you receive no tax relief on your contributions **but** your money benefits from the same tax-efficient growth as a pension fund, and **when you withdraw your money there is no income tax to pay.**

CASE STUDY

Ten years ago Rob Benson was a 47 year-old self-employed window cleaner. Just after he had taken on a junior to increase his business, he bumped into an old mate Tony who was working as an IFA. Tony said it was never too late to start a pension and told Rob to get cracking.

Rob was impressed by the 11% per annum illustrations that placed him on target for a six figure fund at retirement. Tony persuaded him to invest £100 a month into a PPP, which involved considerable personal sacrifice. But Tony reassured him he couldn't lose, especially considering the tax relief. Contributions automatically increased at 10% per year, which became unaffordable when Rob strained his back and was forced to lay off his assistant and stop contributions. He still works occasionally but can't afford to save. He tried to contact Tony for advice but he had moved away.

I only met Rob recently and asked to see his pension statement. As I went through the paperwork, I saw a history of mis-selling and bad advice. Rob was shocked to discover his transfer value of £19,400 even though he'd invested £19,150 over ten years. I could see Rob had never been informed that:

* most of his first two years premiums would disappear in commission and costs
* every time contributions increased, commission would deplete the increase for the next 2 years
* the provider's pension funds were delivering below average returns
* he couldn't access his money, and was unable to top up his income during the period of injury
* if he'd been advised to invest his net income into a good PEP, contributions of around £15,000 would now have accumulated into a tax-free, accessible fund of c.£22,000
* he may have been better off spending the money as he's now in danger of losing state benefits just because he made an effort to save.

Table 1 compares the retirement income you could receive from a pension to an ISA.

Table 1. Income Tax Relief - Pension Vs ISA

Pre-Retirement				
	Pensions		**ISAs**	
Event	Basic-rate Tax-payer 22%	Higher Rate Tax-payer 40%	Basic-rate Tax-payer 22%	Higher Rate Tax-payer 40%
£1,000 Gross earnings	£1,000	£1,000	£1,000	£1,000
Income Tax Payable	£220	£400	£220	£400
Net Investment before Tax relief	£780	£600	£780	£600
Gross Investment after Pension Tax relief	£1,000	£1,000	N.A.	N.A.
(1.) Fund Value after 30 Annual Contributions, Growth 5% per annum	£69,761 (100%)	£69,761 (100%)	£54,413 (78%)	£41,856 (60%)
Retirement Income				
5% Income Withdrawals Gross before Tax	£3,488	£3,488	£2,720	£2,093
(2.) After Income Tax	£2,720	£2,093	£2,720	£2,093

Notes: Table 1 compares a gross investment of £1,000 p.a. into a pension with a net investment of £780 for a basic-rate taxpayer (after 22% income tax), and £600 for a higher rate taxpayer (after 40% income tax), into an ISA. Both plans grow at 5% p.a. for a period of 30 years.

At the end of the investment term, the pension funds are higher by a percentage equal to the tax relief received on the contributions (22% for a basic-rate tax-payer, and 40% for a higher rate tax-payer).

Income withdrawals from a pension fund are taxable. If your personal tax rate remains the same, your gross income is reduced to provide a net income identical to that provided by the ISA, where income withdrawals are tax-free.

At retirement you can withdraw a tax-free lump sum of 25% of the pension fund value. Table 2 examines the effect on a pensioner's income if the tax-free cash is withdrawn and placed in a taxed deposit account. Lower net interest payments will result in the pension providing a similar income to that of the ISA. The remaining 75% is usually used to purchase an annuity – a guaranteed income for life, but it denies the investor access to their capital. Too much depends on the type of annuity purchased, and the rates applicable at retirement date, which are always changing.

Table 2. Pension Income

Retirement Funds		Income p.a. Gross 5%	Income p.a. Net
(1) Cash Fund 25%	£17,440	£872	£680
(2) Remainder 75%	£53,321	£2616	£2,040
TOTAL	£69,761	£3,488	£2,720
ISA Income			
(3) Fund	£54,413	£2,720	£2,720

Notes. Cash / cash ISA invested in a deposit account providing an income of 5% p.a. gross.

The remainder is used to purchase an annuity, which in this case provides a level income of 5% p.a. with no reduction on first death, so a surviving partner receives the same amount. On second death the annuity ceases and the estate receives nothing. (There may be circumstances where an older annuitant could secure a higher income. Rates continually fluctuate which makes retirement planning for those with personal pensions a bit of a lottery.)

Based on these figures there is no advantage for a basic-rate tax-payer to choose a pension over an ISA to provide retirement income.

2.Tax-efficient / Tax-free Savings Plans

Having proved that pension tax relief is a red herring and pensions provide basic-rate tax-payers with no real tax advantages, we must now examine whether there was an option to invest in more suitable alternatives.

Tax-free savings plans have been available since January 1987 when PEPs were introduced to encourage investment in shares and share funds. These were complemented by TESSAs introduced in 1990 to encourage saving into tax-free deposit accounts. From April 1999 no new contributions were allowed into these plans as they were superseded by ISAs.

For ISAs, PEPs and TESSAs you receive no tax relief on your investment, but your money benefits from the same tax-efficient growth as a pension fund. There is no income tax to pay when money is withdrawn from an ISA or PEP.

The amount that could be invested is detailed in Table 3. If your pension contributions were within these limits, you may want to question why the alternatives were not mentioned by your adviser.

Table 3. **Tax-efficient / Tax-free Savings Plans**	
General PEPs	**Amount Per Year**
01.01.87 to 31.12.87	£2,400
01.01.88 to 31.12.88	£3,000
01.01.89 to 31.12.89	£3,000
01.01.90 to 05.04.90	£4,800
06.04.90 to 05.04.99	£6,000
TESSAs	Amount
06.04.90 to 05.04.99	Max £9,000 invested over 5 years
ISAs	Amount Per Year
06.04.99 to Present	£7,000

Between 2 July 1997 to 5 April 2004, ISA and PEP funds were able to claim back the 10% tax credit on dividends (which pension were unable to do), which made ISA/PEP funds more tax-efficient than pension funds. Today no pension or ISA funds can reclaim the 10% tax credit. This is why all-share ISAs must now be described as 'tax-efficient' as they are not tax-free.

What this means is that if you were advised to fund a pension without being informed about the availability of these tax-efficient alternatives, you were probably misled.

3. Tax Credits

The waters have been muddied by the introduction of tax credits which are paid to top up gross income. Their effect on your pension funding depends on how much you can afford to contribute, making it worthwhile for those who can afford to build a large fund (in excess of £100,000), and a waste of money for those whose efforts result in a fund of less than £50,000.

The Benefits – There are two tax credits that affect your pension funding.

Child Tax Credit – was introduced on 6 April 2003 as a payment to support families with children in education up to age18, but reduces if your joint gross income is above £13,910 (2005/06).

Working Tax Credit – was introduced on 6 April 2003 to top up the income of all low paid workers and reduces when your gross income exceeds £5,220 (2005/06).

How Benefits Reduce – It is common for working families with children still at school to claim both credits, but the Government gives with one hand and takes away with the other. For every extra pound you earn, the benefit reduces by 37p, eventually reducing to £545 per year, as demonstrated in Table 4. The bottom line in the table provides the most important figure being the maximum amount of gross income a couple can receive before the majority of the benefit is lost.

Table 4. **Child & Working Tax Credit Benefits 2005/ 06**			
Joint Gross Annual Income	**1 Child**	**2 Children**	**3 Children**
£10,500	£4,160	£5,855	£7,550
£15,000	£2,495	£4,190	£5,885
£20,000	£645	£2,340	£4,035
£25,000	£545	£545	£2,185
Approximate Gross Income where benefit reduces to £545 p.a.	£20,300	£24,900	£29,500

How benefits Increase – The benefit can increase if you make a pension contribution, as the tax credit calculation states that any contribution to an approved pension scheme (personal pension or employer's scheme) reduces your gross income by an equal amount. So for every extra gross pound invested in your pension, your benefit increases by 37p. This is good news as you have already received 22p in tax relief on your pension contribution, and when added to the 37p it costs you only 41p to get £1 invested in your pension (£1 - 22p - 37p = 41p). On the face of it this looks a great deal, but when you retire it may not be – because of the Pension Tax Credit.

Pension Tax Credit – This is a means-tested benefit payable to those in retirement on a low income, who from age 60 are guaranteed to receive the pension credit guarantee, regardless of what they have saved.

Benefit 2005/06	**Single**	**Couple**
Pension credit Guarantee	£109.45 / week	£167.05 / week
State Pension	£82.05 / week	£131.20 / week
Extra Income	£27.40 / week	£35.85 / week

Pension Tax Credit Reduced by Private Pensions – The income derived from your private pension reduces your eligibility to the pension credit guarantee. To match the extra income of £35.85 per week provided by the pension guarantee, a couple would need a pension fund at retirement of £40,000 to £50,000. So while the couple only contributed £410 for every £1,000 invested in their pension, that £410 may have been wasted if the income it generates displaces the income the state would have given them if they had done nothing.

The situation is further complicated by an individual's entitlement to the state second pension and other savings. This is a very complicated subject, and such detail will not be needed when you make a complaint for the ombudsman to assess.

Tax Credit Winners & Losers

Winners – If you can afford to make sufficient contributions to build up a fund in excess of £100,000 to give you an income well above state benefits, AND most of your contributions result in a tax credit award of 37p for every £1 contributed, then a personal pension taken out since April 2003 may be the best way to fund your retirement.

Losers – Many people have been advised to start personal pensions which are not in their interest because:

- The contributions were made before April 2003.
- They are not entitled to tax credits because they have no children, children have left school, or their income is too high.
- They are unlikely to be able to build up a fund sufficiently large to provide an income greater than the pension credit guarantee.

If you are a basic rate tax-payer and recognise yourself in this list, then you need to think seriously about complaining with a view to reclaiming direct control of your money.

Tax Credit Summary – In reality the pension credit system has created a disincentive for low earners to save for retirement. Most people bringing up a family on less than £20,000 a year do not think about paying into a pension as there is no surplus income after paying rent, mortgage and living expenses. If they do save a little, their efforts are cancelled out because the state reduces their retirement benefits. However if you're able to afford to make a contribution, then claim back the money on the pension plan you were mis-sold in the 1980's and '90's and reinvest on preferential terms today by increasing you entitlement to tax credits.

4. You are Denied Access

Before you retire you are denied access to 100% of your fund. When you retire you have access to a tax-free lump sum of 25%, and the remaining 75% must be used to provide you with an income for life. The earliest date you can draw benefits is age 50, which will increase to age 55 from 2010.

Is it reasonable to advise people with limited means to invest in a way that denies them access to such a large part of their savings, especially if they need access in an emergency?

5. Restrictive Retirement Income

At the point of sale, the salesman's pitch focuses on building up as big a fund as possible. Little or no time is spent talking about how the money will be released at retirement. Pensions are a two-stage process: building up a fund, and taking benefits. By concentrating on the former the job is only half done. At retirement you must use 75% of your fund to buy an annuity or draw-down plan which provides an income for the rest of your life. You cannot withdraw 100% of the fund.

Salesmen tend to skirt around this negative aspect of pensions, and most people are subsequently shocked to learn about the restrictions placed on how the money will be drip-fed to them over their lifetime.

6. Loss of Inheritance

After purchasing an annuity on death (or second death if a joint life annuity), your fund is usually lost and your next of kin are likely to receive nothing.

7. Pension Mortgages

Some investors have been advised to buy personal pension plans to produce tax-free cash at retirement to repay the outstanding loan capital on an interest-only mortgage. With an interest-only mortgage, the value of the original loan never reduces and only the interest is repaid. Such plans carry a high-risk of failure that the fund will be too small to repay the loan within the client's timescales. As with endowments, many investors will experience pension shortfalls and will not be able to repay their mortgage. They need to be reviewed and assessed for suitability. Advisers often failed to disclose and evaluate all the extra risks.

Alternative Mortgages – Did the adviser discuss and compare the interest-only costs with a repayment mortgage to enable you to make an informed choice?

Investment Risk – Was it implied (written or orally) that the pension would provide sufficient tax-free cash to repay the mortgage? Were you comfortable with stock market investments? Were you made aware there could be a shortfall? In the event of a shortfall were you advised of your options?

Alternative Investments – If you definitely wanted an interest-only mortgage, did the adviser evaluate and compare the benefits and charges with tax-efficient PEPs / ISAs? As the premiums were higher, the commission was much higher than that paid on PEPs / ISAs. You were disadvantaged as less of your money was invested.

High Premiums & Affordability – The tax-free cash only amounts to 25% of the fund, which requires very high annual premiums to achieve the sum required. A £100,000 mortgage would require a pension fund of £400,000. Over 25 years, assuming a growth rate of 7% you would need to save £6,000 per year. Lenders often insisted on a 25% safety-margin which would require premiums of £7,500 per annum. To tempt investors, plans were often started with a lower premium which increased by 5% to 10 % per year. Often no account was taken of ongoing affordability. This will enable you to make a successful mis-selling claim.

Lack of Access – Was it made clear that you would have to wait until age 50 to access the tax-free cash to repay the mortgage? (This is the earliest age you can draw money from a pension, increasing to age 55 from 2010.) If not, you have a claim.

Lack of Cash – Was it made clear that if there is a cash shortfall, you may be forced to continue working well beyond the expected mortgage redemption date, incurring extra mortgage interest charges? Did the adviser discuss how the plan would cope with a shortfall?

Lack of Flexibility – The plans are inflexible and do not take into account unforeseen lifestyle changes such as redundancy or illness. Generally it was poor advice to recommend such a long-term commitment that could become inappropriate due to a change in circumstances beyond the investor's control.

8. Health & Longevity

If your family has a history of longevity below the national average, you may have special concerns about access and investment. Were these issues taken into account, and was the restricted access explained? If not, you have a case for complaint.

9. Charges

If you were a basic-rate tax-payer at the time you started your pension, and likely to remain so in retirement, taking into account all taxes, denied access, the numerous lifestyle disadvantages, and onerous rules, there are no advantages for a basic-rate tax-payer to fund a pension. So why did the salesman recommend a pension?

The answer, because commission distorted the advice. Paying off your debt pays no commission at all, and regular saving PEPs and ISAs pay very small amounts of commission compared to that paid on pensions in the 1980's and '90's .

A pension plan taken out in the 1980's or '90's would have generated the first year's premium in commission (taken out of your plan), with more commission paid on every subsequent increase in premiums. This incentive was so appealing that salesmen chose the pension option, regardless of your real needs.

Proving Mis-selling

Fortunately the widespread myth perpetuated by advisers *'that the compounding effects of pension tax relief makes pensions a sure winner'* has been exposed as false. If an adviser failed to carry out this analysis they could not possibly have understood your long-term needs and provide you with the best advice. Very few will produce documentation in their favour, which will help your claim.

Fortunately the widespread error of advisers (who talked up the compounding effects of pension tax relief, suggesting your investments would give you significantly more than tax-efficient ISAs), has been exposed. It can now be used as evidence in support of your complaint that the advice you received was unsuitable for someone with your needs and circumstances.

Taking into account the lack of tax advantages and access restrictions, any objective observer would conclude that a personal pension plan is unsuitable for most basic-rate tax-payers, especially those who were recommended pensions prior to the introduction of the child and working tax credit in April 2003. Unfortunately the government is likely to have a different view.

This problem affects millions of people and their families. EVERYONE who is a basic-rate tax-payer, and who was advised to take out a personal or stakeholder pension has potentially been mis-sold that pension, and should complain and have their case investigated. This especially applies to low earners who took out plans and will lose state benefits.

Compensation Claim

When your complaint is resolved, you should have access to net assets as great as you would have had if 100% of your pension contributions had been invested in tax-efficient PEPs or ISAs. As the Inland Revenue will not allow backdated investments into PEPs & ISAs, the compensation should also take into account the considerable loss of <u>future</u> tax advantages had that money been invested in a PEP or ISA. Use complaint Letter 2.

If you are complaining about a personal pension used to support a pension mortgage, use Letter 3.

If the ombudsman recommends that an alternative course of action was preferable to a pension, it can order that the pension is rescinded (cancelled) and your net premiums rebated.

Potentially the industry's bill will be sky high, so we can expect a tough fight. They will look to the government to get them off the hook. We have yet to see whether the supposedly independent ombudsman can resist political interference, as pressure will be applied by the Treasury who will be anxious to prevent a precedent for this type of complaint.

The government will fear being implicated in any mis-selling scandal as it backed numerous advertising campaigns persuading basic-rate tax-payers to invest in personal pensions, which may not have been in their best interests.

TOPTIP

Do not transfer or cease contributions to any old pension before checking to see if there are any guaranteed benefits. See this chapter section e.

c) Contracting Out Personal Pension Schemes

Who is Affected – Anyone who contracted out of the state earnings related pension scheme / second pension.

Background

Since April 1988 people have been encouraged to contract out of the State Earnings Related Pension Scheme (SERPS), now renamed the State Second Pension (S2P). This is the additional pension you receive on top of your basic state pension. Only employed people can contract out.

If you opt to contract out, a proportion of your national insurance contributions are rebated to an appropriate Personal Pension Plan (PPP), administered by a Life Office. The government of the day tinkers with the levels of rebate, making the final benefit difficult to calculate. In my experience the standard of advice to contract out has been atrocious, and in many cases based on faulty premises such as, 'You'll be better off as we'll make your money work harder....You'll gain control of your money....You shouldn't trust the government to pay you anything in the future.' The sales pitch usually ends, 'And it costs you nothing – you don't even have to make a contribution.'

All these points are appealing but INCORRECT. There is every reason to believe that many people will be worse off because they contracted out, and in some cases much worse off.

Reasons why advice is unsuitable

It all went wrong because advisers and companies failed to evaluate all the risks involved in contracting out from SERPS. Most advisers lacked the knowledge to understand the full implications of their advice.

In effect you were advised to transfer your rights from a final salary scheme underwritten by the state (which guarantees to pay you an income linked to your earnings), to a money purchase scheme where there are no guarantees, and you're at the mercy of the markets.

Primary Reason for Contracting In

The volume of evidence produced by several actuaries suggests that if you contract out you are unlikely to get a better pension than that provided by the state. On any reasonable set of actuarial assumptions, the current rebates do not adequately reflect the effect of administration costs on investment returns in a low inflation environment and the cost of increased life expectancy. For this reason you should contract back in.

Actuaries believe that in order to receive a higher contracted out pension than a contracted-in state pension, you would need to achieve a compound annual real return of around 3% above inflation. If inflation is 3% you would need a total return of 6%. If we accept that the risk-free return from cash is around 4%, then after charges you would have to take investment risks to achieve a return of 7% to 7.5%. This is only achievable by investing a proportion of the rebate in shares.

All investments that involve risk should deliver a higher return to help compensate for the extra risk you are taking. As the rebates are insufficient to provide a better pension than that provided by the state *without taking excessive stock market risks* then the majority should be in the state system. **There is NO financial incentive to contract out.**

The government has effectively joined employers in off-loading some of its future liabilities by moving you into a money purchase arrangement today.

As more and more private sector schemes close their doors to final salary schemes, the opportunities for ordinary workers to secure guaranteed income in retirement is dwindling. In our opinion it is important for all employees to acquire as much guaranteed retirement income as possible. If you are contracted out then you need a pretty good personal reason to remain so. If not you should contract back in.

Reasons for Contracting Out

Contracting out could appeal if you want to manage your money, or if you can afford to take a risk. It allows you to take benefits earlier – Since 6 April 2006 you can draw your benefits from age 50, (it was previously 60). And after April 2006, under the new simplification rules, you should be able to take 25% of tax-free cash from your fund.

Perhaps you don't trust the government to keep its pension promises. And if you're married and die prior to retirement, all of the fund must be used to purchase a spouse's annuity. If you're not married, 100% is paid tax-free to your next of kin. If you had remained contracted-in, the State would provide your spouse with 50% of your SERPS pension to date. If unmarried you get nothing.

CASE STUDY

42 year old Jenni McNiven is employed as a Graphics Designer in a UK Engineering firm. Eight years ago she was persuaded by the company pensions adviser that she would be better off at retirement if she contracted out of SERPS and took out a PPP which could run alongside the firm's new money purchase scheme. She was ineligible to join the final salary scheme which had closed to employees who joined after 1997.

The adviser persuaded Jenni that she was still young enough for her fund to grow well, and she was impressed by the prospect of higher retirement income over which she would also have some control.

But the fund is invested in a with-profits fund and to date has performed at an annual return of only 3.4%, a full 4% below the 7.5% needed to ensure Jenni's fund will out-perform SERPS. It now seems likely that when she hopes to retire in 18 years time, her fund will provide an annual income of around £2,500. If she'd remained in SERPS she would be guaranteed around £5,200 p.a. and index-linked into the bargain. Jenni has recently decided to contract back into SERPS.

Contracting Out – Summary

If you remain contracted-in all your working life and acquire the maximum S2P of 20% of band earnings between £4,264 and £32,760 (2005/06) you will receive £5,700 index linked income from age 65 with a 50% spouses pension. To achieve the same income from your contracted out rebates you will need a fund of around £140,000. How is your fund shaping up?

In reality no one knows who will be better off in the future, BUT if you contract out you are taking on risks that may not been fully explained by advisers. There is sufficient evidence to believe that many people will be worse off for contracting out. If you feel the complexities of the state pension and the risks of investment were inadequately explained, and you believe the risks do not reflect your personal attitude to risk, then you may have grounds for complaint.

Whistle-blower believes contracting out in all forms has been a disaster, because the complexity of the system makes it impossible for the public to understand the benefits and deflects resources away from the fundamental need for an adequate state pension.

Compensation Claim

A claim is likely to be successful because salesmen failed to assess fully the risk of a lower retirement income and whether this was suitable for someone in your circumstances, with your risk profile. They may also have failed to keep adequate records justifying the advice as suitable. This gives you the opportunity to have your case investigated.

A claim should be made either to restore your state benefits or have compensation added to your PPP. Use complaint Letter 4.

To avoid the industry being engulfed with contracting out complaints, the government should do the decent thing and offer a 'contracting back in' amnesty where no blame is apportioned. Everyone who has contracted out could repay their contracted-out fund to the Treasury and have the right to an additional state pension restored. The government must knows it is on a sticky wicket, as the problems surrounding final salary pension transfers that led to the first personal pension review could equally be applied to the contracting out scandal.

d) Free Standing Additional Voluntary Contribution Schemes (FSAVCs)

Who is Affected – Anyone who has purchased a FSAVC, especially basic-rate tax-payers.

Background

These pensions were widely sold in the 1980s and '90s as a way of topping up employers occupational pension scheme benefits. All members of occupational pension schemes are currently able to fund a maximum of 15% of their earnings into the main scheme. Most schemes are set up with employees contributing 5%, and they can volunteer to fund a further 10% into an AVC scheme. By law the employer must offer the employee access to an AVC operated by the company. As an alternative the employee can invest their unused contribution allowance into a FSAVC operated by Life Offices.

The FSA recognises there may be a mis-selling problem. They authorised a review of all FSAVCs sold between 28 April 1988 and 15 August 1999 where the employer offered a matched contributions OR an added years scheme. It was a good start, but failed to address whether savers were misled into high-charging contracts, instead of paying off debt or using low-cost alternatives. Where advisory firms are found to be at fault, compensation is based on the costs of reinstatement into the AVC scheme. This is not good enough.

If your contract has been reviewed and you accepted compensation you will have been asked to sign a disclaimer that will prevent you from making a further complaint, regardless of whether it relates to a separate issue.

Why salesmen recommended FSAVCs

Salesmen pushed FSAVCs because they paid high commission and never explored the alternatives fully. They often dismissed the company AVC option (even though most offered better value) as they do not pay commission. They used flawed reasoning:

Portability – FSAVCs are portable, you can continue to fund them if you move to a new employer. You cannot move an AVC scheme. This is true, but:

- You are just as likely to move to an employer where you are not eligible to fund a FSAVC, because they have no scheme or operate a group personal pension.
- As commission is taken out in the early years, if you move you're left with a plan with very little invested.
- Portability is not an issue for employees who are likely to work for the same employer for many years, such as doctors in the NHS.

Early Retirement Funding – FSAVCs allow you to fund early retirement without telling your employer. This is flawed because the charges are usually much higher than the company AVC, so you're less likely to achieve an equivalent fund return, and unable to retire early.

Fund choice – FSAVCs offer more fund choice. This is usually true but very few people exercise that choice. If fund choice is important to you, an alternative ISA would be more appropriate.

The reasons why FSAVCs are unsuitable

Tax – The vital question is whether it was in your interests as a basic-rate tax-payer to be advised to fund either an AVC or FSAVC, instead of a tax-efficient TESSA / PEP / ISA, which is more appropriate and far more flexible, (available from 1987). The perceived tax advantages of pensions are illusory, as the tax relief available on pension contributions at the front end is offset when you draw benefits at the back end, which are taxable. From a tax perspective there is no advantage for a basic-rate tax-payer to have a pension. See personal pensions and basic-rate tax relief Part Two Chapter 10 b.

ISAs and PEPs offer the same tax-efficient growth as pensions without denying you access. Before 6 April 2004 ISA / PEP funds benefited from being able to claim back the tax credit on dividends which pension were unable to do, which made them MUCH more tax-efficient than pension funds.

Company AVC Charges – Many salesmen failed to mention that usually a company AVC charging structure is far superior. Most company sponsored AVC schemes have very low charges that can make all the difference to your fund return, as demonstrated by the figures in Table 1 which compare the returns on an investment of £1,000 p.a. over 20 years, growing at 7% gross. Funding a high-commission FSAVC contract is likely to lead to an investment shortfall of around 20% or more.

Table 1. **AVC Vs FSAVC Cost Comparison**		
Charge	AVC	FSAVC
Initial Commission	Nil	50 % to 120% of first years premium
Initial Investment Charge	1%	5%
Annual Management Charge	1%	1.5%
Effect of charges on £1,000	£38,602 (20% MORE!)	£32,175

AVC Enhanced Terms – Many salesmen also failed to check whether the company AVC scheme offered enhanced terms in the form of matched contributions, (You pay 1% extra and the company pays 1% extra) or enhanced annuities. (Here the annuity rates are better than those available in the general market.) Did the salesman obtain illustrations to compare and evaluate benefits?

Added Years – Salesmen often failed to mention that the employee may have the option of buying added years in the main scheme which provide a guaranteed income in retirement, far superior to the money purchase alternative. Again NHS employees may have grounds for complaint.

Employer Save as You Earn (SAYE) Schemes – Large employers sometimes offer employee savings schemes that run for 3, 5 or 7 years, with a maximum monthly contribution of £250 which can be used to buy shares in the company on preferential terms. If shares are not bought, then the money is returned with interest tax-free. For some people this can be far more beneficial than a pension. Was this option available to you and was it evaluated?

Loss of Pension Credit – This is a means-tested benefit payable to those aged 60 and above on a low income. If the income derived from the personal pension reduces your eligibility to the pension credit, you are liable to an effective taxation rate of 40%.

Stakeholder Personal Pension Plans – Since April 2001 it has been possible for a basic-rate tax-payer with gross earnings of £30,000 or less, who is a member of a company occupational scheme to fund a low-cost stakeholder pension too. This is called 'concurrency'. If you were sold a FSAVC after this date, you definitely have grounds for complaint.

Compensation Claim

In our opinion, 100% of the FSAVC plans sold to basic-rate tax-payers have been mis-sold, and probably up to 90% of the remainder. If you have one then you should think seriously about stopping contributions and complaining. Your complaint should demand compensation based on the loss to you for not using your disposable income to fund an ISA, cash or share-based depending on risk outlook, OR to pay off debt. Use FSAVC Complaints Letter 5.

e) Transfers from Pensions with Guaranteed Annuity Rates (GARs) / Guaranteed Mortality Rates (GMR)

Who is Affected – If you were encouraged to transfer an old pension scheme to a new plan without due consideration of the contractual guaranteed benefits, then you have grounds for complaint.

Guaranteed Annuity Rates (GAR)

These formed part of many with-profits pension contracts, both Retirement Annuity Pensions and Executive Pensions, written between 1970 and 1988. They guarantee to pay you an annuity based on rates at the time which were much higher than those available today, making this a very valuable benefit.

For example a person retiring today age 65 with a pension fund of £100,000 may be lucky to secure a single life, level annuity retirement income of £7,000 (7%) per year, where the GAR may provide an income of £11,000 (11%) per year, an income of over 50% more!

Guaranteed Mortality Rates (GMR)

These were included by some unit-linked pension contracts offered by Life Offices between 1972 and 1988, to compete with their with-profit counterparts. These plans provide a pension based on the mortality rates that existed at the time. Even 35 years ago, actuaries did not expect us to live as long as we do today. Now Life Offices have lowered annuity rates as they expect to pay out an income for a longer period. While not as good as a GAR, this benefit should result in uplift in your income of around 20% over the current market rates.

Poor Advice

Many advisers recommended transfers out using such reasons as improving fund performance, simplifying your plans by consolidating under one roof, and improving death benefits. They failed, through ignorance or incompetence, to pick up on the importance of GARs and GMRs. Some Life Offices are not immune from criticism, they understood the potential cost of these guarantees and sought to reduce their ongoing liabilities by lobbying policyholders to switch to more 'flexible contracts,' in the hope of reducing their ongoing GAR liabilities.

In the 1990's one Life Office ran an ongoing campaign of transferring and consolidating Retirement Annuity Pensions (RAPs), based on the death benefits shortfall. That company was Equitable Life which was undone by its own GARs. While the board press-ganged members into accepting the compromise agreement with a 17.5% uplift in pension fund values (for plans which had guarantees), they cannot remove your right to complain about transfer advice. They are still liable for the advice they gave you to transfer from other Life Offices to the Equitable Life.

Proving advice to transfer was unsuitable

If you have been advised / encouraged to transfer a GAR or GMR policy to another pension without a full transfer analysis taking place, then you have grounds for a complaint. If you still have your old policy document, check to see if the contract contained any retirement guarantees. If not, you could check the details with your old provider. Use the transfer enquiry Letter 6 to obtain details. If you can't find the document, or if the old transferring Life Office refuse to co-operate, then assume that your contract did have GAR / GMR benefits and send the GAR / GMR complaint Letter 7.

Compensation Claim

If you have lost the benefits of a GAR contract, you need to make a claim for compensation based on the likely GAR / GMR income at retirement at normal retirement age taking into account the maximum premiums payable to secure the guarantees AND the actual retirement income based on the value of the transferred fund and current annuity rates.

We estimate that every £1,000 of lost income should result in a compensation payment of at least £15,000.

f) Final Salary Opt Outs and Transfers

Who is Affected

Opt Outs - You were advised to opt out of your company pension scheme and fund a personal pension, forgoing all employer contributions and benefits.

Final Salary Pension Transfers – You were advised to transfer your deferred pension benefit to a personal arrangement.

Opt Outs

Anyone who was advised to opt out of an employer-sponsored final salary pension scheme and switch personal contributions to a Personal Pension Plan (PPP) was badly advised. As both the regulator and industry recognise this as mis-selling, you do not have to prove negligence.

The one issue you need to keep an eye on is your eligibility to join the scheme. Some advisers are defending their positions by claiming that at the time they recommended a PPP, you were not eligible to join the scheme. This may have been the case for a period, but a window to join is likely to have arisen. It should not be used to excuse the advice that you subsequently received which may have been unsuitable for someone in your circumstances and therefore mis-selling. Two scenarios were common:

Temporarily not eligible to join the employer's scheme on the grounds of service / age. The adviser failed to point out that funding a PPP for a short period of time prior to joining the employer's scheme was totally unsuitable for someone in your circumstances as most of the first two years' premiums disappeared in commission. In some cases investors were persuaded to maintain a PPP and not join the employer's scheme, even though they were now eligible. This advice was negligent.

Temporarily not eligible to join the employer's scheme on the grounds of short-term contract. At the time you were advised, you were on a short-term contract, but it was likely to be made permanent, which the adviser was made aware of. On becoming permanent you would be eligible to join the scheme. The adviser played on the nature of short-term contracts advising that it was not in your interests to join the scheme because if you left within two years, you would only be entitled to a refund of your contributions (plus money market interest). The adviser may also have suggested the possibility that you would continue in short-term contracts for the foreseeable future, and needed a flexible plan. The adviser probably failed to point out that funding of a regular PPP for a short period of time was totally unsuitable for someone in your circumstances as most of the first two years' premiums disappeared in commission.

The adviser probably failed to point out that if you had joined the company scheme and left within two years, your returned personal contributions could have been invested into a PPP as a lump sum.

The adviser probably failed to point out that if you had joined the company scheme and left after two years, you would have a deferred guaranteed pension benefit, including employer's contributions that is unlikely to be bettered by any personal pension.

For all these reasons, you should have been advised to save your money in anticipation of joining the employer scheme by investing in a tax-efficient PEP/ ISA.

Use complaint Letter 8 to claim your compensation.

Transfers

Employees who leave an employer are often entitled to a deferred pension benefit. Some people collect a string of deferred benefits never knowing what they are really worth. The salesman has a solution to this and may talk about 'unlocking your frozen pension,' implying that he can make your dead money work for you. This is nonsense as your deferred pension benefit is not frozen but guaranteed to grow by inflation up to a maximum of 5% each year.

Salesmen have also encouraged people to transfer by trading on people's fears of becoming another Maxwell victim. (Robert Maxwell misappropriated funds from The Mirror Group Newspaper Pension Scheme in the 1990's, leaving members with depleted pensions.) Such scandals have been used to encourage people to transfer their pensions away from good schemes. Once you said 'yes', the salesmen would transfer pension funds to either a PPP or Section 32 Transfer Plans.

Briefly the differences are, personal pensions have few investment restrictions and Section 32 Transfer plans must guarantee to protect a part of the transfer which will restrict the investment choices.

FSA Transfer Review

The FSA has been on this case since 1994. They ordered a review of all pension transfer and opt-out business conducted between 29 April 1988 and 30 June 1994 where investors were sold personal pensions. Phase 1 of the review started in 1994 by automatically reviewing high-priority cases including people who had retired or were close to retirement. All other investors formed part of phase 2 and should have received a questionnaire asking whether they wanted their case reviewed. They should have returned the questionnaire to the transferring firm by 31 March 2000. For schemes set up after this date there is also a strong possibility you were misled. The subject is so complex that all who have been advised to transfer should complain and ask for their case to be reviewed by the ombudsman (FOS). (Contact details Part Two, Chapter 7 – Making a Complaint.)

Review Completed

Some people who received review results were advised there was no case to answer. At that stage much depends on what action you took:

Made a Complaint – You had the chance to go back to the company and make a formal complaint, stating that you were not happy with their result. After a further review you would have been offered compensation or had a rejection referring you to the FOS. If you did not contact them within six months of your claim being rejected, they will not assess your case, unless there are extraneous circumstances like a death or illness.

Did not make formal complaint, but enquired to the firm later – If you initially accepted the review result but subsequently realised that there could be a problem and enquired further, a 3 year time clock started from the time you made contact. If you are now outside that 3 year time bar, it will not be possible to complain to the FOS.

Did not complain – If you did not make a formal complaint you can now do so. See below.

Review Complete – Compensation Accepted

Some of you who received compensation in the 1990's may now find it inadequate. Your compensation award, for which you would have signed an acceptance, would have contained a disclaimer clause stating that the award represented a full and final settlement. You cannot make a further claim for losses unless the methods used to calculate the original compensation were outside the guidance provided by the regulator. Check with the FOS.

Who can complain about Pension Transfers?

All those whose pensions were transferred after 30 June 1994 when stricter guidelines came into force.

All those who through administrative blunders were missed off the original pension review list of transfers completed before the 30 June 1994. If you genuinely did not receive notification of the review then you can complain. Some adviser's records were incomplete and they did not keep track of people who moved. However the adviser's firm may claim they have a record proving a letter was sent to your correct address and may reject your complaint under the 3 year time bar. In order to progress your case to the FOS it would be helpful to provide supporting evidence that you had moved, or had post problems. This is a grey area so be prepared so stand your ground.

All those who formed part of the review and did not go on to complain about the findings as they were advised there was no case to answer.

First, make a formal complaint to the firm. The 3 year clock starts from when the complaint is sent. If your complaint is rejected using the original reason 'no case to answer,' complain to the FOS. If you have contacted the FSA and ombudsman there is definitely confusion over your right to complain. If firms reject your claim saying you have missed the pension review deadline, contact the FOS and let them decide.

Reasons why transfer recommendation was unsuitable

After 1994 Life Offices toyed with different methods in assessing transfer valuations culminating in the Transfer Value Analysis Report (TVAR). The report provides details of the critical yield, which is the investment return required on your transferred fund to provide you with a pension similar to that which would have been provided by the ceding scheme. Errors were made along the way. Advisers provided investors with defective and non-compliant advice and reports. Investors failed to understand the implications of the recommended transaction, and were exposed to the risk of the loss of their pension benefits without their informed consent.

CASE STUDY

In 1995 45-year old Robbie Fletcher had been recommended to transfer his deferred final salary pension to a personal pension. His pension on leaving was £6,000 per year, the estimated pension at normal retirement age 65 was £15,920, and the transfer value was £37,000.

Table1. Transfer Comparison

Stay in the Scheme			
Deferred pension at leaving age 45	£6,000		
Estimated pension at age 65	£15,920		
Transfer of £37,000 to a Personal Pension / Section 32 Transfer Plan			
Original Projection	FUND	11% Growth	£298,000
1995 - 2015	PENSION INCOME	6% Annuity	£17,900
Actual Values 2005	FUND	-	£75,000
	PENSION INCOME	4% Annuity	£3,000
New Projection	FUND	7% Growth	£147,000
2005 - 2015	PENSION INCOME	4% Annuity	£5,900
Projected Shortfall			
Income Shortfall	£15,920 less £5,900	£10,020	
Funding Shortfall	Based on fund required to buy a £10,020 index linked income at 65		£250,000

Robbie now needs a staggering quarter of a million pounds to put him back to his original position. My observations when I met him recently were:

- The original projections provided by the salesman showed a projected pension greater than that provided by the scheme, a false hope based on over-ambitious returns which historically had little to no chance of being repeated.
- The actual returns show that the salesman's pitch, 'transfer to unlock your frozen pension and make it work for you' was totally fatuous.
- Robbie was not aware how valuable his pension was. (An entitlement to £1,000 of pension income is probably worth £25,000.)
- Robbie transferred what he considered to be a modest pension and is sitting on huge losses that will require compensation well in excess of the maximum £100,000 awarded by the FOS.

Read Robbie's story carefully and ask yourself whether you're in his shoes.

Complain about Risk

Investors have many reasons to complain around issues associated with risk:

Explanation & Compliance Risk – Was the report compliant and the information correct? Was the recommendation to transfer presented in a clear and logical way that you could reasonably expect to understand? Were all the advantages and disadvantages listed and assessed? Did the adviser make it clear that you were giving up guaranteed benefits for non-guaranteed benefits? In some cases clients were asked to sign 'fact finds' which are hand-written records detailing the investor's financial position and objectives. Advisers have been known to embellish the entries to cover themselves.

Occupational Scheme Risk – Advisers often talked up the prospects of how a pension could be lost or reduced, but failed to carry out any analysis of the financial strength of the scheme. In their reports and fact finds advisers often claim the investor was concerned about the way their scheme was being run, and was prepared to transfer regardless of consequences. In most cases there is no evidence to support these claims, as no analysis of advantages and disadvantages exists. Consumers were deliberately misled.

Investment Return Risk – Advisers' views of investment returns were far too rosy, with little emphasis on potential under-performance. In the 1980's and '90's when inflation and investment returns were abnormally high, salesmen often used the highest projected returns to persuade people to transfer, often using returns of 10% or more, which failed to consider historical averages.

Within their recommendation / suitability letter advisers may have referred to the likelihood of high percentage returns which can be used as evidence against them. Poor investment returns alone are not accepted by the FOS as grounds for a complaint. However promises or implied promises of future returns (not backed-up with investment guarantees) are accepted.

Annuity Risk – Advisers failed to explain that the transferred funds were part of a two-stage investment process and when benefits were drawn, clients would have to buy an annuity with rates that are not guaranteed. They rarely considered the potential impact of lower annuity rates. Most reports failed to cover stage two in any detail, although it was VITAL to the calculation of your final retirement income.

Consumer Attitude to Risk – Advisers failed to analyse fully an investor's capacity for risk. Many used high investment returns and high annuity rates to suggest it was a sure bet. They failed to examine the possibility that the client could end up with a pension of less than 50% of that which they were guaranteed by doing nothing.

Problems arose because advisers had to recommend funds that would beat the 'critical yield', and which were totally unsuitable for the client's circumstances. Many were very cautious investors that only used deposit accounts. The 'Critical Yield' is the estimated compound return required on the transferred fund each year to provide a pension equivalent to that provided by the ceding scheme. To achieve investment returns of 10% per year, advisers would have to recommend risky funds investing in stocks and shares, even though when advisers discussed risk, they found most investors were categorised as low-risk. This leads to a mismatch between the risk level the client was comfortable with to that which the adviser needed to justify the recommendation.

Advisers got around the problem by doctoring the risk profiles or underplaying the risk until clients classed themselves as low or medium risk. Clients with very low-risk-profiles were recommended managed funds and with-profit funds which typically held 60% to 80% of their investments in shares. How can a fund with such a high share content be classed as low-risk?

Impact of Charges – Advisers failed to disclose fully the impact of charges on investment returns and often omitted to disclose the initial charges of 5% to 7% giving them 5% from the fund in commission. These were often disguised in the form of extra unit allocations that made it difficult to assess what was going on. The Life Office would then recover the costs via annual management charges and high early-transfer penalties. They failed to disclose how annual charges of 1% to 2% would act as a drag on final returns. The consumer would incur no such charges if they had remained in the employer's scheme.

Inaccuracies – Adviser reports may have contained misleading information. By concentrating on the critical yield, they were implying you would achieve the same as the ceding scheme. This is misleading. Who would want to take on massive extra risk in the hope of getting no benefit? Clients needed to earn higher returns to compensate for this extra risk, and advisers invested into ever riskier funds so they could claim that the transfer had a reasonable chance of achieving the critical yield. Some advisers use certain Life Offices to obtain free Transfer Value Analysis Reports. They then place the business with another provider. This is clearly flawed as the critical yield calculation was calculated using a different Life Office! Some of the older projection illustrations did not use actual charges but industry average charges which gave a falsely optimistic impression of likely future returns.

Taking all these issues into account, clients could have been misled into making a decision based on a false prospectus.

Other Retirement Investments – Some advisers failed to take into account that you did not have sufficient other assets to provide a decent income in retirement, so the advice to transfer was a gamble. You should have been advised to stay put as it was important to maximise your guaranteed pension income.

Compensation Claim

Taking all the above into account, the recommendation to transfer was both negligent and unsuitable for most working people with low-risk profiles and limited resources.

Reinstatement is the favoured form of redress of the ombudsman. However as this option is entirely at the discretion of scheme trustees, it cannot always be used. In such cases your PPP will be topped up to match as closely as possible the pension you would have received from the employer scheme at retirement.

Be prepared for the salesman's firm to defend their position by producing documents that may have been doctored (e.g. changing your risk profile). Also the recommendation letter on their records may be different to the one you received as the salesman needed to submit a more compliant report to get past his compliance officer. This is rare but fortunately the ombudsman is aware of such practices and places great emphasis on the information that you received (the recommendation report and marketing material).

This subject is complex, but don't be deterred. Use complaint Letter 9 to seek redress.

"HE DOES A SPOT OF WINDOW CLEANING ON THE SIDE."

11

Retirement Complaints

a) Annuities

Background

> Who is Affected – Anyone who has bought an annuity after 29 April 1988.

What is an Annuity? It is an investment that is used to convert a pension fund into a pension income and is guaranteed to be paid to you for the rest of your life. It is in effect a policy that provides insurance against living too long. Once made the decision is irrevocable. Your income is liable to income tax.

How is it calculated? If a Life Office is going to pay you an income for the rest of your life it takes on a liability which it needs to cover and still make a profit. The income is made up of a return of your capital and the income generated from that capital over your expected lifespan. Your lifespan, known as longevity, is estimated using mortality tables produced by the Office of National Statistics (ONS). Life Offices have no idea if you will claim for one year or fifty. To insure against the risk that some people live longer than average, they spread the risk across thousands of annuitants called the 'annuity pool' and those who die early subsidise those who live a long time (the mortality subsidy).

In theory the earlier you buy an annuity, the greater the mortality subsidy. Actuaries have calculated that the optimum time to buy an annuity is somewhere between age 65 and 70. (This is likely to increase due to longer life expectancy which will alter the annuity pool.)

The factors that affect your annuity rate – Put simply, the greater the liability to pay out, then the lower the initial income. Your annuity income will depend on:

- The return the Life Office can make on your money
- Your age
- Your health
- Your sex
- The size of your fund
- Will your income remain level or escalate each year?
- Will the income continue to a partner after your death?
- Do you want income payments to be guaranteed for a period of up to 10 years, payable even after death?

Who buys Annuities? Anyone aged 50+ with a money purchase pension plan can buy an annuity. These include PPPs, stakeholder pensions, retirement annuities, free standing AVC schemes, executive pension plans and all company pension plans that do not

provide an income linked to salary. It was compulsory to use a
pension fund to purchase an annuity by age 75, but after April 2006
it was possible to defer an annuity purchase for the rest of your life
and receive an alternative secured pension income.

What types are there?

- Annuities where the income remains level
- Annuities where the income escalates by a fixed percentage, or
  the rise in inflation (inline with the Retail Price Index (RPI)) or
  the rise in inflation, but capped by an upper limit
- Annuities where the income is linked to an investment fund.

Proving mis-selling

Choosing the right annuity can be quite daunting, especially when
there appear to be so many options, and many people seek advice.
There is usually a knowledge gap between the customer and the
salesman which gives them great scope to mis-sell. To prove mis-
selling you must focus on the key areas of risk, suitability,
information omissions and incompetence.

Access to money denied – When people are sold pensions, very few
are told about the need to purchase an annuity when they retire.
Most people are told about tax-relief, and the tax-free cash at
retirement, but salesmen tend to skim over what happens to your
money thereafter. To many it comes as a shock to find out they are
denied access to their money and must buy an annuity. If you were
not told about this, then you were mis-sold a pension. The salesman
may hide behind the contract 'key facts' and state it was in the
paperwork! But if they did not draw your attention to the key
conditions of the contract and explain those conditions in a way
that you could reasonably expect to understand, then it was mis-
selling. The FSA considers the explanation of access to your money
as a key area to prove suitability. Failure to do so can lead to a just
claim. See Part Two, Chapter 10, Pension Complaints.

Not told of 'Open Market Option' (OMO) – When you decide to
take benefits you are not bound by the quote offered by your
pension provider. You can purchase an annuity from any provider
using the 'open market option'. Life Offices are required by the
regulator to explain this option and if the salesman did not draw
this to your attention, you have been misled. This is more likely to
happen when you deal with tied advisers who only represent one
company (often banks and building societies). They are incentivised
to persuade you to stay with their company at all costs – if you
choose the OMO they get no commission. Steer clear of these
salesmen.

Pension provider annuities ignored – The salesmen chose the
OMO, negligently omitting to consider the higher Guaranteed
Annuity Rates (GARs) and Guaranteed Mortality Rates (GMRs)

LEARNING POINT

Pensions with
Guaranteed Annuity
Rates usually apply
strict conditions as to
when and how the
benefits are drawn and
may stipulate that
benefits can only be
drawn at age 60 or 65
and on a level income
basis (no escalation).

offered by the pension provider. GARs formed part of many with-profit pension contracts, retirement annuities and executive pensions, written between 1970 and 1988. See Chapter 10 Pension Funding Complaints section e.

CASE STUDY

At 58, Andy Pritchard had £100,000 in his pension plan and wanted to retire and take the benefits. He was not aware that the plan contained GARs. His salesman got quotes from the pension provider and another annuity provider, and made a recommendation to transfer, telling Andy, 'You can't take benefits from the old plan until you're 60, so if you want benefits early you'll have to transfer to a personal pension plan. The quote for retiring at 58 from your current provider is poor - it's only £5,000 a year. I've found another company that's paying £6,000.'

I told Andy both statements were probably correct, but what the salesman had omitted to say was that if Andy waited until he was 60, he could secure a guaranteed income of £10,500 per year - 75% more than the salesman's recommendation. Over his lifetime Andy may have lost over £80,000 in pension income and should never have been recommended a transfer. He would have done far better to live off savings for two years (or even a loan), and then trigger his pension. But by the time he came to me, it was too late, he had signed his rights away.

If you have been advised to transfer a GAR pension to another annuity provider without a full analysis of the potential benefits (now or in the future), like Andy you have solid grounds for a complaint. You must claim for compensation based on your lost income. I have estimated that every £1,000 of lost income should result in a compensation payment of around £15,000. (See Chapter 10, section e).

Qualifying for a higher annuity rate because of lower life expectancy

In the same way that Life Offices assess risk when you apply for a life cover policy, the same process can be used to improve annuity rates.

Enhanced Annuities – Most annuity rates are set by looking at average life expectancy. However if you smoke, are overweight, suffer from high blood pressure or angina, you can apply for a higher rate as your life expectancy may be considered to be 3 to 5 years less than average.

Impaired Life Annuity – If you have suffered from a more serious condition, a major heart by-pass operation or cancer, then you can apply for an impaired life annuity. Actuaries estimate your life expectancy to be less than 10 years. This is a sensitive issue and must be handled with care. The bottom line is you need to secure the maximum income from your pension fund to enjoy the rest of your life. The salesman must not evade the subject and must ask you detailed questions about your lifestyle and health. If you fit into either of the above categories and have not been recommended an enhanced or impaired life annuity, then the salesman acted negligently and you have a case for mis-selling.

(With a positive attitude you could change your lifestyle, and live longer than expected, while drawing more money at the Life Office's expense.)

With-profits Annuities

These are a form of investment-linked annuity using a with-profits fund. A claim for compensation can arise if a salesman omitted to define the risks associated with such annuities. (See Chapter 14 With-profits, section a.) Many salesmen wrongly categorise with-profits funds as low-risk. In fact they are riskier than conventional annuities as your income is dependant on the performance of a with-profits fund. The initial income depends on setting the level of Anticipated Bonus Rates, known as the ABR.

If you assume a nil bonus (0% ABR), the starting income will be low. All declared bonuses will result in your income increasing by the declared annual bonus.

If you assume an annual bonus of 5%, your starting income will be higher, but the declared bonuses will have to achieve this every year just to maintain your income. If bonuses fall below this level, your retirement income will fall by an amount equal to the shortfall. For example a 5% ABR annuity would fall by 1% if the declared bonus was 4%. Some Life Offices, including Equitable Life, recommended investors assume bonus levels greater than 5%. Since 2001 this strategy has proved disastrous, as 'with-profits' annuity incomes fell.

Consumers were misled:

- They were inaccurately advised that 'with-profits' funds are low-risk funds. They are not low-risk as they may hold up to 80% of their assets in shares, carry liabilities to other policy-holders, and may be susceptible to bonus cuts if shares take a dive (as they did between 2000 to 2003).
- By recommending an annuity with a high Anticipated Bonus Rate (ABR), it has been possible to deceive investors that they were getting a better deal, as the starting income was higher.

CASE STUDY

This is what happened to Chris Rogers who had a personal pension plan and wanted to retire and take benefits. Chris got a couple of quotes which are shown in Table 1. He was impressed by the illustration with an income of £10,000 per year (A) – £1,000 more than the nearest competitor (B). The salesman told Chris his money would be transferred to a with-profits fund where there was a good chance his income would rise a couple of percent each year. Chris signed on the dotted line.

When I met Chris much later, he was not fully aware that the salesman had recommended a with-profits annuity with an ABR of 5%. For Chris's income to remain at £10,000, the Life Office would have to declare annual bonuses of 5% every year for the rest of his life. If the bonuses fell, so would his income. After the first year Chris had received a statement showing a 3% bonus and his income had reduced by 2%! This was a bolt out the blue as Chris thought his income was guaranteed.

His disappointment is shared by thousands who bought with-profit annuities in the 1990's, unaware of the risks associated with lower bonuses. If he had known, Chris would have chosen quote (B), which guaranteed to pay £9,000 for the rest of his life. I urged him to complain, because if bonuses remain at 3%, by the end of 20 years his income will have fallen 33% to £6,676.

Table 1. Annuity Income – Possible Outcome

Annuity Options	Starting Income	After 5 Years	After 10 Years	After 20 Years
(A) With Profits ABR 5%	£10,000	£9,039	£8,171	£6,676
(B) Guaranteed Level Annuity	£9,000	£9,000	£9,000	£9,000

Spouse's / Partner's benefits ignored

When purchasing an annuity, the salesmen should have impressed the need to include spouse & partner benefits, especially if the pension formed a major part of the family's retirement income. These are called joint-life, last-survivor annuities. Survivor benefits take two forms:

Spouse's pension – Calculated as a percentage of the deceased's income. It can be 100% but is more likely to be two-thirds or half.

Guaranteed Payments. – The annuity guarantees to maintain the income payment at the same level for a term of 5 or 10 years. If the annuitant dies within the guaranteed term, payments continue to the spouse at the same level until the term is over, before reverting to the requested spouse's pension.

Failure to disclose and fully evaluate these benefits can leave the survivor in financial dire straits. If you're the surviving partner or spouse of an annuitant who has died and whose annuity ceased on their death, you should complain and find out why this was allowed to happen. Unless the annuitant declared they wanted the plan to cease on their death it is our opinion that the annuitant was negligently advised and a claim for mis-selling should be made.

Inflation Ignored

When people are confronted with the decision to buy an annuity, they are tempted to choose the one with the highest initial income (which is usually a guaranteed level annuity). Level annuities offer a guaranteed, fixed income for the rest of your life. However they suffer from one great disadvantage; they do not protect pensioners against inflation, as they do not increase.

In our current low-inflationary times it's hard to imagine rampant inflation. But there could be problems ahead if the world's financial system falters, and in the fallout we see a rise in UK inflation. Some hedging against inflation should always be included in your retirement income planning, either via an annuity or other investments like national savings certificates. If the salesmen failed to flag up the effect of potential future problems, then a claim for mis-selling is always possible, unless you stated it was not a concern.

Table 2. **The effect of Inflation on the purchasing power of £1,000**				
Period/Rate	**3%**	**5%**	**7%**	**10%**
5 years	£859	£774	£696	£590
10 years	£737	£599	£484	£349
20 years	£544	£358	£234	£122

Tax-free cash

When you draw the benefits from a money purchase pension, you will have the option of drawing a tax-free lump sum. You should have been advised to take the maximum tax-free cash, as all annuity income is taxable. The only exception to this rule is the availability of GARs that provide a greater income after tax than any reinvested tax-free cash.

If you have been recommended that you forgo the tax-free cash to buy a larger annuity then you have been mis-sold an annuity.

Compensation Claim

This will vary depending on the adviser's recommendation. It is based on restoring your annuity income to the level it should have been if all the annuity options had been considered and the correct one chosen. Use Complaint Letter 10.

b) Mis-selling of Income Drawdown Plans

An Income drawdown Plan is a type of pension plan used by those between the ages of 50 to 75 who want to draw the benefits from their pension fund by taking annual withdrawals of income or capital, while deferring the purchase of an annuity up to age 75. The option to take up to 25% as a tax-free lump sum must be made at the time the plan is started.

Currently the earliest that income can be withdrawn is age 50. From 2010 this increases to age 55. On 6 April 2006 it became possible to continue income withdrawals for the rest of your life, without the need to purchase an annuity.

Background

For years advisers and pensioners had complained about the inflexibility of pension rules that forced holders of money purchase pension plans to use their funds at retirement to purchase an annuity, especially when annuity rates were deemed to be low. As the decision to purchase an annuity is irrevocable, it is not possible to alter the contract should your circumstances change.

The government eventually agreed that it was unreasonable to ask a saver to fund a pension for 30 to 40 years and then force them to buy an annuity on their retirement day, especially when that one decision dictates the level of their retirement income for the rest of their life. So in 1995 The Pensions Act introduced the withdrawal facility, which enabled pensioners to take withdrawals (taxed as income), and postpone their annuity purchase up to age 75 in anticipation of being able to take advantage of more favourable rates.

Mis-selling has occurred because drawdown plans have been sold by advisers who are attracted by the generous commission terms, but fail to inform clients of all the key issues that will affect their retirement income.

Features of Income drawdown Plans

Advisers usually use a combination of the following features to justify a recommendation to invest in an income drawdown plan, as opposed to an annuity. The sales pitch taps into people's emotions and usually follows the line:

'Retain control of your pension and leave it to your heirs if you die'.

Flexible Income – Each year the income can be varied. The initial maximum income is set using government actuarial tables and is supposed to be equivalent to a single-life level annuity. A minimum income must be withdrawn which is 35% of the total. Income levels are reset every 3 years. If the fund has increased in value you will be able to take more income. This is a useful tool to help manage your taxable income and ultimately your income tax liability. However, because the maximum drawdown income can be higher than that provided by a suitable annuity, the drawdown can lead to fund erosion. At the first 3 yearly review, the new income level may be higher or lower than the pre-review level. If annuity rates and fund values fall, the new income levels will be lower, and may be lower than that which could have been secured by an annuity 3 years earlier.

Investment Control – You can retain control of your money and remain invested in a wide variety of investment funds. The freedom to invest is widely talked up, but rarely fully utilised. Money tends to remain in insured funds, with little thought of how best to allocate and invest across a range of asset classes to produce an income stream.

Poor Health & Inheritance of Death Benefits – Drawdown appeals to those who are concerned about their longevity, as it provides an income without the need to purchase a conventional annuity, therefore preserving any unused fund for dependants. Should an investor die before an annuity is purchased the, surviving beneficiaries have three options, to continue drawing an income as before, to withdraw the whole fund as a lump sum payment, subject to an income tax charge of 35% (must be done within 2 years of the death) OR to use the fund to purchase an annuity.

Drawdown provides more options to a survivor than an annuity, and the prospect of a greater inheritance providing death occurs before age 75. Drawdown addresses the short-term fears of those who worry about premature death and the loss of their pension fund to a Life Office. Currently an annuity has to be bought by age 75. From April 2006 it will be possible to defer the purchase of an annuity indefinitely.

Defer Annuity Purchase – You can take benefits in anticipation of securing a more favourable rate. Rates are often perceived to be low, but they may still go even lower.

Tax-free cash – The option to take tax-free cash must be made at the outset. It is in your interests to take the maximum, which is 25% of the fund, as it is not taxable. Tax-free cash is often withdrawn from a tax-free environment and invested into a taxed environment. It is possible to take your benefits in tranches, leaving the remainder to grow in a tax-free environment.

Advisers love Income Drawdown

The main reason why advisers like income drawdown plans is they pay much more commission than annuities. It also gives them two chances to earn commission instead of one, as most people also end up buying an annuity as well. Over the lifetime of an income drawdown contract this can amount to 10 times as much commission, as illustrated below.

CASE STUDY

I recently met Winnie, a retired client who had followed her adviser's recommendations to invest in an income drawdown plan with her pension fund of £278,000. When I calculated the figures, I found to my horror that she had paid her adviser a total of £21,000 in commission. I could hardly bear to answer when she asked me, 'Where did all that money come from?' It had come from her pocket.

Table 1 examines commission costs over a 10 year period.

Table 1. Commission on a Pension Fund of £250,000

Event	Option 1. Purchase an Annuity		Option 2. Income drawdown Plan & Annuity	
	%	£	%	£
Salesman's Initial Commission	1% > 1.5%	£2,500 > £3,750	5% > 7%	£12,500 > £17,500
Salesman's Trail Commission	Nil	Nil	0.5% per year for 10 years	£12,500
Salesman's Annuity Commission	N/A	N/A	1% > 1.5%	£2,500 > £3,750
TOTAL Commission	£2,500 > £3,750		£27,000 > £33,750	

With such a huge commission incentive, many salesmen have persuaded thousands of pensioners to opt for income drawdown plans when an annuity would have been preferable. Some have pre-meditated plans to sell drawdown plans whether you need one or not. Your interests are secondary, their objective is to shoe-horn you into a plan while trying to appear compliant. This is mis-selling.

Proving Mis-selling

It is possible to prove mis-selling where the adviser recommended a drawdown plan and failed fully to analyse and discuss all the risks associated with deferring an annuity purchase. This course of action has been a disaster for a lot of pensioners who have suffered the double blow of seeing their funds fall during the stock market slowdown while annuity rates continue to decrease.

If you were advised by a commission-based adviser (especially between the years 1995 to 2002), you were probably mis-sold a drawdown plan. The following should help you assess drawdown suitability.

Flawed Investment Analysis

The fundamental objective of retirement income planning is to secure an income for rest of your life to replace your income from employment. The choice is between annuities that provide a risk-free guaranteed income, and drawdown plans that provide an income with no guarantees.

The adviser should have provided you with an illustration known as 'Type A Critical Yield'. This is the return required on your fund to purchase an annuity income in the future equal to that obtainable from an equivalent annuity if purchased today. It is a measure of financial viability. This yield should come with a health warning that annuity rates can go up and down as the critical yield only uses today's annuity rates which will change.

Critical yields are likely to have been in the region of 6.5% to 8.5%. The question to be addressed is whether this level of return is achievable. Much depends on the firm's interpretation of returns on various assets, as shown in Table 2.

Table 2. The Industry's Estimate of Asset Returns

Asset	Gross Return	Net Return (After All charges, initial and annual)
Shares	9%	7%
Government Bond Fund	4.5%	3.5%
Corporate Bond Fund	6%	4.5%
Property	7%	5%
Cash	4.5%	3.5%

Here you can see that the only asset class the industry believes has any chance of equalling the critical yield is a 100% share fund.

Having failed to give an investment risk warning, salesmen are likely to have recommended a share-based strategy as it was the only way they could justify a drawdown recommendation with growth-potential to cover costs. Choosing low-risk, low-return assets such as cash and government bonds would not generate sufficient growth and would leave you with losses. This may have resulted in your early exit and would prevent the firm claiming years of trail commission.

Your Attitude to Risk

Did the funds recommended by the adviser fairly reflect your attitude to risk? If you are a low-risk investor there are no low-risk investments that the adviser can recommend that are likely to achieve returns to match the critical yield. If you were relying on the pension fund to provide the majority of your retirement income, then it is vital for peace of mind that you use that fund to secure your income position. If you were advised to invest the majority of your fund in share-based funds then this was negligent as the strategy is unsuitable for someone in your circumstances.

Many investors have been recommended with-profits funds which are totally unsuited for use in a drawdown scheme. Firstly they were wrongly categorised as low-risk, and secondly if you wish to switch at short notice to buy an annuity, you may be liable to a Market Value Reduction (MVR). (See Chapter 14 a) Mis-selling of With-profits Investments.)

Annuity Risks

The adviser may have recommended delaying the purchase of the annuity in anticipation that rates would rise. This was negligent advice unless it was accompanied by a full explanation of the facts.

By the mid 1990's a pattern of falling annuity rates had already started, with level annuities falling from around 14.5% in 1990 to 10% in 1995 as shown in Table 3.

Table 3. Change in Level Annuity Purchase Price for Male age 65			
Year	Purchase Price	Annuity Rate	Annuity Income
1990	£100,000	14.5%	£14,500
1995	£145,000	10%	£14,500
1997	£152,000	9.5%	£14,500
1999	£175,000	8.3%	£14,500
2001	£171,000	8.5%	£14,500
2003	£193,000	7.5	£14,500
2005	£213,000	6.8	£14,500

The adviser would have been aware of these changes and the reasons for them. They would also have known that any drop in long-term interest rates that fed through to a 0.5% drop in the annuity rate would result in the need for a pension fund of 5% to 10% larger just to buy the same level of income.

By deferring an annuity the adviser should have fully disclosed and discussed the following risks which influence annuity rates and whether you were prepared for and could accept further falls.

Known Fact 'Loss of Mortality Cross Subsidy' – Actuaries are the mathematicians who calculate annuity rates. From their mortality tables they are able to increase annuity rates by anticipating the cross-subsidy from those who die early. This is estimated to increase annuity rates by 1% to 1.5%, but its effect reduces the later you buy an annuity as you are entitled to less cross subsidy. Actuaries have calculated that deferring beyond age 70 cannot be justified on a value for money basis, as the loss of cross subsidy is unlikely to be replaced by superior investment returns. Drawdown plans do not benefit from mortality cross-subsidy.

Known Fact 'Life expectancy is improving' – Annuity rates are being pushed lower by improvements in average lifespan over the last 30 years, with life expectancy improving 2 to 3 years every decade. This is likely to continue for the foreseeable future and puts downward pressure on annuity rates as Life Offices expect to pay out for longer.

Known Fact 'Poor Health Annuities' – At one time all annuity policy-holders funds were placed into the same 'general annuity pool' where everyone benefited from the cross-subsidy from those who die early. But now plans identify and remove people from the general annuity pool who are statistically more likely to die early, by offering them special annuities with enhanced rates. This has the effect of lowering general annuity rates. As the availability of poor health annuities becomes more widespread, rates will go even lower.

Unknown Fact 'Interest rate up or down' – Annuity rates can be pushed higher or lower by changes in long-term interest rates. Life Offices invest your money to achieve a guaranteed return to cover their liabilities and tend to use government bonds (gilts - basically IOUs). The rates fluctuate according to inflation, and as global inflation has been subdued, long-term interest rates are low, gilt rates are low and so annuity rates go down.

Trying to second-guess annuity rates is very difficult. Improvements in health and changes in the 'general annuity pool' are putting downward pressure on rates. Any salesman who recommended deferral on the basis that annuity rates would improve has been negligent, as this advice is at odds with the known facts. You have been misled and have a claim for mis-selling.

Income Suitability

Did the adviser cover the following issues:

Lifetime income needs – Did the adviser ask about your likely income needs throughout your retirement, taking into account your other assets and the best way to address those income needs without taking unnecessary risks?

Was there a level of income that you needed just to maintain your lifestyle, and could this be achieved by opting for a guaranteed annuity? If so why were you recommended a drawdown scheme with all the associated risks?

Triennial reviews & Income changes – Were you made aware that at the first triennial review (every third anniversary), your income could go down and continue to go down because your fund and annuity rates were falling? Salesmen often suggest your income will rise as the older you are as the annuity rates are better. Table 3 (above) proves the inaccuracy of such statements.

Highest income – Did the salesman push a drawdown plan because it offered the highest initial income, without discussing the likelihood of fund erosion? Did he say this would only provide a temporary boost as your income was likely to fall after the first review?

Charges & effect of Charges

The full extent of the charges and the effect on growth may not have been fully explained. Were you made aware that a charge of 5% to 7% would be taken directly from your fund? Over the lifetime of the contract the effect of the charges reduce annual growth by 2% to 3%, so if fund growth was zero, your fund would reduce by 2% to 3% a year. This is called the reduction in yield (see glossary). Such a drag on performance gives funds little or no chance of ever beating 'critical yields'. Was this brought to your attention? If not, you were misled and have a claim.

Table 4 illustrates the problem of fund erosion, examining the effect of a 7% initial charge and a 1.5% annual management charge on a fund of £100,000 growing at 5% where annual withdrawals are set at £5,000. The funds available are unlikely to be sufficient to buy an annuity that provides the same annuity income as that available at the outset.

Table 4. Effect of charges on a Drawdown fund of £100,000	
Start	£93,000
5 years	£82,704
10 years	£70,476
15 years	£55,952

Flawed investment strategy

Maintaining control of your investments is often heralded as one of the great advantages of drawdown over annuities where you give up control for an income. However many advisers acted incompetently:

Some had only one strategy; 'The markets are going up!' There was no contingency plan should markets and annuities go down. The salesmen failed to discuss a STOP LOSS strategy used by investment professionals, whereby changes would be made if the combination of falling fund values and annuity rates would result in an annuity income of 10% less than could have been obtained at the outset.

Some proclaimed that shares out-perform other assets over the long-term and showed statistics to prove their point. Such a strategy ignores the basic fact that there may not be sufficient time for you to benefit from or recover from volatility in the market that may force your investments lower. This is definitely the case for anyone within 5 years of purchasing an annuity at age 75.

Finally, there was no coherent asset allocation – The investments were not arranged to meet specific income needs over different timescales. With a bias towards share-based insurance funds you are forced to sell at the bottom of any market to generate an annual income. The income streams should have been secured by cash or low-risk investments.

Passing on your Pension Fund & Inheritance Tax

Passing your money on to heirs is an emotional subject that salesman use to justify recommending a drawdown plan. They usually ask questions like, *'When you die do you want your family to benefit from your pension fund, or the Life Office?'*

That rhetorical question should be counterbalanced with, *'Is it more important that you have a secure retirement income that is not depleted, OR that your heirs may inherit some of your pension fund?'*

Ultimately an annuity provides insurance cover against longevity, while a drawdown scheme does not. To make a fully informed choice, the adviser should have given you information concerning the average life expectancy produced by the Government Actuarial Department (GAD), similar to Table 5 below.

Table 5. **GAD Life Expectancy Tables 2001 to 2003**				
From Age	**Male Life Expectancy**	**Expected Male Life Span**	**Female Life Expectancy**	**Expected Female Life Span**
60	20 years	80	23 years	83
65	16 years	81	19 years	84

Most people in good health could be relying on their pension fund for 20 years or more. If preserving your pension fund for your heirs was really important, did the adviser discuss all your options including phased retirement plans? With a 'phased retirement plan' you draw the benefits in tranches instead of all at once. This is possible because most pensions are divided into 10 and sometimes 100 sub-policies that can be drawn separately. The remainder continues to grow in a tax-beneficial environment and you take what you need to live on using the tax-free cash as income.

CASE STUDY

Bill Wilson is a 65-year old pensioner who is concerned about his health, has £100,000 in a pension plan and needs an income of £5,000 gross each year (equivalent to £3,900 net). His commission-based salesman recommended a Drawdown pension plan and reinvesting the tax-free cash into an insurance bond. My question to Bill was – what would happen to his family if he died after 5 years?

Table 6. Recommendation from Commission Salesman

Pension Fund	£100,000
SPLIT - Insurance Bond	£25,000
SPLIT – Drawdown Fund	£75,000
Drawdown Plan Income	
Drawdown Fund after 5% initial charge	£71,250
Income gross	£5,000
Income net, after 22% income tax	£3,900
Death after 5 years	
What happens to the Drawdown Plan?	
Value after 5 years assuming 5% growth and withdrawals of £5,000 per year	£62,000
Liable to an income tax charge of 35%	£21,700
Net amount forms part of deceased's estate	£40,300
Inheritance Tax 40%	£16,120
Net Drawdown Fund to pass on to heirs	£24,180
What happens to the Bond?	
Bond investment after 5% initial charge	£23,750
Bond value after 5 years assuming 4% growth	£29,000
Inheritance Tax 40%	£11,600
Net Bond Fund to pass on to heirs	£17,400
TOTAL Inherited by Heirs if Inheritance Tax Applies	
Bond	£17,400
Drawdown	£24,180
TOTAL	£41,580
TOTAL Inherited by Heirs if NO Inheritance Tax	
Bond	£29,000
Drawdown	£40,300
TOTAL	£69,300
TOTAL Initial Commission received by Salesman	
5% of £100,000	£5,000

My alternative recommendation was for Bill to take his benefits in stages as the most cost effective and tax-efficient way of securing an inheritance for his family, as Table 7 proves.

Table 7. Recommendation from a Fee-based Planner

Pension Fund	£100,000
Leave in Pension Fund	£50,000
Take benefits	£50,000
Taking Benefits to Provide an income	
SPLIT - Tax-free cash (25% of £50,000)	£12,500
SPLIT – Apply remainder to Drawdown plan	£37,500
Drawdown value after £1,500 fee	£36,000
Gross Income withdrawals from Drawdown plan	£1,800
(A) Net income withdrawals after 22% income tax	£1,400
(B) Use tax-free cash provide annual net income	£2,500
TOTAL net income (A) + (B) = Same as Table 6.	£3,900
Death after 5 years	
What happens to the Drawdown plan?	
Value after 5 years assuming 5% growth and withdrawals of £1,800 per annum	£35,500
Liable to an income tax charge of 35%	£12,425
Net amount forms part of deceased's estate	£23,075
Inheritance Tax 40%	£9,230
Net Drawdown Fund to pass on to heirs	£13,845
What happens to the pension fund?	
Value after 5 years assuming 5% growth – Paid tax-free	£63,814
TOTAL Inherited by Heirs if Inheritance Tax Applies	
Drawdown	£13,845
Pension	£63,814
TOTAL	£77,659
TOTAL Inherited by Heirs if NO Inheritance Tax	
Drawdown	£23,075
Pension	£63,814
TOTAL	£86,889
TOTAL Fees received by Planner	
Fee	£1,500

I wanted to know why Bill's adviser hadn't recommended a phased plan when he knew passing money on was so important to Bill? The advantages are clear below, as heirs receive more, AND you pay less in charges.

Table 8. Compare Results from Tables 6 & 7

	Table 6 Commission Salesman	Table 7 Fee-based Planner
Heirs Inheritance after applying 40% Inheritance Tax	£41,580	£77,659
(£) More		£36,079
(%) More		86%
Heirs Inheritance NO Inheritance Tax	£69,300	£86,889
(£) More		£17,589
(%) More		25%
Adviser charges	£5,000	£1,500
(£) More	£3,500	
(%) More	233%	

Bill was not informed about the advantages of phased plans because the salesman's £5,000 commission came ahead of his best interests. Salesmen don't want to leave money growing in existing plans as that does not earn them commission. They prefer to shift it and generate commission regardless of what is considered best advice.

If you were not informed about the advantages of phased pension planning, you have been the victim of mis-selling.

Tax-free Cash

Salesmen use the emotive phrase 'Let's release the tax-free cash', as if it's trapped and only they can liberate it! They also use it as reason to justify a drawdown by suggesting a drawdown is the best way to obtain tax-free cash. If you need your tax-free cash for essential capital expenditure then use it. But if your adviser has recommended you take the maximum tax-free cash to reinvest you may have been misled and mis-sold to.

It is not in your best interests to withdraw money growing in a tax-free environment and reinvest it in a taxed one. Such advice is unsuitable on the grounds of cost and tax efficiency as proved in Table 9.

Table 9. **Compare Growth of Tax-free Cash**		
	Non Pension 4% Growth	**Pension 5% Growth**
Tax-free cash	£10,000	£10,000
Amount Invested in Insurance Bond	£9,400	N.A.
Value after 5 Years	£11,437	£12,763
(£) More		£1,326
(%) More		11%
Value after 10 Years	£13,914	£16,289
(£) More		£2,375
(%) More		17%

If the money remains inside the pension fund, it is also inheritance tax-free. Some salesmen use elaborate schemes to switch your money to generate commission, perhaps stripping all your tax-free cash to invest into an insurance bond and taking out 5% income to reinvest in another high commission product.

The adviser could have used a 'phased retirement plan' to leave your pension fund and your tax-free cash growing in a tax-free environment. If this was not discussed and evaluated you were mis-sold to.

Servicing

As a minimum your plan has to be reviewed every 3 years (triennial review). Most advisers get out of any contractual obligations to service clients' needs by including a clause in their Terms of Business. However, some do offer ongoing servicing agreements whereby they are committed to service your contracts and will arrange annual meetings. Most salesmen will want to see you and use the drawdown plan as a reason to arrange a meeting to try and sell another policy. Any meeting that you have with your adviser that covers your drawdown scheme should include a check of all the items that supported the original recommendation. These should include:

- Any fundamental change in your circumstances
- A new drawdown illustration and a check on the new 'critical yield' and whether this is realistically achievable using investments that match your risk profile
- A new annuity illustration showing the level of income that could be purchased now. This should be compared with previous illustrations to analyse whether a pattern is developing in interest rates, changes in mortality and whether corrective action is required.
- A discussion of your current and future income needs. Are the levels of income withdrawal sustainable, if not, why not?
- A new analysis of your attitude to risk. Are you comfortable with the level of investment risk? Can you afford to continue taking risks?
- The state of your health and your partner and has it changed?
- Are the investments performing as planned? If not why not?

Failure to cover these essential items is a failure to carry out the level of servicing required to make informed decisions about the future. Remember, the adviser will persuade you to maintain the plan for as long as possible, while they carry on claiming 0.5% trail commission from your fund each year until you buy an annuity.

Why you must Complain

You and your family may have already lost thousands of pounds of income because of bad advice. It is important you don't lose any more. The next two tables show how much you may have lost by examining the income options available to a man aged 65 with £100,000 pension fund.

Both tables compare the level annuity income to a drawdown scheme, where an income equivalent to the annuity is drawn each year. In 1995 this was £10,000 per year and in 2000, £8,000 per year. The drawdown initial charge is 5%. The drawdown fund is invested in share funds. For simplicity I have used the annual returns of the UK FTSE All Share Index. The return does not include the reinvestment of dividends which I have discounted to cover annual charges and the fact that the majority of funds under-perform the index.

This is a rough guide to the position you would have found yourself in if you had been allowed to withdraw the annuity income equivalent each year. In reality the triennial review would have reduced the amount of income that you could withdraw to preserve the fund, and from 1998 onwards your annual income would have been reduced.

Table 10. Annuity Vs Drawdown 1995 to 2005

Year	% Growth in All Share Index	Year Start	Annuity / Drawdown Income	Year End
1995	4.7	£95,000	£10,000	£88,995
1996	15.0	£88,995	£10,000	£90,884
1997	18.1	£90,884	£10,000	£95,477
1998	17.3	£95,477	£10,000	£95,050
1999	11.2	£95,050	£10,000	£88,877
2000	4.5	£88,877	£10,000	£82,247
2001	-12.0	£82,247	£10,000	£63,735
2002	-17.1	£63,735	£10,000	£44,546
2003	-10.9	£44,546	£10,000	£30,780
2004	13.6	£30,780	£10,000	£23,607
Annuity rate for a male age 75 in 2005 = 10%				
Therefore annuity income available in 2005			= £2,361 p.a.	
Lost income in 2005 and every year thereafter Percentage Loss = -76%			= - £7,639 p.a.	

You can see above that anyone who invested in a drawdown plan in 1995 will in 2005 receive an income which is likely to be 50% lower than that they could have secured 10 years earlier.

Year	% Growth in All Share Index	Drawdown Year Start	Annuity / Drawdown Income	Drawdown Year End
2000	4.5	£95,000	£8,000	£90,915
2001	-12.0	£90,915	£8,000	£72,965
2002	-17.1	£72,965	£8,000	£53,856
2003	-10.9	£53,856	£8,000	£40,857
2004	13.6	£40,857	£8,000	£37,326
Annuity rate for a male age 70 in 2005		=	8%	
Therefore annuity income available in 2005		=	£2,986 p.a.	
Lost income in 2005 and every year thereafter		=	- £5,014 p.a.	
Percentage Loss		=	- 62%	

Table 11. Annuity V Drawdown 2000 to 2005

Anyone who invested in a drawdown plan in 2000 will in 2005 receive an income which is likely to be 40% lower than that they could have secured 5 years earlier.

Make YOUR Claim

As far back as June 1999 the PIA (Personal Investment Authority – forerunner to the FSA), flagged up the inadequacies of advisers' record-keeping when selling drawdown plans. It is rumoured that in 2000 the PIA was considering the option of closing down the Equitable pensions operation because of the number of drawdown schemes that it thought were being mis-sold. The Equitable closed for business before the PIA acted.

The good news is that many firms hold inadequate records and are unlikely to be able to prove to the ombudsman that they acted compliantly – which will assist your claim for compensation. Your claim for compensation should be based on converting your current drawdown scheme to an annuity and increasing it to the same income level as that of the annuity available when the drawdown scheme was recommended. You should also receive a lump sum (with interest) to compensate for the difference in income received from the drawdown scheme compared to that which the annuity would have paid.

In our opinion the advice concerning the recommendation and servicing of drawdown plans was so poor (with thousands of pensioners affected by mis-selling), that the FSA should conduct an immediate industry review of all plans since inception. Use complaint Letter 11.

c) Mis-selling of Pension Unlocking

Who is Affected – Potentially all those who have taken their benefits early, primarily to release tax-free cash.

Pension Unlocking is advice to take your pension scheme benefits early in order to release tax-free cash and income. It can take several forms, including taking the benefits from a final salary scheme to provide tax-free cash and an income (See Chapter 10 f), or to a Life Office to take immediate benefits using a drawdown scheme (or purchase of an annuity). It can also be the transfer of a money purchase fund to a Life Office to take immediate benefits using a drawdown scheme or the purchase of an annuity.

Companies like to focus on the tax-free cash. The term 'unlocking' is misleading as it implies the adviser is able to do something special to releases your money. This is not the case; anyone over 50 can draw the benefits from their pensions. The marketing of this type of advice is often targeted towards vulnerable people who are desperate to obtain cash.

Consequences of taking your pension benefits early

It all depends on what you are giving up and whether any penalties are applied.

Final Salary Pension Schemes – These provide an income related to your final pensionable salary and usually provide a pension of 1/60th of your salary for every year of qualifying service. For every year you retire early the scheme is likely to apply an early retirement charge of 4% to 6% (see glossary). If you are lucky enough to be offered a pension without a reduction you should take advantage of the offer.

Money Purchase Pension Schemes – These are pension schemes that are not related to your salary. Contributions are invested into funds that rise and fall. Your final pension income is unknown as your pension fund is used to purchase an annuity, rates of which also rise and fall, making it difficult to plan your retirement income (see glossary).

Possible Losses

If you take your pension benefits early it is likely you will sustain losses because there may be an early retirement penalty (all schemes). Your fund will be smaller as it has had less time to grow (money purchase schemes), and annuity rates will be lower if you're younger, so will provide a lower income (money purchase schemes).

Possible Gains

Even though the advice to take your pension benefits early may have been flawed, it may have worked in your favour by default. If you were a member of a final salary scheme with an employer that has ceased trading and whose scheme was under-funded, it may have reneged on future pensions but maintained existing pensions in payment. If you were a member of a money purchase scheme and bought an annuity early you may have been able to secure an income greater than you would have done today as annuity rates have fallen steadily since 1992.

Proving mis-selling

It is possible to prove mis-selling where a recommendation was made without a full and thorough evaluation of the consequences of taking the benefits early, which has resulted in a lower income.

Objective – Did you really need the money to cover essential spending? If you were encouraged to draw the benefits to indulge in a short-term spending spree, then you may have been misled, as this is unlikely to have been in your long-term best interests. Did the adviser discuss your actual long-term retirement needs and the likelihood that this advice would create a shortfall at your normal retirement date? If so, what plan did the adviser recommend to address the shortfall?

Investments – Was all the cash used to cover essential spending, or was some invested? If it was invested into a taxable plan (e.g. an insurance bond), this is negligent advice to transfer money from a tax-free environment to one where it is taxed. It also undermines the need to take the benefits early. You will have a clear claim to mis-selling. (See Chapter 14, Mis-selling of insurance bonds.)

Cash – Could the money have been raised from another source? Were all sources of cash explored, such as re-mortgaging, or surrendering other investments?

Retirement Income Evaluation – Did the adviser compare the benefits of going early with the potential benefits at your normal retirement age?

With a final salary pension scheme the reduction in income (lost pension) can be considerable. To make a fair assessment of the viability of taking benefits early, the adviser should have valued those benefits using two methods:

Cost of Replacement

The adviser should have estimated the cost of replacing your lost pension entitlement at normal retirement age. If you are entitled to a pension at age 65 of £10,000 per year but were advised to take the benefits 10 years early at 55 and receive only £5,000 per year, how much would it cost to replace the lost pension? Remember all pensions are subject to increases which need to be taken into account. Table 1 illustrates:

Table 1. **Estimated Replacement Pension Costs**		
Pension Options	Take Reduced Pension at age 55	Wait to take Full Pension at age 65
Pension entitlement per annum	£5,000	£10,000
Pension Income Reduction (Lost Pension)	(£5,000)	Nil
Survivors Pension entitlement per annum	£2,500	£5,000
Estimated Pension at 65 assuming 3% pension growth	£6,720	£13,440
Pension Income Reduction (Lost Pension)	(£6,720)	Nil
Survivors Pension entitlement at age 65 (Note1.)	£3,360	£6,720
Cost of replacing income at normal retirement age 65 (Note 2.)		
Annuity Rate	Purchase Price	
3%	£224,000	
4.5%	£149,333	

Note 1: Your spouse or partner is likely to have been far better off if the pension was not transferred, as most final salary schemes pay half to two thirds of the member's entitlement.

Note 2: This is the cost of replacing lost income at normal retirement age and is based on the cost of purchasing an annuity that provides an income similar to that provided by the scheme (to include annual income increases and a survivor's pension). This is the value the financial markets place on your lost pension. This will vary depending on age and rates, but is likely to be in the range of 3% to 4.5%. (To calculate fund required, I have divided the pension income of £6,720 by the annuity rate and multiplied by 100, i.e. £6,720 / 3 x 100 = £224,000.)

The figures highlight how valuable the benefits that you giving up are worth. Were you aware that by taking a reduced pension at age 55 the 'lost pension' of £5,000 is likely to cost you more than £150,000 to replace at age 65?

If you have a partner it is imperative their interests are taken into account. A reduced pension will also reduce their benefits, which may not have been drawn to your attention.

If the evaluation did not take into account your long-term income needs then this would probably be considered mis-selling.

Time to cover Income

The adviser should have estimated how long it would take for the higher pension income (payable at normal retirement age) to cover the accumulated pension income received by drawing the pension early. In our example, a pension of £5,000 at 55, increasing by 3% per year would, after 10 years, provide a total income of £57,319. Remember from age 65 your normal retirement pension would have increased to £13,440, a huge £6,720 more!

Table 2. **Time Taken to Cover Early Pension Income**	
ACCUMULATED early retirement Income	£57,319
Estimated time it will take for the extra pension income at normal retirement of £6,720 to cover the £57,319, assuming the £57,319 had been invested growing at 3% net	10 Years

Loss of Guaranteed Scheme Benefits

If you have an older money purchase scheme the contract may have included guaranteed benefits, such as a GARs. (See Chapter 10 section e.)

Weak Scheme

If you were encouraged to take benefits early because the scheme was financially weak, what evidence did the adviser produce to substantiate this claim? The schemes annual reports and accounts are required including the scheme's last actuarial report. Supposition and hunches are not good enough to support a recommendation.

Compensation Claim

Your claim should be based on restoring you to the financial position you would have been in at normal retirement if benefits had not been drawn early. This will probably require the expertise of the ombudsman to calculate the benefits. However, if you have taken benefits from a final salary scheme where there was no early reduction in benefits then you have NOT been disadvantaged. If you have taken benefits from a money purchase scheme and bought an annuity, you may NOT have been disadvantaged if the annuity was bought before rates fell from 2001.

But regardless of the above, the investment of surplus tax-free cash into high-charging inappropriate investments may still provide grounds for complaint.

Use Complaint Letter 12.

12

Endowment Mortgage Complaints

TOPTIP

Contact the FSA on 0845 456 1555 and obtain the booklet 'Your Endowment Mortgage', published April 2005.

Who is affected – Potentially everyone who is using an endowment plan to repay their mortgage.

An endowment mortgage is an interest-only loan to be repaid using a savings plan known as an endowment. The term of the mortgage and endowment has traditionally been 25 years. In order to work, it relies on the expectation that your investment will grow at a greater rate than the interest on the loan. If it does, you will have a surplus. If it does not, you will have a shortfall.

Current situation

Endowment mortgage shortfalls are the main source of complaints received by the ombudsman (FOS) and will continue to be so. The FOS is concerned at the number of lenders automatically rejecting complaints, which is having the desired effect of encouraging people give up in despair. In May 2005 the Abbey Bank was fined £800,000 for using these tactics. Many providers feel it is worth trying, as they may not get caught.

You must act now

One of the main reasons for writing this guide is to help those who may lose out on compensation because Life Offices are using time bars to reject genuine mis-selling claims. People still believe they can complain when their endowment matures, which will leave millions of them wrestling with endowment shortfalls at a time when they should be doubling their efforts to save for retirement.

When thousands of pension transfers were recommended between 1988 and 1994 on the back of flimsy advice, the FSA declared an industry-wide review. The level of endowment mis-selling is now far greater, but the FSA has now decided against a review. Why? Is it fear of destabilising the industry? Ex-FSA employees are now saying so. Was pressure applied by the Government?

Whistle-blower believes nearly all endowments were mis-sold. If you were recommended an endowment mortgage you have a valid claim for compensation for losses, which could run to thousands.

For endowments sold after 28 April 1988, the FOS must, if asked, examine a complaint. For those sold earlier there is a good chance you will get redress providing the adviser was not an IFA, as most lenders come under the jurisdiction of the FOS.

You can claim even if you have:

- surrendered the policy
- made it paid up (ceased the contributions but keep the plan)
- changed your mortgage, either to a repayment or moved to another lender
- continued with the policy even though you knew there was a problem.

Background

History

Endowment policies are Life Office packaged products that combine life cover and investment in one contract. Old type contracts started before 14 March 1984 benefit from Life Assurance Premium Relief of 12.5%. (For every £100 in premiums paid, you pay £87.50 and the Revenue £12.50.) Some of these policies were known as full endowments as they guaranteed to provide a 'sum assured' equal to the loan, achieved by setting high premiums which almost covered the sum assured over the policy term. The payouts were further increased by large final bonuses.

The low-cost endowment is born

As competition for the business intensified, providers competed on price, unrealistically reducing premiums to gain market share. The low-cost endowment was born, reducing the sum assured (e.g. to £15,000 to cover a £50,000 loan, which left a shortfall of £35,000 to be covered by investment growth / bonuses). While the plans guaranteed to repay the loan on death, on maturity there was no guarantee the investment would be sufficient to repay the loan, as your money was predominantly invested in volatile stock-market investments.

They were sold irresponsibly

Low-cost endowments were used as a way of undercutting repayment mortgages and used investment assumptions out of kilter with historical averages. The maths was flawed and the plans were destined to disappoint. Many Life Offices used a flawed illustration system that used standard charges which did not reflect their much higher actual charges. The plans were heavily promoted by salesmen in the 1980's and '90's. The incentive to sell 25-year endowment policies was so rewarding for salesmen, they were usually sold at the exclusion of all other options. Typically salesmen received 100% to 150% of the first year's premiums in commission.

Low-cost with-profit endowments were heavily marketed

The majority of consumers who were recommended an endowment invested into with-profit endowments. With-profit funds are supposed to smooth and average out returns over the medium to long-term. This proved not to be the case, as bonuses were manipulated to secure positions in promotional tables.

TOPTIP

You must make a claim as soon as possible. The FSA is aware that most endowments have been mis-sold as it was considering a review of all policies but backed down. A full review would have resulted in your endowment being investigated without the need to complain. This book will put pressure on the depleted reserves of Life Offices, so it is in your interests to get your complaint in first. ACT NOW!

Consumers were misled

During the 1980's and '90's consumers were misled into believing endowments were a sure bet. Endowment companies declared bonuses bolstered by cross-subsidies received from applying penalties against the majority of policy-holders who surrendered their policies. Annual bonus declarations were a spectacle, as Life Offices trumped one another, declaring ever higher final bonuses to beat rivals and claim a top five slot. This was misleading as the underlying investment performance could rarely justify such bonuses, but was justified as Life Offices knew they only paid out on a minority of plans that reached maturity.

Advisory firms, including the major high street lenders, used these favourable sales conditions to push endowments and sales soared. It was obvious to many that the market was unsustainable.

Shortfalls are announced

The rot began to set in during the stock market falls of 2000 to 2003 when clients began to receive shortfall letters:

- Green Letter – NO Shortfall. Your endowment is currently on track to pay the target amount at the end of the term.
- Amber Alert – Significant Shortfall Risk. Your endowment may not pay out the target amount at the end of the term.
- Red Alert – High Shortfall Risk. Your endowment will not pay out the target amount at the end of the term.

All the shortfall letter did was highlight to the consumer that there was a problem. If you have been the recipient of such a letter you must decide on a course of action URGENTLY. From 1 June 2004:

You must make a complaint within 3 years of receiving your first 'red' letter, which is deemed to be the day you should have realised there was a problem. This 3 year date is known as the 'final date', after which the complaint is time barred.

The 'final date' can only take effect if you received a letter within the 3 year period and at least 6 months before the 'final date.' It must explain that the time within which you must complain will expire on a specified final date.

You can still complain

If you have not received a 'final date' letter you can still complain, even if more than 3 years have elapsed.

If you have received a letter and deny receiving one the Life Office may have difficulty proving you did, unless it was sent by registered post. Make sure you give reasons why the letter did not reach you, e.g. moving house, or postal problems within your area.

Important Considerations

Regardless of what letter you hold, it is the prevailing investment conditions between now and the maturity of your policy that will dictate whether you end up with a shortfall. No one knows what the final outcome will be. However two facts are known:

If you have an endowment mortgage you are leaving the repayment of your mortgage to chance. There are no guarantees that the endowment will cover the debt. You can move to a position of certainty by switching to a repayment mortgage.

If you want to use a savings plan to repay an interest-only mortgage, you should use a low-cost, tax-free, flexible ISA which is far superior to an endowment.

TOPTIP

If a firm rejects your complaint on the grounds that you are 'time barred' (outside the 3 year limit), your legal rights are not affected. It is possible to complain to the small claims court. Some in the industry believe it is difficult to impose this ban so it needs to be challenged. See Small Claims Court Part Two, Chapter 7, Step by Step Guide.

b) Grounds for Endowment Complaint

If the risks associated with an endowment policy were not fully explained by the person who sold it to you, you have grounds for complaint.

When I took out my first mortgage in 1986 I do not remember the adviser discussing repayment mortgages, but I do remember the tables. Reams of them showing me how many times Company 'A' had claimed a top 10 place compared to Company 'B'. 'A' had recently paid out more than 'B', but 'B' had been more consistent. The salesman used the 'alternative close,' suggesting they were both good, but as 'A' was slightly cheaper, I should opt for that one. The mortgage choice I was offered was - Did I want an endowment mortgage with Company 'A' or 'B'? The real choice I should have been offered was – Did I want a repayment mortgage or an interest-only mortgage, and if an interest-only mortgage what was the best plan to repay the loan? The risks of endowment mortgages were not explained. Repayment shortfalls and action to cover a shortfall were never mentioned. Instead, surpluses got a big mention!

If this scenario sounds familiar and the risks associated with the purchase of your endowment mortgage were not fully explained, then you have grounds for complaint. The key point to remember is that complaining about a shortfall will not result in a successful claim, but complaining about <u>the unexplained risks that caused the shortfall</u> will.

Fortunately, poor record keeping should come to the aid of those who complain. Many in the industry were so busy chasing the next sale, that they failed to complete accurate records. Many firms find it difficult to prove that their advice was suitable because they failed fully to analyse the following:

Risk

The FOS upholds complaints if an adviser failed to explain fully the investment risks of a plan that was unsuitable for someone with little or no previous experience of investing. For example, if the adviser:

- failed to explain this was predominantly a stock market investment, with 60% to 80% of the fund invested in volatile shares which are volatile
- failed to point out the strict condition of the contract that the plan could not guarantee to pay off the mortgage
- failed to explain what would happen to the mortgage in the event of an endowment shortfall.

Whistle-blower is concerned about how the FOS is dealing with risk and how salesmen are defending their positions. This is happening because the FOS questionnaire asks about other investments such as shares or Personal Equity Plans. The FOS considers that if you hold other equity investments then you were may have been aware of the investment risks. Salesmen are using this in their defence but the argument is flawed because it fails to recognise that people apply and accept different risk strategies for different objectives. It's perfectly reasonable to accept a high-risk approach to funding a possible holiday home, while wanting a no risk / low-risk strategy to repay the debt on the home. You may have been sold the equity investments by a salesman who also failed to define and explain the risks. Perhaps you inherited or were given the investments, or the investment decision was made by someone else.

If for any reason the FOS decides the endowment suited your risk profile, it is still possible to claim the endowment was mis-sold because a lower cost, flexible tax-free PEP would have been a far more suitable product. See below.

Other Mortgage Options

The adviser failed to evaluate fully or mention other mortgage options such as repayment mortgages. Salesmen usually dismissed these by saying endowment mortgages were cheaper. This is misleading and factually incorrect and there is often no documentation to prove a full analysis was completed.

Other Investment Options

In the event that you wanted an interest-only mortgage, you should have been recommended a PEP to repay the loan. Some lenders actively discouraged them although they were available from 1 January 1987. (They were superseded by ISAs from 6 April 1999. Full details of PEPs and ISAs are to be found in Chapter 10 Pension Complaints, section b.) They were far superior to endowments because they are flexible. You can stop / start premiums and encash at any time, usually without penalty. Endowments tie you in for 25 years. Also, the money grows tax-free, where endowment funds are taxable.

Unsuitable Contract

Endowments were unsuited to most people's lifestyles as their inflexibility failed to take into account events such as divorce, unemployment and ill health. It is unreasonable to recommend that someone pay a fixed amount for 300 months, when a failure to do so will result in huge penalties.

Contract Incorrectly Set-up

Advisers were prone to extending the life of the contract to claim extra commission. This can be easily proved where:

- The maturity date was set beyond your retirement age, with no analysis of affordability. A check of your retirement income would have proved you could not afford to continue with the premiums.
- The endowment was set up to mature after the mortgage ceases, the consequences of which were not made clear at the time.
- You were advised to extend the life of the mortgage to tie in with a longer endowment policy.

TOPTIP

When you were recommended the endowment, if you had never invested in shares, and held your savings in a building society, you're on safe ground to complain as you clearly did not want to take risks. If you did own share investments you can use the same reasons, but make it clear you wanted to take a no risk / low risk strategy with the repayment of your mortgage.

Which? Magazine's dedicated endowment web-site includes some excellent background information on how to make an endowment complaint, including a drafted multi-choice letter. Visit www.which.net/endow mentaction

Policy Churning

You were advised to cease and surrender an old plan and start one larger policy. The salesman probably said it was easier and simpler to have just one policy, but in actual fact was seeking extra commission. Policy churning is absolutely taboo and on its own will justify compensation.

Misleading Information

The salesman provided misleading information. This could be particularly helpful if it was provided in writing. You may have received undertakings or guarantees in writing that the fund would be sufficient to pay off your mortgage. Perhaps the salesman said there would be a surplus at maturity sufficient to go on holiday or buy a car. All these points are covered in Complaint Letter 13, Endowment Mortgages.

Completing the Financial Ombudsman Service Endowment Mortgage Questionnaire

After you receive a rejection letter from the firm, you must complain to the FOS by completing their standard complaint form, which is covered in Chapter 7, and an endowment mortgage questionnaire. You may require assistance on the following:

Section A: About You

Question 4 – Asks for details of other investments, including share-based investments such as Personal Equity Plans (PEPs) held at the time you bought the endowment.

The FOS must investigate whether you understood the market risks. Before completing this question read Risk in the previous section. If you had never invested in shares and your savings were held in building society accounts, say so here. But if you did own share investments you must make it clear you did not want to take risks by adding the statement, *'I did not want to take risks with the repayment of my mortgage and wanted to adopt a no risk / low risk strategy'*.

Question 5 – Details of other death benefits and life policies.

The FOS is trying to establish whether you had any other life cover or death benefits which may help prove that the life cover provided by the endowment was superfluous to requirements. You may not have started any personal policies, but your employer may have provided death benefits, sometimes referred to as 'death in service benefits', of 3/4 times your salary, which could have been used to repay the mortgage.

Questions 6 & 7 – Expected retirement date and income? If the adviser was aware that it was your intention to retire earlier than the endowment maturity date, and your retirement income would be insufficient to cover mortgage payments, then on the grounds of ongoing affordability you have a very strong case. Whether that age has changed is not the issue, it was the age you stated at the time you were advised that is important.

Section B: About Your Endowment policy

Most of this information will be available on your policy document and statements.

Question 7 – Were you advised to take out an endowment and did the adviser arrange the loan? In the 1980's some estate agents found selling endowments so lucrative that it became more profitable than selling houses. I heard many stories of first time buyers being advised to start endowments before they had even applied for a mortgage or even found a house on the grounds of 'being ready.' This is balderdash. If it happened to you tell the FOS as it is clear mis-selling to advise you to take action before even discussing your loan requirements, on the presumption that endowment was the best option.

Question 11 – (first part) Are you still planning to use the endowment to repay the mortgage? Tick 'NO'
(second part) If you have changed your mortgage but kept the policy why are you still paying into it?

Possible answers:

• You did not know what to do for the best.
• You thought it may be required as a condition of making a claim.
• You were told there were heavy penalties for stopping.

Section C: About the Advice you were given

This section is vital and backs up what you put in your complaint letter, so you must make sure you are consistent with your reasoning.

Question 1 – What were you told about what would happen if the endowment did not pay off your mortgage? Most people were told nothing about endowment shortfalls. They were told, or it was implied that the endowment was guaranteed to pay off the mortgage. Salesmen often implied there would be a surplus, so a shortfall was never raised as a possible outcome.

Question 2 – What concerns did you raise about making sure the mortgage was paid off? Most people were not concerned because they did not think it was an issue - the salesman had implied / guaranteed the mortgage would be repaid by the endowment.

Question 3 – What were you told about the costs of an endowment mortgage compared to a repayment mortgage? Most people were told nothing. They were given no choice.

Question 4 – If you had not taken out an endowment what would you have done instead? A repayment mortgage should be most people's choice.

Question 10 – What was the reason for taking out a mortgage that extended past your intended retirement date? Some people were unaware their policy was set up in this way, as they failed to check the policy documents, or the salesman increased the term without informing the client. Where it was flagged up as an issue, the salesman may have incorrectly estimated your retirement income as being sufficient to pay the loan interest. Or they may have suggested that there would probably be sufficient in your endowment plan to encash it early and repay the loan.

Questions 11 & 12 – Ask about affordability to maintain payments after retirement. Be consistent with your answer in question 10.

Section D – About Your Mortgage

You will find all the details on your mortgage policy document. If you are unsure about any of the questions be honest and write, 'I am unsure'. Sign & send with the general complaints form and copies of your letters.

c) Advice on Your Future Endowment Options

Once the complaint procedure starts, you must decide what you want to do with the existing endowment. Whistle-blower recommends the following action with a view to securing the repayment of your mortgage:

Complaint Sent

Surrender – Do not surrender your endowment until the complaint review is complete.

Additional Payments? – Under no circumstances should you pay additional premiums into your existing endowment or take out an additional endowment to cover the endowment shortfall. DO NOT throw good money after bad. If you have been advised to do this, then this advice should form part of your complaint, or a new complaint.

Switch Mortgages – Switch to a flexible repayment mortgage which will guarantee to repay the mortgage at the end of your chosen term. Flexibility is desirable that will allow you to make lump sum repayments without penalty. Consult our other guide 'Mortgages'.

Life Cover Quotes – If life cover is required, obtain life insurance quotes to cover the outstanding mortgage. At this stage you are only assessing the cost.

Complaint Review Complete

At the end of a successful review, compensation will be calculated based on the current endowment surrender value. You can now objectively consider your options on merit. (Note: if you can get more than the surrender value then you will be better off).

Reduce Mortgage – Use the compensation to reduce the outstanding mortgage.

Enquire for more Information – Having switched to a repayment mortgage, the endowment can now be evaluated as a stand-alone investment. First find out more about the policy by using Letter 14 – Endowment Enquiry. There are some key areas you need to check out before you make the decision to surrender.

Compare Projections – Compare the Life Office 4% return maturity projections to the surrender value growing at 4%. For this you need to use a financial calculator or Appendices 1 & 2, which are manual compounding calculators. If the Life Office projection is much greater, then assume the surrender value is lower than the current value and a penalty is being applied.

Make Paid-up? – It may be possible to make the plan paid-up, whereby you cease premiums and leave the plan in place. This may be helpful if you want to keep the plan but cannot afford the premiums.

Check Bonus Levels – You need to know what with-profit bonuses have been declared over the last 5 years, both annual and terminal bonuses for contracts similar to yours, to see if a pattern is emerging. You need to ask the Life Office for their 'Principles and Practices of Financial Management', (PPFM) document which describes how they run their with-profits business. It includes details on how it formulates its investment strategy, the calculation of bonuses, charges & expenses and how it manages its inherited estate. These have been available to all policyholders since 30 November 2004. A consumer-friendly version known as the CFPPFM is now also available.

Guaranteed Growth Rates – Some old with-profits contracts benefit from guaranteed growth rates, if so how much? Remember you are looking for a total net return after tax equivalent to the interest you are paying on the loan.

Exit Penalties – Is your Life Office applying exit penalties to with-profit contracts known as Market Value Adjustments (MVAs)? These supposedly reduce the surrender value in line with the drop in underlying assets to protect investors who remain in the fund. Suffice to say it's a penalty that reduces your value, which is not transparent and the regulator is unwilling to intervene.

Ownership – Do the proceeds belong to you? Lenders used to demand that contracts were charged to them as security against the loan, to protect their position in the event of default or death. If so, the plans need to be released back to you. The contract could have been placed in trust for someone else to benefit. This would be very rare but you should check.

Other Benefits – You need to check whether the policy has any other benefits, which will be paid for out of your premiums. They would only prove important if your health had deteriorated and you wanted to protect your family.

- Critical Illness Benefit – pays out lump sum on diagnosis of critical illness. Rare with older contracts.
- Terminal Illness Benefit – pays out a lump sum if death is likely within 12 months.
- Waiver of Premium – An insurance that covers the cost of premiums in the event you have an illness or accident.

Charges – What are the current investment and annual charges? These are likely to be much higher than a tax-free ISA. Sometimes plans offer loyalty bonuses and charge reductions.

Surrender Taxation – Will the surrender of the policy give rise to a taxable chargeable gain? (See below)

Windfall Bonus! – If a mutual organisation is likely to de-mutualise (e.g. Standard Life), you need to consider whether it is worth holding on for any potential windfall pay out.

Unit linked – If you have a unit-linked endowment policy which is directly linked to stock market funds, you should surrender the policy. Only retain if you are in poor health and need the life cover. Use the proceeds to reduce your mortgage.

With-profits – Whistle-blower believes with-profits endowments represent poor value and there are better ways for consumers to save (such as tax-free ISAs). You should only consider keeping a with-profits endowment if:

TOP TIP

Life Cover - Do not surrender a policy if you're in poor health as you may not be able to secure alternative cover under normal terms. If you're in good health and need to cover your liabilities, make sure you set up replacement life cover prior to the surrender.

TOP TIP

Sell DON'T Surrender - If you decide you don't want to continue funding a with-profits endowment, or need to check if a valuation is fair, DO NOT surrender without first obtaining two separate quotes from traded endowment policy companies that may want to buy your policy for more than the surrender value. See next section for procedure.

- The exit Market Value Adjustment penalty is high, for example over 25%. It is worth asking every 6 months to find out if it is reducing.
- You need the life cover as your health has deteriorated.
- You are within 5 years of maturity and you believe there is a good chance the surrender value is too low and does not fully factor-in all the terminal bonuses.
- You expect to receive a demutualisation windfall payout.

Note: You can check on the fairness of the surrender value by obtaining a traded endowment policy quote.

> If you received endowment compensation based on the endowment surrender value, you now have the chance to come through this ordeal with a profit, by selling your contract to Traded Endowment Company for more than the surrender value. See next section.

Consider taking their offer if it is 10% above the surrender value. This is possible because their valuation will make an allowance for a higher terminal bonus than accounted for in the surrender value. But take note - if someone is willing to pay more for your policy, they believe there is profit in doing so. Some of you may interpret this as a hold signal to continue with the plan, others will get out on preferential terms as future bonuses may reduce. If you are offered less, this is an indication that they do not rate your endowment and you should surrender it.

Taxation of Surrendered or Sold Policies

There is no tax to pay if you receive less than the contributions you have paid, or if you have maintained the policy for 10 years or more.

For 10-year term policies there is no tax to pay providing the contract is maintained for more than 7.5 years. If you have maintained the policy for less than 7.5 years and you receive more than your premiums paid, the extra is classed as a chargeable gain and is taxable. As the Life Office has been taxed on its funds, this gain comes with a non-reclaimable 20% tax credit. The gain is added to your income, and if you remain a basic-rate tax-payer, there is no more tax to pay. If you are a higher rate tax-payer, there will be a further 20% tax to pay. Ask your tax office for help.

d) Traded Endowment Policies (TEPs)

Before you surrender your with-profits endowment, you must obtain valuation quotes from two separate companies that trade in second-hand endowment policies. These companies buy policies to be sold on to institutions. The new owner will continue to fund the policy with all the benefits assigned to a third party.

FAQs

Q. Why should I consider selling to a third party?

A. Because you may receive 10% to 20% more than the Life Office surrender value.

Q. How can they pay more?

A. Life Offices offer lower surrender values than the current value because they withhold a large percentage of the accumulated terminal bonus. But TEP companies have access to the latest information concerning the Life Offices' financial strength and bonus history and can make a more accurate assessment of the current value and what your plan is likely to be worth at maturity. They are still taking a risk on future returns, but are willing to pay you more than the surrender value now.

Q. What sort of policy can I sell?

A. Companies set their own criteria but most are interested in with-profit endowments which have been in force for at least 7 years OR 25% of the policy term and are within 10 years of maturity, and have a surrender value of greater than £1,500.

Q. How do I get a quote?

A. At the end of this section are contact details of the major traders that deal with the public. You can get an instant indicative quote and a firm offer will be made within a week after the company has verified the facts. Get at least 2 quotes. Alternatively you can go to a broker that specialises in the market to get a quote for you.

Q. What information do they need?

A. Your latest statement / bonus notice, your policy document and Life Office reply to your endowment enquiry, see Letter 6.

Q. Who do I use?

A. The one with the best quote.

Q. How long will it take before I get my cheque?

A. Up to 2 months. Some companies may complete in 1 month if there are no problems.

Q. What are the common problems?

TOPTIP

Don't be afraid to bump up your surrender value by 3% to 5% to ensure they come back with their best price. (They would give an adviser 3% to 5% commission, so should have some slack in their figures.) They will need to beat your surrender value by about 10% to make it worthwhile for you to accept their offer.

A. Policies were often set up by lenders who took a charge on the policy as security against the loan. The TEP company should be able to liaise with the lender to have it released, which may add a couple of weeks to the process. Alternatively you can ask the policy to be released. This should be quite simple if you have converted to a repayment mortgage.

Q. Are there any hidden charges?

A. No – the contract offer price is what you will get. All legal fees are paid by the TEP company.

Traded Endowment Companies

Company	Services	Remarks
Absolute Assigned Policies T.I.S House, Spring Villa Park, Edgware, Middlesex HA8 7EG Tel: 0800 072 1994 www.aap.co.uk Email: glwebvaluations@aap.co.uk	Will deal direct with the public. Hope to complete deal within a month. Phone or email details to get indicative quote.	Largest Market Maker in buying and selling second hand endowment policies. Regulated by the FSA.
1st Policy 845 Finchley Road London, NW11 8NA Tel: 020 8455 1111 www.1stpolicy.co.uk	Will deal direct with the public. Hope to complete deal within a month. Phone or email details. Aim to get contract quote issued in 24 hours.	Market Maker Regulated by the FSA.
Policyplus International Kings Court, Bath, BA1 1ER Tel: 0845 055 3055 www.policyplus.com	Will deal direct with the public. Hope to complete deal within a month. Phone or email details. Aim to get contract quote issued in 48 hours.	Market Maker Regulated by the FSA.
The Association of Policy Market Makers The Holywell Centre 1 Phipp Street London, EC2A 4PS Tel: 020 7749 3400 www.apmm.com	Trade body for Traded Endowment Policy market makers. Web-site provides details of market makers.	Offers some reassurance as to the standards that TEP companies should aspire to. All APMM members must be regulated and carry professional indemnity insurance.
Integrity Financial Solutions Ltd Silvester House Silvester Road Waterlooville Hampshire PO8 8TD Tel: 08701 287 333 www.bestpriceendowment.com	Specialist Adviser who trades second hand endowments across the whole market, searching for deals from the major market makers.	Broker. Regulated by the FSA.

13

Mortgage Complaints

Who is Affected – All those with a mortgage, especially those who have re-mortgaged.

a) Mis-selling of Mortgages (General)

What is a Mortgage? A mortgage is a loan against a property whereby the lender (mortgagee), can take possession of the property in the event the borrower (mortgagor), cannot repay the debt in accordance with the terms stipulated in the contract.

Scope for mis-selling – In a 2005 survey conducted by Lloyds TSB Staff Union, 39% of mortgage specialists felt they were pressurised to sell products that they knew consumers did not need or could not afford. 92% felt the company was only interested in sales. And these are only the percentages they're prepared to own up to! Because the market is so large, the scope for mis-selling is huge. Around 70% of mortgages are re-mortgages where the scope for churning contracts to generate commission is increased.

Mortgage advisers would like you to re-mortgage every 2 or 3 years as this generates new commission. They are loath to consider longer term contracts such as lifetime base-rate trackers, as this gives them little scope to recommend future re-mortgages. Many advisers in the mortgage market are struggling to comply with the new regulated market, as proved by the poor advice uncovered by the FSA and 'mystery customers' used by the consumer organisation Which?

Can I complain? Mortgages became regulated from 31 October 2004. All mortgages sold prior to this date are not covered unless the organisation was covered by the Mortgage Code Arbitration Scheme. Advice received directly from most lenders should be covered, but advice from mortgage brokers and IFAs will not.

Proving mis-selling – Initially it would appear very difficult to prove mis-selling as advisers can hide behind over 8,000 deals in the market, which are always changing. They defend their position by stating they provided the best deal in a moving market. Rates do change, but a few fundamentals need to be addressed before the final deal is chosen.

Exclusions – The following are exempt from mis-selling complaints: 'Buy to Let' mortgages, and some mortgage switches with the same lender from mortgages started before 31 October 2004.

Reasons to Complain

There are a few fundamental rules a salesman should have followed to make sure that you got the most suitable deal for your needs and circumstances.

Regulatory Failures – This is one of the FSA's main causes of concern, compliance visits have revealed that large numbers of cases are incorrectly documented. This may involve breaches that would result in a successful mis-selling claim.

- **The Initial Disclosure Document (IDD)** – Did you get one at the first contact with the adviser? Did the adviser disclose their status and whether they deal with all mortgage providers, some providers or just one provider? Many of the highest charging advisers represent just one lending company and are uncompetitive. Was this made clear? If not the adviser breached the rules.
- **Key Facts Illustration (KFI)** – Did you get one? Did the adviser clearly explain all the charges and fees associated with starting and redeeming the mortgage? These should all be detailed in the Key Features Illustration. Some advisers also make further charges which may not be immediately obvious. Does the information in the KFI match the workings of the mortgage? If not the adviser breached the rules.
- **Recording Suitability** – Advisers often fail to record adequately why the recommendation was suitable and appropriate for the client's needs and circumstances. Request a copy of your personal file held by the firm, to which you are entitled under the Data Protection Act.

Repayment or Interest-only – In the first instance, all borrowers should be recommended a repayment mortgage as this is the lowest risk option. Interest-only mortgages carry extra risk as the debt is still outstanding at the end of the mortgage term. You are forced to rely on investments that may or may not pay off the debt. They should only be used at your insistence.

Investments backing up Interest-only – Some advisers recommend investments to repay the debt on interest-only mortgages. Many investments will fail to deliver a net return after tax equivalent to the interest payments. Endowments, are NOT tax-efficient and will fail many investors. The mis-selling of endowment mortgages is comprehensively covered in Chapter 12.

Amount – Did you need to borrow as much? Did you have other assets that could have been used to reduce the initial loan?

Term – Why did you sign up for a loan term of 25 years? It may be traditional, but may bear no relation to your personal objectives, and should have been ignored if you could afford to repay a debt sooner. Best advice dictates you should repay all debts as soon as possible.

Inappropriate Protection Policies – Salesmen like to piggy-back protection policies on to a mortgage as it can earn far more commission than the mortgage loan. Their recommendations are often inappropriate. Never buy protection policies from a commission-based mortgage adviser. See Chapter 14, Investment and Protection Complaints.

Re-mortgaging costs – Did the salesman disclose all the re-mortgaging costs? Did they provide evidence to prove that by switching you would be better off within a stated period because:

- The monthly savings covered all the re-mortgaging costs over the timescales expected.
- At the end of the deal period, the outstanding debt is the same or lower than the amount that would have been outstanding under the original mortgage loan.

Often the extra re-mortgaging costs are so high that the salesman bundles them in with the existing loan. While your monthly repayments may initially be lower, the outstanding loan is higher. At the end of the deal period you may find yourself in the position of having more debt.

Table 1 identifies the charges you could encounter when re-mortgaging.

Table 1. **Re-mortgaging Costs**	
Old Lender's Charges	
Redemption Penalty	If you accept a special deal and you repay (redeem) your mortgage at any time prior to the end of the mortgage deal term you may have to pay certain fees or an interest penalty. Most mortgages that plod along at the Standard Variable Rate (SVR) can be moved without penalty.
Redemption Penalty Overhang	Some have extended redemption penalty tie-ins. This means that the penalty charges will extend beyond the initial fixed or discounted period.
Interest Penalty	On ending a mortgage some lenders may charge interest for the whole month, regardless of when the change is made. If this applies the change should have been made at the end of the month.
Exit Fee Administration Charge/ Deeds Release Fee / Sealing Fee	Basically this is the exit fee to cover the release of your Property Deeds to the new lender. As it can be varied at any time some lenders, especially the banks are profiteering and abusing this privilege to hike up their charges to extortionate levels. Variable up to £200, and rising. Such practices on their own a justify a complaint as it infringes the Financial Services Authority (FSA) 'Treating Customers Fairly' principles.
New Lender's Charges	
Booking Fee	Used to secure the deal – not refundable. Not always applied. Variable up to £250.
Valuation	£200 to £500 depending on size of property.
Legal Fees	Estimate £250 - £1,000.
Arrangement Fee	Variable Payable to the lender £200 - £500.
Telegraphic Transfer	Transfer of funds between lenders £20 to £30.
Adviser Charges / Fees	Variable 0.5% to 1.5% of the advance which is usually accounted for in the lenders rate. Some also charge an additional advice fee.

CASE STUDY

The Atkins family had a 20-year repayment mortgage of £100,000, subject to an interest rate of 6.5% when a salesman told them he could save them over £1,000 a year by switching to a 5% fixed rate for 2 years. Mr Atkins decided to re-mortgage:

Table 2. Salesman's Pitch

	After ONE Year		After TWO Years	
	Current £100,000	Proposed £100,000	Current £100,000	Proposed £100,000
Total Annual Repayments	£8,947	£7,919	£17,894	£15,839
Total Repayment Savings	None	£1,027	None	£2,055
Loan Outstanding	£97,479	£97,013	£94,789	£93,873
Loan Reduction	-	£466	-	£916
TOTAL Savings (Repayments & Loan Reduction)		£1,494		£2,971

The salesman advised that all the additional costs could be added to the mortgage, so the Atkins didn't have to find the extra money. Table 3 examines the true re-mortgaging costs, including penalties, amounting to £3,000.

Table 3. Actual Costs

	ONE Year		TWO Years	
	Old £100,000	NEW £103,000	Old £100,000	NEW £103,000
Total Annual Repayments	£8,947	£8,157	£17,894	£16,314
Total Repayment Savings	None	£790	None	£1,580
Loan Outstanding YEAR END	£97,479	£99,923	£94,789	£96,689
Loan Reduction Savings	£2,444	None	£1,900	None
TOTAL Savings (Repayments & Loan Reduction)	£1,654	None	£320	None

When I met Ron Atkins I pointed out that he should have waited until the end of the mortgage term to avoid the £1,800 redemption penalty. This deal was just an exercise in commission generation for the salesman that has left Ron £320 out of pocket.

For any re-mortgage to be classed as best advice it must place the borrower in a more advantageous position, after taking into account all the re-mortgaging administration costs, the loan outstanding and the monthly repayments. If not, the salesman is 'churning' to generate commission.

Re-mortgaging using existing lender – Salesmen are keen to rebroker your mortgage with a new lender, as this generates commission. They often fail to ask your existing lender for details of their best offer, which would save switching costs, and may provide a better deal.

Affordability – Safety margins should always be built into repayments to make sure you can continue to afford them if interest rates rise, or to cover the probable rate increases at the end of a deal period.

Short-term deals & Standard Variable Rates (SVR) – Most salesmen encourage you to take out deals for 2 or 3 years, where the interest rate is fixed, discounted or capped below the SVR. However, at the end of the deal period most revert to the lender's SVR which is usually uncompetitive, often set at 1.5% to 2% above base-rates, giving the salesman the chance to re-mortgage again and again, making commission and charges at your expense.

> Whistle-blower believes this practice is irresponsible and therefore mis-selling as it assumes that there will always be a better deal to switch to and that the customer wants to switch. By failing to consider long-term deals, these recommendations do not take into account the long-term needs of most people.
>
> Whistle-blower believes best advice dictates that all consumers should always be recommended mortgages that revert to a 'Lifetime Base-rate Tracker', capped at no more than 1% above base-rates. This is a mortgage where the interest rate follows the movement in the lending base-rates set by the Bank of England. (It may be possible to secure 0.5%.) It should be the benchmark against which all mortgages are measured, as it caters for the majority who do not regularly switch.

Sub-Prime Mortgages – These are mortgages for borrowers with impaired or low credit ratings. Such borrowers tend to be more vulnerable and are taken advantage of by unscrupulous salesmen. See Section b) Mis-selling of Sub-prime mortgages. Use complaint letter 16.

Pension Mortgages – These are interest-only mortgages that use the cash from a pension scheme to repay the loan. The pension scheme most often used is a personal pension plan. This is a high-risk strategy that can lead to a mortgage repayment shortfall as the associated risks were not fully explained. See Chapter 10 b. Use complaint letter 3.

Claim for Mis-selling

This should be based on the extra costs you incurred because the salesman recommended an unsuitable mortgage for someone in your circumstances and with your risk profile. You need to be restored to the position that you would have been in if you had taken the best repayment mortgage tracking at no more than 1% above the Bank of England base rate. Those reasons are:

- You were recommended an interest only mortgage and savings plan when a repayment mortgage would have been more suitable.
- You have paid too much interest because you were recommended the wrong deal, as the salesman failed to take into account other assets, greater affordability, reduced term, lifetime base rate tracker deals and the existing lenders options.
- The re-mortgaging savings were incorrectly calculated leaving you in a loss situation as the recommendation was based on a false prospectus.

If you feel you have been misled, use Letter 15 and seek redress.

b) Mis-selling of Sub-Prime Mortgages

Who is Affected – All those with have applied for a sub-prime mortgage, especially those who have consolidated other debts.

A Sub-Prime Mortgage is a mortgage for borrowers with impaired or low credit ratings who are unable to obtain a mortgage under normal terms and conditions from a traditional high street lender. These are also referred to as non-prime, non-conforming, non-status or adverse credit mortgages.

Impaired Credit Rating – This will apply to borrowers who are ex-bankrupts, or have defaulted on loans or have County Court Judgements (CCJs) against them.

Low Credit Rating – This will apply to borrowers who do not have sufficient credit history, through multiple jobs, short contract work or who are self-employed and do not have a trading record of 3 years.

Sub-prime mortgages are categorised according to risk. Higher risk results in higher interest charges which vary depending on the 'loan to value' (LTV), which is the amount you want to borrow as a percentage of the value of your property.

Categorisation

Sub-prime mortgages are categorised according to risk. Higher risk results in higher interest charges. These vary depending on the borrower's credit history and the size of the loan. Don't imagine the lender is doing you a favour. With sub-prime mortgages, lenders need to cover the extra risk with higher interest rates and tighter conditions. They are making a commercial decision to lend you money with your house as the security and will start court proceedings and seek a 'possession order' if you fail to keep up the loan repayments. Categorisation depends on the impact of different types of debts as detailed in Table 1 below.

Aspects of Sub-prime Mortgages

Bankruptcy – You are declared bankrupt if you make a petition, or a creditor makes a petition to a court that results in a bankruptcy order. Then an official receiver is appointed who takes control of your property and deals with your creditors. You will be automatically freed from bankruptcy (discharged) after one year. After being satisfactorily discharged you can apply for a mortgage, albeit at high rate. If you wait a year the rates will reduce.

County Court judgements (CCJs) – These are notices served by a county court ordering a debtor to repay a debt. Initially a creditor will approach the court and file a claim, then the court sends the debtor a 'claim form' and the debtor has 16 days to reply. At the court hearing, if the judge agrees with the creditor, a CCJ is issued against the debtor. When you apply for a mortgage a lender will be looking at CCJs of no more of £1,000 for the best sub-prime rates to unlimited CCJs for the highest rates.

Individual Voluntary Agreements (IVA) – These are formal agreements made between a debtor and a creditor to restructure debt repayments. A debtor may be close to insolvency but to avoid being declared bankrupt, may apply for an interim order preventing creditors from proceeding with a bankruptcy petition. A meeting is called whereby if at least 75% of the creditors (by amount owed) vote for the proposal, the agreement is binding on all creditors. When seeking a mortgage the borrower will usually have to provide proof that the payments have been satisfactorily paid for 6 months.

Loan to Value (LTV) – Is the amount you want to borrow as a percentage of the value of your property, i.e. an £85,000 mortgage is against a property valued at £100,000 = 85% LTV. The lower the LTV, the lower the interest rate.

Mortgage Arrears – The number of months that a borrower has failed to repay their mortgage. When seeking a sub-prime mortgage, a borrower with no more than 2 missed payments in the last 12 months will secure the best rates. Some lenders are willing to accept unlimited arrears, but at very high rates.

Self Certification – Prospective borrowers are able to vouch for their own income to apply for a mortgage where there is no history of steady regular income, which may be the case for contract workers or those new to self employment with less than 3 years accounts. When seeking a sub-prime mortgage, lenders will apply a premium to the interest rate to cover the extra risk. Some advisers are guilty of encouraging or even entering false information to secure a mortgage to earn commission.

Table 1. Categorisation of Sub-prime Mortgages

Description	Bankruptcy	IVA	CCJs	Mortgage / Rent Arrears	Max LTV	Adviser Commission
Mainstream	Not Acceptable	Not Acceptable	Not Acceptable	Not Acceptable	95%	0.35% to 0.5%
Self Cert	Not Acceptable	Not Acceptable	Not Acceptable	Not Acceptable	85%	0.4% to 0.7%
Near Prime	Not Acceptable	Not Acceptable	Max £1,000 Satisfied None in last 12 months	Satisfied None in 12 months	90%	0.5% to 0.7%
Extra Light / Low	Discharged for 1 Year	Satisfied for 1 Year	Max £3,000 None in last 6 months	1 in 12 months	90%	0.5% to 0.7%
Light / Low	Discharged for 1 Year	Satisfied for 1 Year	Max £5,000 None in last 6 months	2 in 12 months	90%	0.5% to 0.1%
Medium	Discharged for 1 Year	Satisfied for 1 Year	Max £7,500	3 in 12 months	85%	1%
Heavy	Discharged	Satisfactorily Conducted	Max £10,000	6 in 12 months	80%	1% +
Unlimited	Discharged	Satisfactorily Conducted	Unlimited	Unlimited	75%	1% +

NOTES

1. This is a general guide, different lenders apply different criteria. That which is categorised as near prime by one lender is considered extra light by another.
2. Mortgage rates vary according to the LTV. For example if you were to borrow only 50% of the value of your property the interest rate would reduce by at least 0.5%
3. A borrower who applies for a sub-prime mortgage and who also needs to self certify their earnings can expect the interest rate to increase by a further 0.25% to 0.5%.

Scope for mis-selling

It is estimated that 1 in 5 people are rejected by high street lenders because of concerns over credit. In this large sub-prime market the scope for mis-selling is huge. Sub-prime borrowers tend to be more vulnerable to mis-selling because they may have been rejected more than once and some are desperate for someone to say yes. Their family circumstances may have changed and they need a loan because they need a home, and some applicants lack financial literacy skills that caused the original credit problems. Unscrupulous salesmen take advantage of borrowers' vulnerability and make unsuitable recommendations to earn commission.

Can I Complain?

Mortgages became regulated from 31 October 2004. Mortgages sold prior to this date are not regulated unless the organisation was covered by the Mortgage Code Arbitration Scheme; most lenders would have been, but advice from intermediaries such as mortgage brokers and IFAs will not be covered.

Proving mis-selling

Initially it would seem difficult to prove mis-selling as advisers can hide behind the volume of deals, which are always changing. They defend their position by stating they provided the best deal in a moving market, BUT a few fundamentals should have been addressed before the final deal is chosen. The adviser must treat you fairly and place your interests first. They should make recommendations suitable for your needs and circumstances. Many do not.

Reasons to Complain

Regulatory Failures

This is one of the FSA's main causes of concern. Compliance visits have revealed that over 60% of sub-prime cases are incorrectly documented. This may involve breaches that would result in a successful mis-selling claim.

The Initial Disclosure Document (IDD) – Did you get one at the first contact with the adviser? Did the adviser disclose their status and whether they deal with all mortgage providers, some providers or just one provider? Many of the highest charging advisers represent just one lending company and are uncompetitive. Was this made clear? If not the adviser breached the rules.

Key Facts Illustration (KFI) – Did you get one? Did the adviser clearly explain all the charges and fees associated with starting and redeeming the mortgage? These should all be detailed in the Key Features Illustration. Some advisers also make further charges (e.g. 2%

– 3% of the advance as a set up fee) which may not be immediately obvious. Does the information in the KFI match the workings of the mortgage? If not the adviser breached the rules.

Recording Suitability – Advisers often fail to record adequately why the recommendation was suitable and appropriate for the client's needs and circumstances. Request a copy of your personal file held by the firm, to which you are entitled under the Data Protection Act.

Unsuitable Sub-prime Mortgages

The FSA states that a suitable mortgage contract must satisfy ALL three of the following conditions, that you can afford to enter into the contract, that it is appropriate to your needs and circumstances AND it is the most suitable contract available from the lender from the service they provide.

Most sub-prime lenders do not deal direct with the public so borrowers have to use intermediaries. The recommendation to use a sub-prime mortgage may not have been properly assessed as the intermediary failed to use the search and underwriting systems correctly. Some advisers categorise borrowers incorrectly and recommend higher risk sub-prime mortgages to increase their commission. Some lenders operate 'cascade underwriting systems' where the adviser logs into the lender's web-site and inputs client details so the system can analyse client needs and recommend according to risk. Advisers who override the recommendation and opt for an alternative may be acting unscrupulously.

We can only guess how often this has happened. A complaint to the ombudsman will expose any mis-selling. Where a better deal was available but ignored, compensation for the difference in interest payments should be claimed.

Consolidating Loans

Nearly 60% of sub-prime mortgages involve the consolidation of debt. If the adviser can encourage you to consolidate your debts and increase your mortgage they make more commission. Many fail to carry out a comprehensive evaluation to assess whether consolidation is appropriate. This omission will help you to make a successful mis-selling claim.

Secured Vs Unsecured – A mortgage is a loan secured against a property, and if something goes wrong, the debt can be collected. Most personal loans and credit card debts are 'unsecured loans', as they are not secured against your property. Were you made aware of the differences and the consequences of increasing your secure loans? If not, you have a case for mis-selling.

Renegotiate Debts – If you were experiencing repayment problems, did your adviser recommend renegotiating the terms of the loan with the original lender? If so what was the outcome? Most advisers fail to explore this option fully and you may claim mis-selling.

Lower Outgoings? – Were you misled into believing the adviser could save you money by reducing your outgoings? Did the adviser explain the consequences of extending the loan term? Were there redemption penalties and how were they taken into account? Were they hidden within the lower monthly outgoings?

CASE STUDY

Ali Jenkins had a personal loan of £10,000 fixed at 8% for 5 years (see Table 2). After 2 years she was struggling with her debts and had defaulted on a payment. A salesman recommended consolidating the personal loan within a sub-prime mortgage with a variable interest rate of 7.5% (0.5% lower), but he failed to carry out the necessary assessment.

When Ali came to me she was totally unaware that the extra 17 years' interest payments and the redemption penalty would cost her a further £6,389!

Table 2. Loan Consolidation Analysis

Original Loan	£10,000
Monthly Repayment – fixed 8% for 5 years	£203
TOTAL Repayments after 5 years	£12,166
TOTAL Interest Payments at end of 5 years	£2,166

Salesman recommended consolidating the personal loan within a sub-prime mortgage with a variable interest rate of 7.5%, which is 0.5% lower but failed to carry out the following assessment.

Event	Continue with Loan	Consolidate Loan
Loan Outstanding	£6,471	£6,471
Redemption Penalty (3 months interest)	-	£609
Total Loan	£6,471	£7,080
Loan Terminates	3 Years	20 Years
Monthly Repayments	£203	£57
TOTAL Repayments over term	£7,300	£13,689
TOTAL Payments above £6,471	£853	£7,218
Extra Payments made (£)	-	£6,389
Extra Payments made (%)	-	750%

If the salesman had asked the original lender to renegotiate the loan, Ali could have extended the term by 3 years, reducing her monthly payments to £114, which she could afford.

Ali has grounds for a mis-selling claim and compensation.

Higher Purchase (HP) / Conditional Sale Agreements – These are loan agreements often used to buy goods (furniture and cars) where you never own the goods until the last payment is made. Until that time, the creditor (usually a lender, not the retailer) owns the goods. Interest payments can be much higher than for personal loans.

CASE STUDY

My previous neighbour Jon had a HP agreement on a car for £10,000 for 5 years. The effective Annual Percentage Rate (APR) was 15%. After one year a salesman persuaded Jon to consolidate the loan with a sub-prime mortgage paying 7.5% interest. The monthly repayments were lower, and Jon asked me what he should do.

Table 3. Monthly Repayments Comparison

HP Agreement @ 15%	£238
Consolidation Mortgage @ 7.5%	£92
Monthly Savings	£146

With HP agreements, monthly repayments are fixed for the term of the loan. If you repay the whole loan you simply pay off ALL the outstanding payments early and don't make any savings in interest payments. You are simply giving the creditors back their money early as detailed in Table 4.

Table 4. Schedule of HP Loan Payments

Period	Monthly Payment	Annual Payment	Outstanding	Redemption Amount
Start	£238	£2,856	60 months	£14,280
After 1 Year	£238	£2,856	48 months	£11,424
After 2 Years	£238	£2,856	36 months	£8,568
After 3 Years	£238	£2,856	24 months	£5,712
After 4 Years	£238	£2,856	12 months	£2,856

After one year, the recommendation to consolidate the HP loan would result in the outstanding £11,424 being repaid early instead of spreading the cost over 4 years. The salesman had made the situation worse because Jon would now be paying two sets of interest charges on the same borrowed money, 15% from the original HP loan, and 7.5% on the mortgage making 22.5%! See Table 5.

Table 5. Mortgage Interest on £11,424

Year 1	£848
Year 2	£828
Year 3	£807
Year 4	£784
TOTAL	£3,267

I advised Jon to leave the HP agreement in place and reduce his other outgoings.

Switching between Sub-prime Mortgages – Did the salesman disclose all the re-mortgaging costs? Did they provide evidence to prove that by switching you would be better off within a stated period because the monthly savings would cover all the re-mortgaging costs over the timescales expected? And evidence that at the end of the deal period, the outstanding debt would be the same or lower than the amount that would have been outstanding under the original mortgage loan?

As extra re-mortgaging costs are so high, the salesman will bundle them in with the existing loan. While your monthly repayments may initially be lower, the outstanding loan is higher. At the end of the deal period you may actually BE IN MORE DEBT.

For re-mortgaging costs, refer to Table 1 in Chapter 13 a, Mortgage Complaints.

Self-certified Mortgages & Falsifying Information – Advisers still close deals by asking people, *'Shall I fill out the paperwork for you?'* Some will embellish the borrower's self-certified earnings to secure a higher loan, with or without the borrower's knowledge. It is a criminal offence to falsify or to be party to the falsification of information. Such practices ignore the need to assess affordability now and in the future. The adviser should have recommended the borrower consider a smaller loan. If you are struggling to manage your debts as you were advised to borrow too much by an adviser who falsified your earnings, you have a claim for mis-selling.

Inappropriate Protection Policies – Salesmen often piggy-back protection policies on to a mortgage as it can earn them far more commission than the mortgage alone. Their recommendations are often inappropriate. (See Chapter 13 d, Mis-selling of Loan Payment Protection Insurance, and Chapter 14 Investment & Protection Complaints.)

Claim for mis-selling

This is based on the extra costs you have incurred because a salesman recommended an unsuitable mortgage for someone in your circumstances, with your needs and risk profile. You need to be restored to the position you would have been in if you had been recommended the most suitable mortgage, which should also take into account the decision to consolidate any other loans. A successful compensation claim will help reduce your debt problems.

Conclusion

The market for sub-prime mortgages is likely to grow as more consumers struggle and fall into debt. Regrettably, the most vulnerable consumers are the least likely to contact the regulator when things go wrong. Instead they may seek advice from a salesman who recommends a sub-prime mortgage linked to debt consolidation. Whistle-blower believes the regulator has a duty to protect the weakest consumers and should send a clear message that the FSA will not tolerate the mis-selling of such mortgages by announcing a review of every sub-prime mortgage sold since 31 October 2004.

We suspect the FSA will not initiate such action. To help the most vulnerable, we have prepared Letter 16. Use this to claim compensation.

Need Help?

If you're struggling with mounting debts and mortgage problems, do contact one of the many charitable or government organisations that offer free, independent confidential advice. Help is only a free phone call away. Contact the organisations listed below.

Table 6. Debt Counselling Organisations / Information

Sources of Information	Remarks
National Debtline Freephone: 0808 808 4000 www.nationaldebthelpline.co.uk	Charity dedicated to helping people with debt problems by providing a free confidential phone service.
Citizens Advice Bureau Local number in phone book www.adviceguide.org.uk	Citizens Advice Bureau web-site with practical advice to addressing debt problems.
Shelter Freephone: 0808 800 4444 www.shelter.org.uk	Charity dedicated to preventing homelessness and helping the homeless. Web-site includes clear guidance and help on repossessions.
Consumer Credit Counselling Service Freephone: 0800 138 1111 www.cccs.co.uk	Industry sponsored charity that offers free advice on how to manage debt problems.
Money Advice Scotland 0141 572 0237 www.moneyadvicescotland.org.uk	Set up by the Scottish Consumer Council to provide free and confidential debt advice.
www.insolvency.go.uk	Department of Trade & Industry (DTI) web-site with numerous helpful guides.
www.direct.gov.uk	UK Government web-site with very helpful search facility on all subjects.
Community Legal Service Direct Tel: 0845 345 4345 www.clsdirect.org.uk	Direct advice to help you find the right legal information. Sponsored by the Legal Services Commission who look after legal aid in England & Wales.
The Home Repossession Page www.home-repo.org/	Consumer 'underdog' web-site. Needs updating but provides information to those who have had or are having their home repossessed.

c) Mis-selling of Equity Release Plans

Who is affected – Those of you who have used the equity in your house to raise money, while continuing to live in the property.

Background

There are 2 types of equity release plans whereby the lender takes a first legal charge over your home.

Lifetime Mortgage – You take a mortgage against your house and make no repayments, while interest rolls up within the loan. You can either take one lump sum or withdraw money in tranches to suit your annual income needs. On death your house is sold and the mortgage repaid. These plans became regulated from 31 October 2004.

Home Reversion Plans – You sell a percentage of your house in exchange for a lump sum or income. You pay no rent on the portion sold. On death the purchaser acquires that percentage of the house sale proceeds, regardless of its value. These plans are currently not regulated as they are considered to be sale and purchase agreements and not a financial product. It is unlikely that they will be regulated before 2007.

Plans of Last Resort

Lifetime mortgages are plans of last resort as the compounding effect of the interest will rapidly increase the size of your debt and erode your wealth. Most offer very poor value, with fixed mortgage rates of around 6% to 7%. Your money would have to grow at 9% gross just to maintain your position, an almost impossible target in the current climate of low inflation. (Some plans taken out in the last 5 years may even have used rates of 7.5% and 8%.)

Current rates are far too high compared to other mortgages, sometimes 1% to 2% above the standard variable rate. Lenders say they need to apply a higher rate to cover the guarantee of 'no negative equity,' (where the loan is greater than the value of your house). With this guarantee you can never owe more than the value of your home, regardless of the size of the eventual loan.

Why not Different Rates?

Whistle-blower believes the industry should set two rates, one for small loans where there is virtually no chance they could exceed the house value, and one for larger loans where there is a little more risk.

Lender's Flawed Risk Assessment

It seems perverse that lenders are prepared to lend 90% to 95% of the value of a house to a first-time buyer who has limited assets (and where there is a risk of negative equity) at interest rates below

5%. In contrast a home-owner with equity of £100,000s is locked into a lifetime contract by high redemption charges, and charged 7% annual interest or more. This looks like exploitation of the older borrower. You should not be persuaded or advised to sign up to these terms. Rates are now coming down to 6% and will go lower, so wait.

The Effect of Extortionate Rates

See below how a typical lifetime mortgage of £50,000 on a house valued at £300,000 can escalate to levels that wipe out the wealth of an entire lifetime of work.

Table 1. Lifetime Mortgage of £50,000 – Amount Owed		
Term	Current Rate 7%	Top Fair Rate 5.5%
5 years	£70,128	£65,348
10 years	£98,358	£85,407
15 years	£137,952	£111,624
20years	£198,484	£145,888
25 years	£271,372	£190,670
30 years	£380,613	£249,198
35 years	£533,829	£325,691

Regulation

If you were advised to take out one of these plans before they were regulated, you cannot complain to the ombudsman about the specific contractual terms, and if the adviser / provider has become insolvent you are not covered by the FS compensation scheme. If the equity release company is a member of the trade body called Safe Home Income Plans (SHIP), they will try and resolve the dispute or bring in an independent arbitrator. However, the advice on investing the lump sum IS regulated, and you can complain about the investment of money which was unsuitable for someone in your circumstances, because you were recommended to invest in risky funds where the returns are unlikely to cover your mortgage interest payments.

The FSA is Concerned

In May 2005 the FSA flagged up concern over these contracts following an investigation using mystery shoppers who uncovered a catalogue of mis-demeanours. The industry claimed the investigation used too small a sample, but neutral observers disagree. As with all mis-selling, we must analyse the suitability to your needs and circumstances – paying particular attention to the risks.

Reasons to Complain

Stay in your Own Home OR Trade Down – The main reason advisers give for recommending an equity release plan, is that the client stated they did not want to move so trading down was not an option. But were you made aware of the likely cost and associated risks of all the options? If not, you were being asked to make a major investment decision based on insufficient information.

Trading down is a low-risk strategy. Equity release is a high-risk strategy, as demonstrated in Table 2. Lump Sum Equity Release plans come out second best after trading down. Equity release will only work if house prices continue to rise. If these tail off or reverse over the next decade, some investors could see their lifetime assets wiped out in less than 20 years. It would help if the FSA made it compulsory to show how long it would take to wipe out your assets under different investment scenarios, which would make consumers think about the true cost of equity release.

Table 2. Income Options

	Equity Release	Trade Down
House Value	£350,000	£350,000
Lifetime Mortgage 7%	£100,000	N.A.
New House Purchase (Allow £15,000 Costs)	N.A.	£235,000
Free Cash	£100,000	£100,000
Position after 10 YEARS if house inflation is 2% above inflation		
Cash after £5,000 withdrawals	£50,000	£50,000
House Growth 4%	£518,085	£347,857
Lifetime Mortgage	£196,715	-
NET Assets / Family Inheritance	£371,370	£397,857
Position after 20 YEARS if house inflation is 2% above inflation		
Cash after £5,000 withdrawals	Nil	Nil
House Growth 4%	£766,893	£514,914
Mortgage	£386,968	-
NET Assets / Family Inheritance	£379,925	£514,914
Term to NET Assets = NIL	45 Years	Never
Position after 10 YEARS if house inflation is equal to inflation		
Cash after withdrawals	£50,000	£50,000
House Growth 2%	£426,648	£286,464
Mortgage	£196,715	-
NET Assets / Family Inheritance	£279,933	£336,464
Position after 20 YEARS if house inflation is equal to inflation		
Cash after withdrawals	Nil	Nil
House Growth 2%	£520,082	£349,198
Mortgage	£386,968	-
NET Assets / Family Inheritance	£133,114	£349,198
Term to NET Assets = NIL	26 Years	Never

The bottom line of the equity release column provides a sobering thought, for after 26 years the loan is worth more than your house! A working lifetime scrimping and saving to buy a house is wasted, because your house is now owned by the mortgage company and the money released has all been spent. You have nothing! How are you going to manage?

Lifetime Mortgage Options – If there was no other choice than to opt for equity release, did the adviser consider all the equity release options? In the past advisers encouraged home-owners to take a large lump sums and ignored the option of annual income withdrawals.

In Whistle-blower's opinion, every consumer who was recommended a lump sum equity release plan, (where some or all of the proceeds are invested, and where investment returns fail to cover the mortgage interest), has been a victim of mis-selling. This is a high-risk strategy totally unsuitable for most elderly investors. The bad advice is further compounded by the use of Life Office bonds where initial charges of up to 7% place your investments at an immediate disadvantage. A lower risk strategy using a drawdown plan to take income on an annual basis should have been recommended.

This alone is sufficient to make a claim for compensation based on the difference between the drawdown and lump sum options.

If you need a lump sum to cover expenditure like an operation or lifetime holiday you should have been advised to take what was needed and no more. Building societies will allocate you an allowable mortgage against which you draw on an annual basis. See below how much better off you would be with a draw-down lifetime mortgage compared to a lump sum.

Table 3. Lifetime Mortgage Options – Comparison

	Lump Sum	Draw-down
House	£350,000	£350,000
Mortgage @ 7% interest	£100,000	£5,000 per year
Investment Bond after Charges	£94,000	-
Income	£5,000	£5,000
Position after 10 Years		
Mortgage	£196,715	£73,918
Bond (4% net after Charges)	£76,711	-
NET Debt	£120,004	£73,918
Position after 20 Years		
Mortgage	£386,968	£219,326
Bond 4% after Charges	£51,120	-
NET Debt	£335,848	£219,326

After 10 years you could be £46,086 better off (£116,522 after 20 years). This extra capital could be used to make further advances, or provide a greater inheritance for the family.

Risky Investments – Were you recommended to take more than you needed for the immediate expenditure? Was that extra money invested in share-based investments where the returns can rise and fall and are lower than the mortgage interest? Unless you insisted, then such a high-risk strategy was mis-selling. You should have been recommended to withdraw the money in tranches, to reduce the accumulation of debt and avoid high-risk investments.

> The initial euphoria of going on holiday or the security of having a little extra in the bank could soon be replaced by the insecurity of a runaway debt and an investment that has failed to deliver, making the last years of your retirement a misery.

Lack of Regulatory Support – Was it made clear to you that the advice you were receiving was not regulated and that this may restrict your compensation options?

Misleading Interest Rate Information – When the adviser quoted an interest rate, was this the annualised rate? If not you may have been misled as a headline rate may look good, but compounded over a year it may be 0.3% higher than you were told.

State Benefits – Did the adviser carry out a full analysis of your income? One of the reasons for releasing cash is the need for extra income. If you did not have enough to live on, you may be entitled to means-tested state benefits such as pension credit and council tax reductions. Were you advised to discuss your position with the Department for Work & Pensions, your District Council and charitable organisations like Help the Aged, who are familiar with all entitlements for the elderly? Sometimes plans are started prior to full retirement before retirement income is known. If your income is low, acquiring a lump sum could have the negative result of reducing your entitlement to state benefits.

Taxation – Equity withdrawals are tax-free, as are proceeds from selling your main residence. Were you made aware that by taking a lump sum and investing it, you were moving money from a tax-free environment to a taxed one? Again, annual equity withdrawals would have been preferable.

Home improvements – Advisers often recommend equity release to improve your home, but may not have informed you about local authority or charity grants. Some councils operate their own Home Reversion Plans, whereby they will carry out improvements to your property and then allow you to continue living there, taking a percentage of the sale proceeds. There are also charities and agencies that give grants, details of which are in the FSA Factsheet, 'Raising money from your Home'.

Inheritance Tax Planning – Equity release plans are sometimes sold to release cash to carry out inheritance tax planning. This usually involves the money being invested in a life insurance bond, with 5% withdrawals providing an income or paying for a life policy. These schemes rely on the bond to deliver a certain return and for the life cover premiums not to increase. They are complicated, with too many unknowns, so carry a high probability of failure. You could have gifted the money or just spent it! In most cases theses are just exercises in commission generation. A £100,000 bond where the 5% withdrawals are use to fund a life policy could generate immediate commission of £12,000, with £500+ a year thereafter, which is taken from your money.

TOPTIP

Health – Did the adviser consider the consequences of declining health or the loss of a partner which may force a move to a smaller property or sheltered housing? Usually equity release schemes are transferable, providing the new property is acceptable, but may exclude sheltered housing. If you are forced to repay the loan, you may not have enough money to buy the house you want. If you go into residential care, your house will be sold and the mortgage repaid, which may not leave you enough to secure a place in a home of your choice.

Charges – The adviser may have failed to draw to your attention to the extent of investment charges and early surrender penalties such as the loan arrangement fee of up to 2.5% added to the loan. Were you made aware that if you redeemed the mortgage within the first 5 years there is likely to be an Early Redemption Charge of 5% of the capital repaid? In some cases these charges extend well beyond 5 years.

Why Salesmen like Equity Release

Lifetime mortgages are a means to an end, and commission-based contracts may be piggy-backed on to the loan. If you borrow £50,000, the salesmen may get £300 to £500 in commission. But if you are persuaded to invest £40,000 into a life insurance bond paying 7% commission, this increases their commission 600%. The motivation to sell inappropriate equity release plans is to generate commission. There are no clearer examples of how commission distorts advice than the sale of equity release plans to fund risky share investments. Only a removal of commission will make consumers safer, especially the elderly and vulnerable.

Why you must Complain

An equity release plan should be no more than a mortgage in reverse. In the same way that interest-only mortgages linked to investment plans (notably endowment plans), are now acknowledged as totally inappropriate, the same conclusion will be drawn about lump sum equity release plans.

If is best advice to repay a mortgage by reducing the loan capital year by year, so in reverse, it is best advice to increase the loan capital by a small amount each year by releasing a little equity year by year.

Sometimes an equity release plan has been agreed by a family member who is reluctant to admit they were wrong. Family members should be questioning the advice given to their elderly parents, especially where incorrect advice may lead them into financial hardship in the future, as well as depriving beneficiaries of their inheritance.

Many advisers will have failed to keep adequate records of why the recommendation was suitable, and this will lead to a successful mis-selling claim. Use complaint Letter 17.

Useful Contacts & Addresses

Organisation	Services	Remarks
Department of Work & Pensions Benefit enquiry line: 0800 88 22 00 www.dwp.gov.uk	Details of state benefits. Ask about benefits on a low income and how a lump sum may affect them.	
Age Concern Freephone 0800 00 99 66 www.ace.org.uk	Charity campaigns on the welfare of the elderly.	Obtain Factsheets FS12 Equity Release schemes FS13 Repairs to your Property.
Help the Aged Freephone 0808 800 6565 www.helptheaged.org.uk	Advice about state benefits and old age.	
SHIP (Safe Home Income Plans) PO Box 516, Preston Central, PR2 2XQ Tel: 0870 241 6060 www.ship-ltd.org	Trade body for equity release companies promoting those providers whose plans with a 'no negative equity guarantee'.	
Home Improvement Agencies (HIA) Tel: 01457 891 909 www.foundations.uk.com	Help and advice in arranging home improvements, including grants.	Will direct you to your local agency. There are separate organisations for Scotland, Wales & Northern Ireland.
The Home Improvement Trust Freephone: 0800 783 7569 www.hitrust.org	Non profit Organisation that facilitates equity release plans.	
Council of Mortgage Lenders Tel: 020 7437 0075 www.cml.org.uk	Industry trade body. Web-site provides a lot of useful information, including details of lifetime mortgages.	

d) Mis-selling of Loan Payment Protection Insurance

Who is Affected – All those who have taken a loan and may or may not be aware that their repayments are protected by insurance, including old loans that have been repaid.

Loan Payment Protection Policies insure the cost of your loan repayments in the event of redundancy or incapacity to work. The cover usually lasts for 12 months and very occasionally extends to 24 months.

Regulation

Only contracts purchased from 14 January 2005 are definitely covered by the ombudsman. Policies sold prior to this date should be covered providing the firm was under the General Insurance Standards Council (check your documentation). The Financial Services Compensation Scheme pays out if the firm is no longer trading, but only covers plans purchased after 14 January 2005.

The Sales Approach

The industry uses three names to describe the same policy. These are:

- PPI – Payment Protection Insurance – usually attached to personal loans.
- MPPI – Mortgage Payment Protection Insurance – usually attached to mortgages.
- ASU – Accident Sickness & Unemployment cover – used as general cover.

These policies often generate far more commission than the loans they are covering, and are tagged on to the end of a sales pitch. They tend not to require underwriting, and profit margins are high compared to other insurance policies as claims are relatively low. They are sold as a 'one size fits all', which of course it doesn't. When completing loan application forms salesman may persuade you to tick the box by hyping up the fear that a failure to maintain repayments could lead to your home being repossessed. The salesman may even tick the box without telling you. As the cost of the insurance is bundled up with the loan repayments, some people do not even know they have it. Other customers are misled into believing protection is a condition of the loan and are obliged to buy it from the lender.

Reasons to Complain

Misleading interest rates

Customers may be provided with misleading rates when they need a personal loan. Quotes must show the Annual Percentage Rate (APR) which includes all costs (both interest and administration), over the term of the loan. To appear more competitive, salesmen sometimes provide quotes excluding the cost of the payment protection insurance.

Deceitful practices are sometimes used by loan consolidation companies who want to bundle all your debts under one roof, 'cancelling' them into one big debt with them.

Ignore adverts using celebrities on day-time TV who tell you to sign up. The maths simply doesn't stack up. If you have debt problems, contact your local Citizens Advice Bureau (CAB) or another debt-counselling organisation from the list earlier in this chapter under sub-prime mortgages.

They provide inadequate cover

The salesman may not have given prominence to strict conditions in the contract that affect any claim, such as:

- The special conditions that apply to the self-employed and the cessation of trade.
- As the policy only covers the loan repayments (which probably amount to less than 25% of your monthly expenditure), how will you pay the other 75%?
- Cover usually lasts 12 months and only covers short-term needs. If you are seriously ill or injured, there is a high probability that you will be unable to return to work within 12 months. What will happen to your home when the payments stop?
- The premiums are not guaranteed and can increase at any time after giving 30 days notice.

High street lenders apply extortionate rates

Buying on the high street is often twice as expensive as buying direct. Banks are some of the worst offenders and offer poor value, taking from a captive audience who feel obliged to buy. This is not allowed within the 'Treating Customers Fairly' rules, and the FSA should insist on reviews of all cover sold on all loans.

Other income protection options ignored

The salesman may ignore other protection options, failing to mention the advantages of Income Protection Policies (IPPs), also known as Permanent Health Insurance (PHI) policies. In the event of a claim following an accident or illness, these plans pay a tax-free income of up to 60% of your earnings to age 65. These policies are not a quick sale, usually requiring completion of a 20-page application form and need underwriting. They are more hassle, and often go un-mentioned. Best advice does not come into the equation. If the lender does not sell pure income protection policies, but there is a clear identifiable need for such protection, they should refer you to the type of organisation that does provide such a service. If they fail to refer customers they are guilty of mis-leading, and of mis-selling an inappropriate product.

Refunds are overlooked

Some lenders sold contracts where borrowers paid an up-front lump sum premium, which is added to the loan and runs for the life of it. Where the loan is repaid early or transferred, the borrower should be entitled to a refund of the premium covering the unused period. Sometimes lenders forget to make refunds, so a retrospective claim can be made. In 2005 Barclays Bank started making refunds of premiums after this administrative error. Although helpful, do not be fobbed off with a partial refund of contributions when 100% return (plus interest) should be claimed, as you may have been mis-sold a contract that was inappropriate for your needs.

Making a claim

Everyone who has taken out a personal loan should examine the contract. A claim for compensation should be based on the fact that the plan is inadequate to suit your needs and you claim a return of your contributions plus interest. Use Letter 18.

14 Investment & Protection Complaints

a) Mis-selling of With-profits Investments

A flawed proposition

The marketing of with-profits funds is built around the flawed proposition that 'you can have your cake and eat it', to the extent investors are promised higher returns than a cash deposit account from a share-holding fund without the usual market risks. This is impossible as with-profits funds cannot defy gravity! During prolonged periods of poor investment returns, they can only disappoint.

Investors have been misled

Investors have been lulled into a false sense of security, in the same way that Titanic passengers were reassured by seeing so many lifeboats. They took it for granted there would be enough to go around. In the same way, with-profits investors are not made aware that if the market went down 50% and stayed down, there would not be enough to go around, and your investment would also crash.

An appealing concept

As a concept, with-profits has appeal. If someone introduced you to a fund that smoothed and averaged returns from a mixed portfolio of assets and declared guaranteed annual bonuses, you would probably be interested. You may be persuaded to invest if you were guaranteed to get back your original capital after 10 years, plus annual bonuses and a terminal bonus that in the past has resulted in investors doubling their money. This spin has sold millions of with-profits policies.

Undermined by commission

The truth is that as providers competed for market share, they declared unsustainable bonuses, and introduced contract guarantees. At the same time, commission was increased to motivate the salesmen. The small print went un-noticed, in case it got in the way of a good sale. For as long as the stock market went up, the party could continue, with everyone a winner.

Doomed to failure

Nobody asked what would happen when the markets went down and stayed down. With-profits funds will fail to meet investor expectations in prolonged, flat economic conditions, because after expenses, investors are unlikely to receive returns as good as cash returns. Millions of ordinary working Britons have been enticed into investing in pseudo low-risk funds, and are now incurring losses. Most of the investors cannot afford to lose money, so how did it happen?

With-profits risk

It all comes down to interpretation of risk. The industry likes to claim that with-profits funds are low-risk funds, and presents simple risk scales placing with-profits just ahead of cash and just behind other mixed asset funds, as demonstrated below:

Table 1. **Industry With-profits Risk Comparison**			
Risk Scale		**WITH-PROFITS Categorisation**	**Other Investments Categorisation**
0	NO Risk		National Savings, Cash Deposit Accounts
1	Low-risk	Industry	Short-term Gilts
2	Low / Med Risk	Ombudsman *	Longer term Gilts / Mixed funds - low equity content, around 40%
3	Med Risk	Ombudsman * Consumer	Large Company Share Funds, Mixed Funds - High Equity content around 80%
4	Med / High-risk		UK smaller Companies, International Funds
5	High-risk		Emerging Markets

Appealing to 'No Risk' investors – The industry uses this format to target customers with money on deposit, who are currently risk averse. Time and again salesmen said, *'Let us make your money work for you,'* knowing they could not persuade 'No risk' savers to consider mixed funds with 60% to 80% invested in shares. But a fund that is 'guaranteed' not to go down, and may produce better returns than cash can entice people, especially if you give it a profitable sounding name!

Consider Table 1 and ask yourself, is it a fair reflection of with-profits risk, relative to other investments?

Whistle-blower says, NO!

Note to Table 1.

*the ombudsman has not defined with-profits on any risk scale as it would cause an avalanche of complaints if they were to set a precedent. They will only analyse risk on an individual case-by-case basis. However having spoken to staff at the FOS, they would, off the record, categorise with-profits as a 2 / 3 on such a scale depending on the fund.

This is excellent news for consumers as they know that any claim for mis-selling that involves the recommendation to invest in a low-risk, with-profits fund will be dealt with sympathetically. The FOS is currently more aligned with the consumer's attitude to risk.

Table 2 reflects consumers' simple attitude to risk which advisers may ignore.

Table 2. Consumer Attitude to Risk

Risk Scale		Description
0	No Risk	Will not lose money, have instant access, get a little interest each year
1	Risky	Could lose some of my money. up to 10%
2	Very Risky	Could lose a lot of my money. No more than 50%

The Ombudsman's (FOS) position. Why does the FOS take a different view to the industry? It looks not only at what the provider and adviser say, but also at the construction of the contract and how it really works. If the provider has misled the adviser that is not your problem. In law, omissions are proof of negligence.

True Definition of Risk

'With-profits' funds are mixed, managed funds with in-built liabilities that restrict investment freedom. This would make them at least a 2 and probably a 3 on the industry's investment scale. If you have been misled into making an investment in a with-profits fund on the basis it was low-risk, then you have grounds for complaint.

Salesman's Omissions

Here are a few details about with-profits funds that the salesman may have failed to mention:

High Share Content = Higher Risk – From 1980 right up to 2002, most with-profit funds held 60% to 80% of their assets in shares. There is no objective investment analyst anywhere in the world who would categorise a fund with this level of equities as low-risk. Did the salesman inform you about this, and the effect it could have on the fund? Since 2000, with-profits funds that are still open to business have reduced their share holding to 40% to 60% of the fund.

Aligning Personal Attitude to Risk and Fund Risk – If you WERE fully informed that the fund had 80% in shares, you may be disappointed to learn that the fund has now reduced its equity content to 50% and is now lower risk.

Or, by accepting the salesman's word that it was low-risk you may have gone on to invest new money in even riskier funds in the false belief that your 'with-profits' fund was secure and would grow steadily, thus distorting the overall risk of your portfolio.

Liabilities in the Fund – Did the salesman inform you that with-profits funds carry liabilities to pay out guarantees? These are hard to quantify because the funds are not managed transparently. The Life Office can withhold bonuses from you to cover up past mistakes. This is happening today as the current with-profit funds policyholders pay the penalty of nil returns for the excesses of the last two decades.

Asset Allocation & Liabilities – Did the salesman tell you that the Treasury and FSA insist that Life Offices reserve assets to cover liabilities? The managers have to arrange their asset allocation based on covering guarantees and meeting obligations. Investment decisions are actuarially driven, not market value driven. This increases the risk of the fund being mis-managed, as managers cannot take advantage of market opportunities and apply the investment maxim 'buy cheap' and 'sell expensive'. On the contrary, in the recent down-turn, many funds were forced to sell shares cheaply, only to buy back more expensively a year later.

Market Value Adjustments (MVA) can apply at any time – This is also called Market Value Reduction (MVR). Did the salesman inform you that if you bought a with-profits pension, there is only one day during the life of the contract that you can access your money without penalty? And that if you bought a with-profits bond there may be no time you can exit without penalty, or perhaps only on the 10th anniversary? At any other time your money is exposed to a potential MVA which is applied at the discretion of the managers. This is a penalty applied to reduce the value of the contract inline with the performance of the underlying assets.

<u>In effect, with-profits funds actually operate in the same way as a unit-linked mixed asset fund which is rated higher on the risk scale.</u> This one penalty clause nails the myth that with-profits are low-risk funds.

If you examine your statement it will show a current fund value that is likely to be more than the amount you invested. This is a notional value only and is used to disguise costs and true performance. The important value is the surrender value that reflects the value of the underlying assets. You could invest £10,000 in a with-profits bond (£9,500 after charges), and find that in 10 years time the fund still has a statement value of £10,000 as no bonuses have been applied.

As the market has dropped 50%, a market valuation of 30% is applied and on surrender you will receive £7,000. At no point (now or in the future) are you guaranteed to get your money back. The fact you could have received 3% net per annum in a building society and your fund would have been worth £13,500 highlights the risks you are taking. Some analysts believe the arbitrary way in which MVAs are applied, and the need to reserve for liabilities, make with-profits more risky for the consumer than unit-linked funds. At least with unit-linked funds you can access your money at any time, on current market valuation terms.

The FOS is particularly keen on MVAs. Salesmen defend themselves by drawing investors' attention to the fact that MVAs can be applied. However if your investment time horizons are short, and you have few other assets, your money should never have been exposed to the prospect of MVAs at all. This is especially so if there is no MVA-free guarantee day, or the MVA free day is the 10th anniversary, which falls after you are likely to need the money. Under such circumstances it is clear that with-profits was inappropriate and you have a case for mis-selling.

More Proof of Risk Mis-categorisation

There can be no clearer proof that the industry failed to categorise with-profits risk correctly than the number of with-profits funds that have had to close to new business because they got their sums wrong, just as the salesmen got their risk rating wrong. If those risk assessments were correct, such funds would be flourishing today because we have the exact economic conditions in which the marketing men claimed 'with-profits' could deliver consistently good returns. But they have not flourished, many are failing. They have been exposed for what they are, medium-risk funds deceptively trying to persuade investors they are low-risk.

The demise of the Equitable Life with-profits fund from 1998 proves that the general public was misled. No-one would have invested in that fund (or in any other that has closed since 2000) if they had been provided with all the facts.

Grounds for Complaint

The following can be included in any complaint letter where you were advised to invest in a product using a with-profits fund which was classified low-risk. If the product was a pension, a Life Office bond or a whole-of-life contract, there are usually other reasons to make a complaint, but you can use this on its own to claim compensation. Be prepared for the firm to produce their risk scale tick boxes and reject your complaint. As soon as you receive your rejection letter, send a complaint to the ombudsman. Use complaint Letter 19.

- The salesman failed to give prominence to strict conditions in the contract that would affect my investment returns.
- The salesman failed to inform me that the fund originally held 50% to 80% of the assets in shares. This is equivalent to a medium risk fund. The fund was wrongly categorised. I would never have consented to expose my money to such risk if I had been told all the facts.
- (With-profits Bond) The money was originally held on deposit (OR it was the tax-free cash from my pension which I was going to put into the building society), but I was persuaded to move to a with-profits fund which the salesman said was low-risk, my money was guaranteed and the bond would deliver returns above deposit accounts. This was misleading and incorrect.
- (With-profits Bond) I am a pensioner / close to retirement and this was recommended as a safe way to provide retirement income for me when I did not want to take risks. This was misleading and incorrect.
- The salesman failed to explain the MVA fully, and (if pension) how I can access my money on only one day during my retirement without penalty OR (if a 'with profits' bond or endowment) there is only one day being the 10th anniversary / maturity date that I can access my money without penalty. At any other time I am exposed to a MVA which is applied at the discretion of the Life Office. As this charge can be applied at any time during the period access was required, or likely to be required, with-profits was inappropriate for my needs.
- The salesman failed to inform me that at any time the managers can withhold growth to cover their liabilities.
- The salesman failed to inform me that the managers have to arrange their asset allocation based on covering liabilities and meeting obligations. Investment decisions are actuarially driven and not 'market value' driven. The fund is at risk of not being able to take advantage of market opportunities.
- The salesman failed to point out that the fund manager can change or be forced to change the investments in such a way as to alter the investment profile of the fund, breaking any link with the original assessment matching the fund to my attitude to risk. My attitude to risk has not changed but the risk profile of the fund has.

- Through no fault of my own I find myself forced to move my money to funds that suit my risk profile, but to do so, I am potentially liable to a market value adjustment.
- (With Profits Bonds) The salesman failed to point out that I could have achieved the same or better returns at a far lower cost using a different investment mix, of cash funds, national savings and low-cost tracker funds.

These points shows that on the grounds of flexibility and risk the recommendation to invest in with-profits was totally unsuitable for someone in my circumstances with my risk profile.

Special Mention – closed With-profits funds

Some with profits funds which have closed to new business are known in the city as 'Zombie Funds' because of their resemblance to the walking dead. They paid out too much and could not afford to take on any more liabilities, unable to absorb new sales costs which were putting undue strain on weak solvency margins. Closure was inevitable.

Information on closed funds

Since April 2004 all companies operating with-profit funds are required to publish their Principles and Practices of Financial Management, (PPFM), describing how they run their with-profits business. These include details on investment strategy, the calculation of bonuses, charges & expenses and have been available to all policyholders since 30 November 2004. A consumer-friendly version known as the CFPPFM was available after 31 December 2005.

Can we trust Life Offices?

The future management of all with-profits funds needs to be closely monitored by regulation. In January 2005 the FSA issued a Policy Statement 05/1 on *Treating With-profits Policyholders Fairly* which attempts to make the current system work better. It does not go far enough and fails to protect the millions of policyholders trapped in closed with-profits funds. I remember an Equitable Life policyholder comparing her ordeal to the plight of a mushroom, *'They keep us in the dark and feed us shit!'* Her uncharacteristic outburst was borne out of sheer frustration with the Equitable's board, but aptly sums up how the industry and government have dealt with this affair.

The future of closed funds is bleak

Closed funds exist to enable Life Offices to run off their liabilities while providing management with the opportunity to make money at your expense. The liabilities are the contractual guarantees (promises) usually made to holders of mainly older policies that tie up a disproportionate part of the fund's assets at the expense of other policyholders who feel unable to exit because of charges. They are locked in with large MVAs.

Some companies believe there is profit in managing closed funds, which they are aggressively accumulating. They take 1% annual management charges, plus 10% of the declared bonuses on £billions under current management. Over 90% of many funds are invested in government and corporate bonds and require little management. After expenses, clients will be lucky to get 3.5%, (perhaps less than 2% after liabilities). This is an absolute disgrace.

Why common sense will not prevail

Many funds that are classed as solvent are not if calculated on a buy-out basis (similar to rules applied to winding up a final salary pension scheme). If all the closed with-profits were forced to unitise, I suspect many would provide valuations at less than 90% of the notional current fund value and would be declared insolvent. The Financial Services Compensation Scheme (FSCS) would have to pick up the compensation bill. The FSCS is funded by the industry which could refuse to pay the extra £billions needed. To prevent this scenario, I suspect the Treasury, Regulator and industry chiefs have decided to let these closed funds limp on, relying on millions of unsuspecting policyholders not to complain when they receive next to nothing at fund maturity. This will be like premium bonds without the prizes, but you'll be lucky to get your stake money back, regardless of how long you wait.

So you must complain. As you cannot rely on the authorities to help, you must go it alone and complain about any with profits investment sold on the basis that it was low-risk.

With-profits – Conclusion

The fundamental risk assessment of with-profits funds is incorrect. The provider's marketing literature may have stated it was low-risk, and the adviser agreed because they both had the objective of removing money from no risk deposit accounts. If they had said, *'Come and invest! Our fund has 80% in volatile shares but on one single day in the next decade we'll give you your capital back, with no guarantees of growth'*, I suspect they wouldn't have convinced us!

There are some strong with profits funds in existence that defy the above statements. But on the grounds of initial costs, ongoing expenses, transparency, security, tax and investment returns, investors can have their money managed better elsewhere. The term with-profits is a misnomer. Such funds should more accurately be renamed 'Little Profit' funds, or 'With Losses' funds. Steer Clear.

Use letter 19 to seek compensation and get justice.

b) Mis-selling of Life Office Insurance Bonds

Who is Affected – Everyone who has bought an Insurance Bond.

Life Office insurance bonds are packaged lump-sum investment products offered by Life Offices. They are technically life insurance contracts as on death they pay a small element of life cover (usually 101% of the premiums paid). Money from all investors is pooled to diversify across a range of investments. While they are unsuitable for 90% of investors, 90% of investors with lump sums to invest who have sought advice from commission-based IFAs have probably got one.

Superior Alternatives

Most investors would be better suited to lower cost options or better-performing funds at the same cost. Here follows a summary of the main retail funds:

Unit Trusts – A legal trust collectively managing a portfolio of shares and bonds, where investors are issued units. The trust is open-ended and can expand and contract by issuing or cancelling units. Typical initial charges; initial 5%, annual 1.5%. Typical commission; initial 3%, annual trail 0.5%.

OEICs Open Ended Investment Companies – A limited liability company set up to collectively manage a portfolio of shares and bonds, where investors are issued shares. Open-ended and can expand and contract by issuing or cancelling shares. Charges as for unit trusts above.

Investment Trusts – Companies listed on the London Stock Exchange that invest in the shares and securities of other companies. The trust is close-ended (a fixed number of shares are on offer). The fund expands and contracts as the shares rise or fall. Typical initial charges; initial 1% - 2%, annual 0.9%. Typical commission; initial nil, annual trail nil.

These three types of fund benefit from no internal capital gains charges on transactions. (Capital gains tax applies on the growth of an asset.) Small investors can avoid capital gains tax by using their personal capital gains tax allowance, currently £8,800 in 2006/07. All income distributions are taxed, assuming you are a basic-rate tax-payer. By contrast, high commission Life Office insurance bonds offer poor value for money BUT they are the most popular investment sold by commission-based advisers.

The FSA is well aware of the commission anomalies (insurance bonds pay 6% where a unit trust / OEIC pays only 3% and an investment trust 0%). Advisers must recommend the most suitable product / investment as stated in the FSA Conduct of Business manual, COB 5.3 'Suitability': *'An Adviser must not recommend a packaged product if they are aware of another more suitable product that is generally available'*.

Even salesmen with rudimentary qualifications are aware of the existence of unit trusts, investment trusts and OEICs, and are capable of sourcing funds with lower charging structures and superior performance. Sadly, most salesmen do not adhere to this rule and use flawed reasoning about flexibility of income, tax and simplicity to push bonds above all else. This has led to 100,000's of consumers being mis-sold bonds instead of more appropriate investments.

Grounds for Complaint

Quality of Investment Advice

The performance of most Life Office funds is average to very poor. The most talented fund managers prefer to work for dedicated fund management companies, not Life Offices, so most funds are not actively managed. The management team prefers to hug indexes and stay with the herd, buying most of the shares that make up the FTSE 100 share index. True tracker funds will charge less than half that of actively managed funds, so you are being overcharged.

Many Life Offices recognise their investment failings, and offer external fund links, whereby their bond will mirror the performance of a recognised unit trust or OEIC. After charges and internal tax, the bond is at a disadvantage, which begs the question why didn't the salesman invest in the funds direct? Most IFAs are salesmen, and prefer to sell bonds as they pay double the commission. (See Part One, Chapter 2.)

Most consumers' money is invested into managed funds, such as with-profits, distribution, cautious or balanced managed funds. These are all mixed asset funds which spread your money across a range of assets, including shares, government gilts, corporate bonds (IOUs), property and cash. No individual thought or planning goes into the process. If you had £100,000, it would be unwise to invest it all with one manager. Even commission salesmen belatedly recognise you should not put £100,000 into one with-profits bond. Unfortunately all too often they just split it and invested £50,000 into two with profits bonds.

If you recognise this scenario you must ask yourself why the adviser made a recommendation at odds with the cardinal investment rule that:

> Your money should be spread across a wide range of managers and assets, as this spreads the risk while maximising your long-term returns.

Money should be spread across very good managers of property funds, corporate bonds, national savings / gilts, and very good share-fund managers. This is called Asset Allocation and is a skill that most salesmen fail to use. If your adviser ignored more appropriate funds then they acted negligently and you were mis-sold an insurance bond.

Effect of Charges

Table 1 compares the cost and returns from a portfolio of individual assets with that of a bond. Did the salesmen explore the cost and effect of the costs on your portfolio and the impact on likely long-term returns? If not, then the bond was mis-sold. On the grounds of cost and likely performance, a basket of mixed assets is likely to out-perform a Life Office bond. The bond was unsuitable as lower cost, lower risk options were ignored.

Table 1. Investment of £100,000 – Cost & Return Comparison

Investment	A. Commission Driven Salesman (Salesman gets £6,000 Commission)			B. Fee-based Planner (Planner charges £1,000 Fee)		
	Amount	Initial Charge	Annual Charge	Amount	Initial Charge	Annual Charge
Insurance Bond	£100,000	£7,000	£1,500	Nil	-	-
Cash	Nil	-	-	£20,000	-	-
National Savings	Nil	-	-	£20,000	-	-
Share Tracker Funds	Nil	-	-	£20,000	£250	£100
Share Funds (Active)	Nil	-	-	£20,000	£1,000	£300
Commercial Property Fund	Nil	-	-	£10,000	£500	£150
Corporate Bond Fund	Nil	-	-	£10,000	£250	£100
TOTALS	£100,000	£7,000	£1,500	£100,000	£2,000	£550
TOTAL Invested	£93,000	7%	1.5%	£98,000	2.0%	0.6%
Value after 5% Gross Return		More (£)	More (%)		More (£)	More (%)
5 Years	£110,055	-	-	£121,368	£11,932	10%
10 Years	£130,238	-	-	£150,308	£20,837	15%
20 Years	£182,387	-	-	£230,537	£49,327	26%

Ignored Other Fund Managers

Salesmen are often culpable of ignoring collective funds such as unit trusts, OEICs and investment trusts. They fail to spread the risk across a range of the best fund managers and investment companies.

Table 2 proves the point. Would you prefer to have your money invested in one fund, managed by a Life Office, or 10 funds managed by more accomplished fund managers with lower charges?

Table 2. Collective Funds OR Insurance Bond?

10 x £10,000 into Collective Funds			1 x £100,000 Bond	
	Initial Charge	Annual Charge	Initial charge	Annual Charge
5 x Unit trusts / OEICs	£3,000	£750	£7,000	£1,500
5 x Investment Trusts	£1,000	£500		
TOTAL	£4,000	£1,250	£7,000	£1,500

This alone should be enough to prove that you were mis-sold a bond, as the adviser did not act in your best interests, but their own.

Income Withdrawals

If you were advised to invest in a bond to take tax-free income withdrawals of 5% per year, this is incorrect as no income is tax-free. You can make capital withdrawals of 5% of your original investment, and defer the higher rate income tax liability until the date the bond is surrendered. After 20 years of withdrawing 5% per year, all withdrawals are classed as chargeable gains and are potentially taxable.

Many people are misled into believing that withdrawals are income, an amount over and above the capital growth. This is misleading and incorrect as it is a capital withdrawal and in poor investment conditions your capital will be eroded. If this is not made clear, you have been mis-sold a bond.

Taxation

Life Office insurance bonds are liable to income tax, and funds are subject to internal taxation of 20% of their income and realised growth. On surrender the chargeable gain (over and above the initial investment) is liable to income tax. If you are a basic-rate tax-payer there should be no more tax to pay as this is accounted for by the internal taxation. As a higher rate tax-payer you will have to pay a further 20% being the difference between basic and higher rate tax. Non tax-payers and 10% tax-payers cannot reclaim any tax.

There are two aspects of taxation to consider where alternatives would be more suited to your needs and circumstances.

Personal Taxation – It is accepted by all tax professionals that the combination of using your personal annual capital gains allowance of £8,800 in 2006/07 and capital gains taper relief makes Unit Trusts / OEICs / Investments Trusts more tax-efficient for the majority of investors than insurance bonds. Some higher rate tax-payers who become basic-rate tax-payers may under certain circumstances be better off using the bond taxation system. However any potential taxation gains may be undermined by below average investment returns. If you are a non-taxpayer or a 10% income tax-payer you should not have been recommended a bond as you are being charged tax which you cannot reclaim which will have the effect of reducing your total return.

Tax-free Investments – There are more tax-efficient options than a high charging bond. For smaller funds you should first have used your annual allowance of £7,000 into a tax-free ISA (£14,000 for a couple). For larger investments above £7,000, the salesman may have ignored your ongoing ISA allowances by failing to set aside sufficient today to cover future investments of £7,000 every year.

Did the salesman also ignore national savings certificates where it is possible to invest £15,000 into each tax-free issue? There are currently four issues, so an individual can invest £60,000 and a couple £120,000.

Churning of Investments

Churning is the process where you are advised to change investments for questionable reasons which include:

Increasing Tax-free Withdrawals – Salesmen are making the shocking recommendation that investors switch bonds every 5 years to take advantage of higher 5% 'tax-free withdrawals'. For example: If you had invested £100,000 five years ago, you could take 5% (£5,000 a year). Today the bond is worth £130,000 and the salesman recommends a new bond to increase the 'tax-free withdrawals' to 5% of £130,000 equal to £6,500. Some salesmen genuinely believe this is good tax planning! There is nothing to be gained but lots to be lost through extra charges! This product churning generates commission of 5% to 7% which is taken from your fund. It is recognised by the FSA as unethical, even though it may have been dressed up using other reasons. If this has happened to you, you have definite grounds for a mis-selling claim.

Place your money in Trust – Most Life Offices provide in-house trusts, which probably included your old provider. If not, a solicitor could create a trust and assign the bond to the trust. If these options were not explained to you, then you were mis-sold.

Switch to another individual – This does not require reinvestment and can be achieved by maintaining your existing bond and completing an assignment form.

Better performance – If this was important, why weren't you recommended better performing unit trusts, OEICs or investment trusts? Salesmen usually have a catalogue of spurious reasons used to back up their recommendation to churn products. They tend to ignore the option of free internal switches as they generate no commission.

Inheritance Tax Planning

Trusts – Salesmen will try to legitimise their recommendation by wrapping a trust around the investment bond to remove it from your estate, without fully evaluating all your options. Few salesmen are properly qualified to deal in this area and often omit to disclose:

- That some schemes are not guaranteed to save you tax, new legislation could make the plan tax inefficient, by keeping the money in your estate.
- The same tax savings could be achieved by asking a solicitor who specialises in estate planning to rewrite your wills at a fraction of the cost of the commission on your bond.
- The charges and risk of poor performance could reduce the value of the investment to the point where there is no tax liability, OR the net amount to be inherited by the beneficiaries will be less than if you had done nothing.
- You have lost control over your money, because of the restrictive access.
- The importance and joy of gifting, which is free, is ignored.

No Trust – Sometimes bond trust wrappers can help reduce tax. The salesman may omit to recommend a suitable trust which would have been appropriate to help avoid inheritance tax. This will result in the delayed use of the seven-year rule, where gifts are exempt from inheritance tax after 7 years.

Flawed Risk Assessment

If you were advised to switch money from no or low-risk investments to a 'with-profits' bond (incorrectly categorised as being low-risk), your money has been exposed to far more risk than you wanted, and has led to losses. See separate with-profits complaint.

Other Reasons why the Insurance Bond is NOT suitable

There are numerous reasons why a bond may not be suitable. Here are two examples of poor advice which will help substantiate your mis-selling claim:

Policy Feeding – You were advised to invest in a bond and strip out the 5% withdrawals to feed another policy, thus doubling the salesman's commission on the same money. The first 4 or 5 years' contributions should have been left on deposit, to avoid incurring initial charges of 5% to 7%.

Debt Repayment – You were advised to invest the money instead of paying off a debt or loan, where there is no realistic prospect that the bonds net investment returns after charges will be sufficient to cover the interest payments / repayment of loan capital.

Reasons to have a Bond

There are some genuine reasons for having a bond, provided that charges and internal taxation costs do not erode the advantages. Never let the tax tail wag the investment dog. A bond is valid if it was proposed by the trustees of a trust, as part of a comprehensive inheritance tax plan, where all possible solutions were evaluated and where the potential saving in 40% tax could not be covered by gifting or other low-cost means.

In very limited cases a bond is suitable where a higher rate tax-payer wants exposure to high income-producing assets, and wants to defer that income tax liability knowing they will be a basic-rate tax-payer at the time the money is withdrawn.

Investors who switch funds regularly, on a weekly or monthly basis, would benefit from a free switching facility, without any capital gains liability. A bond is also suitable for a pensioner who wants to avoid the reduction in their 'Age Allowance'.

Conclusion

Everyone who was advised to invest in a Life Office bond without clearly stated taxation reasons, without full evaluation and comparison with ALL other possible investment solutions, has probably been mis-sold a bond.

Proof of Poorer Bond Performance.

Other tax advantages need to be compelling to take into account the loss of growth caused by a higher charging and higher internally-taxed bond, when compared to unit trusts, OEICs and Investment Trusts.

If you examine the returns in financial magazines you will find that bonds consistently under-perform unit trusts (see Table 3 comparing performance of the same fund in and outside a bond). The Fidelity Special Situations Fund is managed by Anthony Bolton, who is recognised in the industry as an investment guru. For the last 25 years he has consistently out-performed the UK indexes. These figures also ignore the likely higher initial bond set up costs.

Table 3. **Unit Trust V's Insurance Bond − £1,000 Invested**			
Investment	Fund	*5 Years	*10 Years
Unit Trust	Fidelity Special Situations	£1,779	£4,386
Bond	Skandia Fidelity Special Situations	£1,643	£3,521
Unit Trust Superior Performance %		8% more	25% more

Note: Values at 1 May 2005, units on a bid to bid basis − Moneyfacts / Lipper Data

CASE STUDY

Pete Morgan invested £100,000 in a bond 10 years ago and his salesman put his money in the Skandia Life Bond. When I met Pete recently, he asked why his salesman hadn't recommended the Fidelity fund, which would have made him £86,500 better off? I explained that Skandia would have paid 6% of Pete's money in commission while Fidelity was only paying 3%. Poor Pete had paid an extra £3,000 in commission, for the privilege of losing £86,000!

Best advice does not always enter the equation. Salesmen are motivated by commission and they like bonds which pay out 0.5% of the fund each year as a servicing charge, even though many offer no structured ongoing service. And the contract is also laden with high penalty charges that prohibit transfers in the first 5 years!

FSA's Lack of Policing

This begs the question why the FSA has allowed the industry to flog bonds for so long, when their sale contravenes the 'Principles for Business', as listed below:

Principle 1 requires that a firm must conduct its business with integrity.

Principle 2 requires that a firm conducts its business with due skill, care and diligence.

Principle 6 requires that a firm pays due regard to the interests of a customer and treats them fairly, which means a firm must not make excessive charges.

Principle 9 requires that where a relationship of trust exists between the firm and the customer, and where the customer relies on the firm's judgement, the customer is entitled to advice that is suitable.

It also falls foul of the FSA directive on 'Treating Customers Fairly'. How can it be fair to overcharge a client for an inferior bond at the exclusion of lower charging better-performing investments?

Make Your Claim

Now is your chance to reclaim some of your lost thousands. The basis of your claim for compensation will depend on your attitude to risk:

If you are averse to risk, then a claim for compensation should be based on claiming the difference between the surrender value of the bond and the return on a high interest deposit account / cash ISA.

If you accept some risk, then your claim should be based on claiming the difference between the surrender value of your bond and a portfolio of above-average collective funds, national savings and high interest accounts.

If you wanted to be fully invested in the markets, then you should claim compensation for the difference between the surrender value of your bond and the performance of ten collective funds (unit trusts, OEICs and investment trusts) with above-average performance.

Use letter 20 for general complaints about Insurance Bonds and letter 21 for complaints about 'With-profits' Bonds.

The table shows how much you can reclaim based on the payment of 0.5% trail commission:

Table 4. Trail Commission Rebates

Contact	Annual Rebates after £35 Charge	
	Amount Invested	Rebate
Intelligent Money Ltd	£10,000	£15
20 Fletchergate	£25,000	£90
Nottingham, NG1 2FZ	£50,000	£215
T: 0870 1166117 or	£100,000	£465
0115 9477570	£250,000	£1,215
www.intelligentmoney.com	£500,000	£2,465
	£1,000,000	£4,965

The most high-profile firm is Intelligent Money Ltd, which charges £35 per year to claim back and rebate all ongoing commission on all contracts. But be aware that some salesmen have been pushing through bonds taking an enhanced commission. This is based on taking the servicing charge up-front, claiming 7% commission and no trail commission, instead of 5% and 0.5% trail. Unfortunately if this has happened there is no trail to claim.

The more you learn about commission, the more you may agree with us that it must be abolished – the only way to stop ongoing abuse of consumers.

TOP TIP

With immediate effect I recommend you transfer the agency of your bond, and the right to collect commission, to a commission rebating company and claim back your money.

Most insurance bonds are set up to give the adviser 0.5% trail commission, which is taken from the bond as part of the annual management charge. It rubs salt into the wound to think they're taking more of your money every year for servicing a mis-sale!

Most provide very little or no ongoing service. Don't confuse a chat to 'see how you are' with a sales call to see if you have any more to invest!

Consult Table 4 and claim your money.

c) Mis-selling of Precipice Bonds (High Income Bonds)

Who is Affected – People who bought contracts probably between 1997 and 2001, who now find they have lost money or are likely to lose money and as yet have not taken action. You do not have to wait for the bond to mature to make a complaint.

The term 'precipice bonds' was created by the press to publicise the problems associated with high income bonds, where investors' money fell faster than the markets, like a fall from a cliff. The bonds provided an income and the return of capital linked the performance of certain major stock markets.

False Promises

High-income bonds proved popular with investors in the late 1990's as they promised a high annual income percentage – often 50% more than the best high-interest cash accounts. On the back of these headline grabbing rates, salesmen were set loose on a public eager for higher income in an era when interest rates were declining.

Unfortunately some salesmen failed to emphasise that the investor's capital would only be returned at the end of the investment term if the stock market did not fall (usually measured against the UK FTSE 100 share index). If the stock market had fallen, then your losses could escalate. In some cases capital fell by twice the fall in the corresponding index, which left open the prospect of your capital being wiped out.

Some Promises are Hard to Understand

As competition hotted-up, providers became more creative and offered higher income. Providers started linking the return of capital invested to two or three international indices, such as the European Euro Stoxx 50, German Dax and the US Dow Jones, NASDAQ 100 and S&P 500 indices. These were usually accompanied by charts that emphasised the certainty of gains.

Problems arose from 2002 when large numbers of plans came to the end of their 5-year term during a decline in world stock markets. Investors found their capital had been reduced by 50% or more. Investors were not prepared for the losses. These bonds are complicated structured products that take bets on the movement of markets. There was always going to be a mismatch between provider knowledge and investor expectation.

Providers use computer models to calculate the odds in their favour, while marketing offices use advertising to raise your expectations and entice you on-board. Investors were not fully informed about how the products operated in all market conditions. Where there were risk warnings, they were not given the prominence that was needed.

Mailshots

Many of these products were bought on the back of direct mailings. These should have provided enough information to enable you to make an informed assessment, but to be compliant the information should:

- Be clear, fair and not mis-leading
- Give a fair and adequate description of the nature of the investment
- Outline the commitment required
- Outline the risks involved.

If your mailing did not, then you may have grounds for complaint.

Grounds for Complaint

Most complaints revolve around a mismatch between the clients' attitude to risk (which tends to be low), and the product risk which tends be higher than that outlined by the salesman or sales literature.

Literature Based

Marketing literature often failed to provide sufficient detail of the risks and fell foul of the regulator for the following reasons:

- The risk was not explained in a way that could be easily understood.
- The contract was inaccurately described as low-risk and suitable for cautious investors. The good news is that the ombudsman believes that any investment where the return of your capital is linked to a stock market index cannot be classed as low-risk.
- The contract was accurately described as medium to high-risk by the product provider, but sold as low-risk by the advisory firm.
- It failed to provide sufficient information on the indices used and the probability of achieving the required returns over the same timescales as used in the contract. It was not possible for you make a fair comparison of the risks.
- Where there was mention of risk, it was marketed as 'Low Downside Risk'. The small print stated that the downside risk kicked in after a certain percentage fall of the index, usually 20%. At this point your capital falls by a multiple of the fall in the corresponding index, which still left open the prospect of your capital being wiped out. This was not made sufficiently clear and cannot be classed as low-risk.

It is very difficult for a customer to assess fairness, and whether the product literature complied with the regulator's rules. For this reason you must complain to the ombudsman who will make the assessment for you.

Other Reasons

Complexity – The product was too complex to understand for someone with your investment experience and knowledge.

No Risk Options – The adviser failed to evaluate no risk and low-risk options.

Tax-free Investments ignored – You were aware of generic market risks and were recommended a high-income bond as opposed to other more tax-efficient investments such as PEPs (before 6 April 1999), and ISAs (after the 5 April 1999). This amounts to £7,000 for an individual and £14,000 for a couple.

Designated low-risk money – You were aware of generic market risks, but this was an investment made on the basis of reshuffling your low-risk money within the low-risk part of your portfolio. While you own share investments, you did not want to increase your overall exposure to higher risk assets. You must emphasise that you wanted a low-risk product.

Tax Unclear – The literature did not make the tax position clear.

Charges Unclear – The adviser did not make the charges clear. As these are built into the contract, they are lost in the literature, encouraging some advisers to imply that there is no initial charge. This is incorrect. The total initial charges probably amounted to 6% to 7% of your investment, with commission of 3% to 5% paid to the salesman.

Access Denied – The salesmen failed to take into account your lifestyle needs and that you may require access to the money prior to the expiry of the 5-year term. You now realise that you can only access your money after incurring high surrender penalties and exit charges.

The key fact to remember is that the FSA does not regulate products, it only regulates advice. Providers can create and market poor investments which continue to be sold. You can only complain if the adviser failed to advise properly of its suitability, taking into account your needs and circumstances. Sales literature forms part of the advice process. To its credit, the FSA's own monitoring unit has been pro-actively investigating the marketing of these products for many years, trying to head off possible problems by insisting providers change their sales literature.

Making a Complaint

These products were unsuitable for most investors as they were mainly sold to no risk investors as low-risk products. Most of the investors' money originated from deposit accounts and they just wanted a little extra income with low risk. In December 2003, Lloyds TSB were find £1.9 million and asked to pay £98 million in compensation as they were found guilty of indiscriminate selling of high income bonds. Many were sold to elderly people, for whom income is important but who have no scope to replace lost capital.

Suitability is the key to a successful complaint. Taking into account your asset base, your other income, your investment experience and your current attitude to risk, did the investment sit comfortably alongside your other investments? Was it suitable after the salesman had explained what could happen to your capital in the best and worst case scenarios? And if you bought after receiving a mailshot, did the product perform exactly as you expected, and as presented in the marketing literature?

If the risks were not fully explained, then you have grounds for complaint.

Just be aware that the ombudsman (FOS) will look sympathetically at cases where you bought after receiving a personalised mailshot or newsletter, sent to your home address, even if the advisory firm classed the sale as 'execution-only'. An execution-only investment is one where you signed a declaration to say that you had not sought or received advice. The FOS view will be that you were encouraged to enter into the contract by the adviser, who having assessed the product, may have used advisory statements like, 'this would suit the cautious investor'. Such statements are likely to be interpreted by you as confirmation that this was a low-risk investment and as advice to invest.

If however, you made the first move and bought 'off the page', by responding to an advert and buying on an execution-only basis, then you are unlikely to receive compensation as you made the initial contact.

If you feel you were misled, use complaint Letter 22 to complain about the advice received, and Letter 23 to complain about the mailshot received where there was no direct advice. Use the ombudsman to assess your complaint and seek justice. Your claim for compensation should be based on the difference between the surrender value of the bond and a high interest deposit account.

d) Mis-selling of Corporate Bond Funds

Who is Affected – Anyone who has invested into a corporate bond fund, especially high-risk bonds known as junk bonds.

Corporate Bonds are funds that invest in fixed interest loan stock (debts) issued by companies when they want to raise capital. They are in effect IOUs. As an investor you are lending money in return for a fixed interest payment. To spread the risk managers have created funds usually holding over 50 different bonds.

There is a great deal of difference in the quality of bonds issued by companies. Those with the best credit ratings issue bonds classed as 'AAA'. They are lower risk as there is less chance of the company defaulting, and therefore pay lower interest. Companies whose credit rating is poor, issue bonds that the market names 'Junk Bonds'. These pay much higher levels of interest, to reflect the greater level of risk.

Popularity

The popularity of corporate bond funds increased after 2000, following the stock market downturn. They gave salesmen the chance to earn 3% to 5% commission on selling alternative investments, when investors turned their backs on share funds. Like share funds, the risks associated with corporate bond funds was (and continues to be) poorly explained.

The Problem

Problems arise because advisers and investors start chasing higher income from funds paying the highest interest. This can only be achieved by investing in low-investment grade riskier bonds. Investors may have been misinformed as to the exact risks involved with such funds. When interest rates are low and corporate profits are high, the conditions for bonds are good, but the converse is also true. Any increase in interest rates or a squeeze on credit will lead to big drops in bond valuations.

We have an accident waiting to happen. Economic conditions can easily change, and if interest rates doubled, it could lead to bond valuations halving!

Over time these funds may spawn a mis-selling scandal where consumers claim they were not informed of the inherent risks.

Risks to Capital & Income

- Were you advised that your fund was a low-risk fund?
- Was the adviser talking generically about all bond funds, or specifically about your fund?
- Were you aware that both the capital and income are at risk?

There are several reasons why you may not get back as much as you expected.

Interest Rate Risk

The primary risk of corporate bond funds is interest rate risk, as these funds buy debts that offer a fixed rate of interest. These interest payments provide an income known as the yield. (A fund yielding 6% is producing a 6% income.) The yield provided by the fund moves in line with market rates. As the interest rate on the underlying corporate bonds is fixed, the fund yield can only change if the value of the underlying bonds rises or falls. If investors want higher yields, then bond prices must fall. Your capital is at risk.

Think of bond values and interest rates as opposite ends of a seesaw. If interest rates move down, the value of bonds increase. This happens because an investor is initially willing to pay more for an investment paying above market rates. But if interest rates move up, the value of bonds decrease. This happens because an investor wants a market return and will pay less for an investment paying below market rates.

If the risks of capital loss were not made clear and interest rates rise, then you have a case for mis-selling.

Bond Redemption Risks & Yields

Most bonds are dated, which means they have a redemption date when the debt is repaid. Bonds are issued and redeemed at the same price (known as the 'nominal' or 'par' value, usually in lots of £100). Most managers do not hold their bonds to redemption, but trade them. The price of the bond will vary depending on the movement in interest rates. If interest rates move lower, managers will pay more for bonds that pay a higher interest.

All advisers should inform investors that there are two yields that need to be considered:

Running / Flat Yield – This is often the headline yield quoted by salesmen or marketing literature and is calculated by simply dividing the income by the price paid for the bond. It does not take into account capital depreciation caused by redemption losses.

Redemption Yield – This is the more accurate yield and takes into account the gains and losses when the bonds are redeemed. It is usually a lower figure.

If the redemption yield is lower than the running yield, the only way the fund manager can avoid future capital losses is to hope interest rates continue to fall or to switch into ever riskier low grade investment bonds.

If you were persuaded to invest into a corporate bond fund having been quoted a higher running yield, you have been misled and have a case for mis-selling. This is especially the case where the money originated from a deposit account and the salesman falsely compared the fund's running fund yield to the rate available from the best deposit account. It is also the case if you made a transfer from another fund where the quoted lower redemption yield was wrongly compared with the new funds higher running yield.

High Income Funds (Junk Bond Funds)

The chance of capital appreciation and depreciation is likely to be magnified in a 'high income fund' that invests in low-grade investment bonds called junk bonds. These have a poor credit rating and there is a greater possibility of credit default and they can be very volatile especially during times of economic instability.

Many investors do not even realise they are invested in funds that are so risky. Using the salesman's risk scale of '0' to '5' (0 being no risk), such funds tend to be classed as risk scale 2. Many should be classed as a 3 or 4. If the risks associated with 'high income funds' were not explained and your capital depreciates, then you have grounds for complaint.

Risk of Capital Depreciation Through Charges

The charges levied by the fund managers can be charged against either capital, income or against both. Many bond fund managers deduct charges from capital to make the bond yield look more attractive, and therefore easier to market. Salesmen then tout the higher rate without fully discussing the impact of the charges on your capital. This can be very misleading and is likely to affect those who were persuaded to invest to receive a higher income where the money originated from:

- A deposit account because the salesman falsely compared the funds yield before charges to the rate available from your deposit account.
- Transfer from another fund where the salesman recommended a fund with a higher yield because the charges were drawn against capital.

If you were misled into investing on the basis of a false prospectus, then you have a case for mis-selling.

Risk of Capital Gains Tax

Those with large holdings in corporate bond funds may be liable to capital gains tax when they sell, which could have been avoided. If a gain on an investment exceeds your annual capital gains tax allowance, you may be liable to capital gains tax up to 40%.

This could have been avoided by buying the corporate bonds direct through a stockbroker and holding them in your own name. Any gain on the sale of a qualifying corporate bond is capital gains tax-free, potentially increasing your overall profit. If this was not brought to your attention, you could have been misled and have a case for mis-selling.

Claim for Compensation

Even though the current trading conditions for bonds appears benign, you should be prepared for sudden swings which may leave you with losses. You may have bought into a fund under false pretences as shown here:

Table 1. Presentation of Corporate Bond Funds – Effect on Income

Description	Salesman's Pitch	The Truth
Running Yield	6% p.a.	6% p.a.
Redemption Yield (Taking into account capital depreciation)	Not quoted	4.5% p.a.
Annual Charge	Taken from capital	1.25% p.a.
Yields	Quoted = 6% p.a.	Actual = 3.25% p.a.
Difference compared to a Deposit Account Rate of 5%	1% more	1.75% Less
Exaggerated Income (The Deception Cost)	2.75% p.a.	-

Do you think you were correctly advised to move your money from a deposit account paying 5%, into a fund with risks paying 3.25%! If you are a no / low-risk investor your claim should be based on restoring your capital to the value it would have if it had been left in a high interest deposit account. If you are suffering from capital losses from a fund that you were recommended as low-risk, then use Letter 24 to claim compensation.

If you have such an investment and have made a profit, you may want to reflect on whether such a fund suits your risk profile. Remember you cannot claim compensation for losses you have not incurred. If you are ahead, this may be a good time to reconsider your position.

e) Mis-selling of Life Office 10-Year Savings Plans

Who is Affected – Everyone who has bought a Life Office 10-year savings plan, especially since January 1987.

These plans are regular premium savings plans sold by Life Offices that combine a small amount of life cover with investment, into a managed fund, often a with-profits fund. Savers are guaranteed a sum assured which is basically their money back. They are technically known as 'qualifying' policies as they should avoid higher rate tax if maintained for 10 years or three-quarters of the term. They are subject to internal Life Office taxation of 20%.

Life Offices have gone out of their way to market the plans as tax beneficial, using titles like 'cash maximiser', 'cash accumulator plan' or 'cash builder'. Regardless of their names, they are all just short-term endowment plans.

Background

These plans were popular with former industrial Life Offices whose salesmen went door to door to collect premiums. They were tied advisers representing just one company and emerged in an era when this was the only way for many to save outside the post office. To encourage people to save and take out life cover, the premiums benefited from tax relief known as 'life assurance premium relief' (LAPR). This was abolished for all policies affected after 13 March 1984.

They were popular with salesmen as they paid high commission. In many cases the commission was most of, if not all the first year's premium.

Mis-selling Uncovered

Since January 1987 it has been possible to save into more tax-efficient savings plans, at a lower cost (which many salesmen have ignored because they pay very little commission). Those plans are Personal Equity Plans (PEPs) launched in January 1987, which allowed access to shares and share-based funds, Tax Exempt Special Savings Accounts (TESSAs) launched April 1991 as tax-free deposit savings plans and ISAs. In April 1999 ISAs replaced both PEPs and TESSAs. Since 1999 it has been possible for an individual to invest £7,000 per tax year.

Prior to January 1987 a salesman should have used unit trust regular savings plans or investment trust regular savings plans, as only the distributions (income) are immediately taxable. Most savers will be able to offset any capital gains against their annual capital gains allowance.

Scale of the Problem

The scale of the mis-selling problem is huge. Salesmen have persuaded thousands of people to invest into inferior higher-charging 10-year savings plans instead of superior lower-cost tax-free alternatives.

It is probably not far behind the mortgage endowment scandal and affects most working families who came into contact with Life Office salesmen.

Many people were persuaded to start saving using such plans at levels that were unsustainable and doomed to be abandoned. Many salesmen's only objective was to ratchet up premiums and commission. If you have ceased or surrendered your plan it is still possible to claim, as most of the unnecessary costs were incurred in the first two years. Even if the salesman represented a company that did not offer the option of tax-efficient savings plans, the salesman should have made the generic recommendation that you use your tax-efficient savings allowances. By failing to do so they failed to act in your best interests.

Reasons to Complain

Unnecessary Tax – Taxation will affect your investment growth. The money within life funds is subject to internal taxation of 20% and should have been placed in a tax-efficient PEP or ISA, where money grows almost tax-free. For larger contributions, the maximum should have been invested into tax-efficient savings plans before considering alternatives.

Unnecessary Charges – You were not made aware of the high charges associated with the 10-year savings plans, and that lower-cost alternatives were available.

Unnecessary Life Cover – Within all 10-year savings plans there is a small amount of life cover that has to be paid out of your premiums. Why pay for something that is not required and reduces the amount invested?

Risk – The salesman failed to explain fully the investment risks. The plan was unsuitable for someone with little or no previous experience of investing. The adviser failed to explain that this was predominantly a stock market investment, with 60% to 80% of the fund invested in shares, and you could end up with just the sum assured, which is basically your money back.

Access Denied – 10-year savings plans are inflexible. If saving was important, access to those savings could be equally as important. 10-year savings plans do not allow access unless you cancel the plan in part or in full, an event which usually triggers exit penalties and possibly a tax charge. ISAs and PEPs offer immediate tax-free access, usually without penalties.

Poor Investment Choice – Why did the adviser invest your money in a mediocre Life Office fund when there was a choice of investment firms with a long history of delivering above average returns?

Debt Repayment – Did the salesmen fail to consider the repayment of all debts as a viable use for your disposable income?

Make a Complaint

Under the 'Suitability – know Your Customer Rules', it is the adviser's duty to take into account your current financial position and allocate your disposable income in the most tax-efficient way. Failure to do so is a clear breach of the Conduct of Business Rules and a claim for mis-selling can be made.

By recommending an inferior 10-year savings plan, the salesman has lost you money which you must claim in compensation. Table 1 shows how much this has cost you. It compares difference in fund values of a 10-year savings plan and a PEP/ISA, investing £1,000 per annum for 10 years, using assumed investment returns of 5% for the life fund, and 6% for a tax-efficient PEP/ISA.

Table 1. 10-year Savings Plan V's PEP/ISA (PLAN is COMPLETED)

Plan	1 Year	2 Years	3 Years	4 Years	5 years	10 Years
10-year Savings Plan	£0 (Note 1.)	£998	£2,045	£3,145	£4,299	£10,999
PEP/ ISA	£1,007	£2,074	£3,206	£4,405	£5,677	£13,273
Difference (Compensation Claim)	£1,007	£1,076	£1,161	£1,260	£1,378	£2,274

Note: The first year's investment of the 10-year savings plan is usually lost, as it is used to cover commission and other set up costs.

Table 2 shows the compensation you can claim assuming the premiums were stopped after 1 and 2 years, and the amount you should have if your money had been invested, based on £1,000 per annum.

Table 2. 10-year Savings Plan V's PEP/ISA (PLAN CEASES)

Value after ceasing the plan after 1 Year		5 years later	10 years later	15 years later
10-year Plan	£0	£0	£0	£0
PEP / ISA	£1,007	£1,348	£1,803	£2,413
Difference (Compensation)	£1,007	£1,348	£1,803	£2,413
Value after ceasing the plan after 2 Years				
10-year Plan	£998	£1,274	£1,626	£2,179
PEP / ISA	£2,074	£2,775	£3,714	£5,269
Difference (Compensation)	£1,076	£1,501	£2,088	£3,090

Compensation should be based on your attitude to risk. If you are happy to invest into shares, then base your claim on the returns you would have achieved if the money had been invested into a PEP or ISA. If you are a cautious saver, then your claim should be based on the returns you would have achieved from saving into a cash TESSA or ISA.

Use Letter 25 to seek compensation.

f) Mis-selling of Whole-of-life Plans / Flexible Protection Plans

Who is Affected – Potentially all those who bought life cover plans with an investment link since c.1975.

Mis-selling on a Grand Scale

The inappropriate sale of whole-of-life plans is a scam that has been going on for 30 years. It continues today, and like all mis-selling practices is fuelled by commission.

After endowments and pension transfers, this is the next biggest mis-selling scandal that has yet to be fully publicised.

Hundreds of thousands of consumers have been mis-sold these plans. The industry and thousands of salesmen continue to get away with it. Now Whistle-blower hopes to help tens of thousands of people claim millions in compensation.

What are they?

These plans pay out a sum assured on death. They can continue to provide cover for the rest of your life, providing you can afford the premiums. They combine both life cover and investment in one contract. Premiums are initially invested into a unitised investment fund, where units are cancelled to cover the cost of life cover. The older plans offered little flexibility. The newer plans were marketed as flexible; it is possible to increase or decrease the level of life cover within certain limits.

As you get older, the cost of life cover increases. This requires the cancellation of more and more units to cover the increased cost. At some stage the life cover costs may exceed the premiums paid. The extra cost is paid out of the investment pot, or by an increase in premiums. There are regular premium reviews, with the first usually at the 10th anniversary (more frequently if you are older). This can lead to an increase in premiums, which are not guaranteed to remain level for the life of the contract.

To make plans more attractive, salesmen may vary the level of life cover between a minimum and maximum sum assured. For example for a premium of £100 per month it may be possible to choose any level of life cover between £15,000 and £500,000. The higher the life cover, the lower the investment, and the greater the likelihood premiums will have to increase to maintain the cover.

CASE STUDY

Janey Baker came to me with her policy into which she was paying £100 per month, investment units cost £1 each.

Table1. Life Cover Costs

Year 1.	
Event	Costs
Premium	£100
Investment Cost 5%	£5
Amount Invested (95 x £1 units)	£95
Cost of life cover	£80
Investment Remaining	£15
Year 11.	
Premium	£100
Investment Cost 5%	£5
Amount Invested	£95
Cost of life cover	£120
Covered by Investment Fund / Premium Increase	-£25

Janey asked me why the Life Office didn't deduct the cost of the cover before her money was invested? This would save her the 5% charge of £2.50 on the units that were cancelled to cover the life cover cost of £50, which would have left more in her investment fund. I had to explain to Janey that the Life Office was aiming to make money for its shareholders, executives and salesmen, not for her.

Background

Like Janey's policy, most were mis-sold in the 1980's and 1990's when standards were even lower than they are today. They were very popular with all commission-based salesmen, especially tied advisers (who represent just one company). Those companies included Allied Dunbar, Abbey Life, Albany Life, Barclays Life, Colonial Mutual, Cornhill Insurance, Crown Life, Laurentian Life, Liberty Life, General Portfolio, Pearl Assurance, Refuge Assurance, J Rothschild Assurance (now renamed the St James's Place Partnership), United Friendly and many more. I remember in the 1990's seeing a sales league table that showed some salesmen earning over half a million a year! This level of income could only be achieved by selling high commission plans.

Many were sold to unsuspecting working people who have subsequently ceased the policy and written it off as a loss. You may have made a mistake 15 years ago, but don't make another one today by failing to claim an amount that is rightfully yours.

You can still make a considerable claim for compensation if:

- The policy was made paid-up, (you ceased the premiums)
- The policy lapsed without worth, (you ceased premiums and the Life Office advised there was no surrender value)
- You surrendered the policy and received a fraction of what you had paid in premiums.

Reasons to Complain

Let's examine the main areas where it's easy to prove mis-selling. Don't worry if it happened 17 years ago and your memory is hazy. That doesn't matter. In fact you're more likely to receive compensation, because the Life Office / firm have probably destroyed your records and the salesman moved on, making it difficult to disprove your claim.

Unsuitable Life Cover.

Many people need life cover to protect their family but are recommended costly whole-of-life plans instead of cheaper fixed term assurance and family income benefit plans. Term assurance pays out a tax-free lump sum on death covering fixed term, and family income benefit pays out a tax-free annual income on death. Both of these are preferable to whole-of-life cover as they cover the period of most need, and premiums are guaranteed to remain level. As a 30-year old do you know if you will need life cover in 50 years time? If not, why pay three times the cost for something you may not need? The difference in costs can be considerable as shown below:

Table 2. Life Cover Cost Comparison

Cover	Monthly Premium	Commission	Annual Cost	Cost after 10 years	Cost after 15 years	Cost after 20 years
Whole-of-life	£50	£750	£600	£6,000	£9,000	£12,000
Term OR Family Income Benefit (25 years)	£15	£225	£180	£1,800	£2,700	£3,600
Difference	£35	£525	£420	£4,200	£6,300	£8,400

Anyone who was sold whole-of-life instead of being given the opportunity to compare the costs of cheaper alternatives which are more appropriate to their needs, has been the victim of mis-selling.

Sold as a Savings Plan

Over the years I have met numerous people who want a life policy that gives them some money back, wrongly believing they are getting something extra. This myth has been perpetuated by salesmen who use it to help them close the sale.

Inefficient – To clarify the situation, if life cover cost £15 per month and you are paying £50 per month, then you're paying £35 too much. Some of this disappears in costs and commission before being invested. It is far better to keep the cover and savings separate.

More Tax – Taxation will also affect the investment growth. The money within life funds is subject to internal taxation of 20%. The extra £35 should have been saved into a tax-efficient savings plan such as a PEP or ISA, where money grows almost tax-free. Prior to January 1987, a unit (or investment) trust regular savings plan should have been used.

Access Denied – If saving was important, access to those savings should be equally as important. Whole-of-life plans do not allow you to access your money unless you cancel the plan in part or in full, which usually involves exit penalties. ISAs and PEPs offer immediate access, usually without penalties. Whole-of-life plans are inflexible.

Poor Investment Choice – Why did the adviser invest your money in a mediocre Life Office fund when for the same or lower cost there was a choice of investment firms with a long pedigree in delivering above-average returns?

Real Needs Ignored – Protection is needed to cover the shortfall in income until your assets are sufficient to make you financially independent. Spending too much on protection policies is counter-productive as it prevents you from building up your assets (freeing you from the need for life cover, as you have a ready reserve to use in an emergency). A virtuous circle is created where the more you save the less life cover you need.

Unsuitable – Under the 'Know Your Customer Rules', it is the adviser's duty to take into account your current financial position and allocate your disposable income in the most tax-efficient way possible. On a tight annual budget, squeezing the most out of your savings is essential. Best advice dictates that you should have been advised to plan to cover your essential protection needs, with the excess saved tax-efficiently. By mis-selling a whole-of-life plan as a savings plan, the adviser has probably lost you thousands of pounds which you must claim in compensation. Table 3 shows how much this deceit has cost you. It compares difference in fund values of a whole-of-life plan and a PEP/ISA, where term assurance is purchased, using a monthly budget of £50, equal to £600 per year.

I have assumed initial investment charges of 5% per annum and the investment returns of 4.5% for the life fund and 5% for a tax-efficient PEP/ISA. With most whole-of-life plans there is little or no surrender value in the first two years. In the early 1990's one company called General Portfolio did not offer a surrender value on some of its contracts until you had made 5 years contributions.

Table 3. Whole-of-life V's PEP/ISA – Fund Value Comparison

Plan	Premiums	1 Year	2 Years	3 Years	4 Years	5 years	10 Years	15 Years	20 Years*
Whole-of-life Policy	£600	0	0	£300	£732	£1,182	£3,760	£6,973	£10,976
Term Assurance & PEP/ISA	£180 Life cover £420 Savings	£420	£861	£1,324	£1,810	£2,321	£5,283	£9,063	£13,888
Difference = Compensation Claim		£420	£861	£1,024	£1,078	£1,139	£1,523	£2,090	£2,912

Note: *The 20 year PEP / ISA amount is a projection, as these tax-efficient plans have only been available for 18 years. In reality whole-of-life plan expenses, both for life cover and administration costs, tend to be much higher than the best low-cost term assurance. These figures probably flatter the whole-of-life plans. Hopefully after the ombudsman has worked out your compensation you will be pleasantly surprised.

Misled by Commission

Were you informed about all the costs? Were you aware that most of your first two years' contributions would be used to pay commission and administration costs? In 1995 The PIA (forerunner to the FSA) introduced new disclosure illustrations detailing costs in the first five years. The rules were not watertight and they were abused. Some organisations tucked them into the back of the small print sent to customers, or left them out all together! Suffice to say many salesmen did skirt around the issue.

They were helped by the way Life Offices covered costs, in the form of capital and initial units. (These are described in Part Two, Chapter 10 section a, Commission Manipulation.) The money taken in commission can be astronomical, as many whole-of-life plans are sold to people with large inheritance tax liabilities who are persuaded they need cover. Table 4 will give an idea of commission costs.

Table 4. **Commission Costs**	
Policy Premiums	**Likely Commission**
£1,000	£1,000 to £1,200
£10,000	£10,000 to £12,000
£20,000	£20,000 to £24,000
£50,000	£50,000 to £60,000
£100,000	£100,000 to £120,000

If you were not told about the full extent of commission costs, you were mis-sold the policy. Many of these large contracts are sold by IFAs who have developed partnerships with accountancy and law firms. Many of them take advantage of their privileged position to sell high commission inheritance tax plans to clients. If you recognise this scenario, you must set aside your personal relationship with your accountant and your solicitor and make a complaint.

Reviewable Premiums & Affordability

Many people were never told that their premiums were reviewable and that they can increase at any time at the discretion of the Life Office.

After a review they are shocked to find (usually at the 10th anniversary), that their premiums have increased. You shoulder all the risk, as the Life Office can increase your premiums to cover its own claims experience, regardless of how well your investments have performed.

If you are retired and living on a fixed income, the hike in costs can make these plans prohibitively expensive. It is not unusual for a couple in their 70's to find their premiums have increased more than 100% and are forced to cancel the policy. In effect all premiums to date have been a waste of money. This is blatant mis-selling. If you were recommended a whole-of-life contract without being informed that the premiums could increase, and the possible extent of those increases, you have solid grounds for complaint. If you were told premiums were reviewable, but the extent of the possible increases was not made clear, then you still have grounds for complaint as the salesman did not take into account ongoing affordability against your future income.

The problem can be compounded if life cover is needed to cover an ongoing liability like inheritance tax. The adviser should have provided you with details comparing the costs of both reviewable and guaranteed premium plans. Salesmen often fail to do this because in a competitive situation they know that lower premiums are likely to secure the business.

A claim for compensation can be complicated as it may not be possible to secure life cover at the level that guaranteed premiums could have secured at the outset. Under such circumstances a full return of all premiums plus interest should be demanded.

Churning Contracts

This usually happens when salesmen carry out new client reviews and recommend a switch of provider to secure lower premiums. Unfortunately in order to present lower costs, the salesman may have misled you by recommending a change to generate commission.

You may have been advised to switch from a superior guaranteed premium policy to an inferior lower cost reviewable premium policy. Old guaranteed premium contracts are worth keeping, as the premiums for new guaranteed policies have increased considerably over the last 5 years with a number of providers withdrawing from the market.

Alternatively, you may have switched from a reviewable premium contract set up on a standard sum assured basis (where a large proportion of the premiums are invested), to another reviewable premium contract set up on a maximum sum assured basis (where a much smaller percentage of the premiums are invested). The second plan appears cheaper but this is illusory, as at the first review the premiums are likely to be increased above the level of the original plan.

If a switch has been recommended on the back of a false prospectus, churning has happened and you have a definite claim for mis-selling.

Investment Choice & Risk

Salesmen often pay little attention to fund choice and risk, fearing this may draw attention to the fact the premiums are not guaranteed. The cost of the life cover and the investment performance are equally important, as good investment performance will have the effect of keeping the premium review costs down and vice versa. Salesmen often choose default funds, such as with-profits and managed funds, which fail to address your needs. If the salesman failed to discuss the fund risks and your attitude to risk, then you have a case for mis-selling.

Trusts

If a whole-of-life plan was sold without it being placed in trust, you have grounds for a mis-selling complaint. A trust is a legal arrangement that controls the direction of the property within the trust. The trust owns the property so it does not form part of the deceased's estate. This is important as it avoids inheritance tax, charged at 40%. If a close member of your family had one of these plans, which was not written in trust, and the proceeds were liable to inheritance tax, then you have a definite claim for compensation to cover the cost of the tax incurred.

Whole-of-life / Flexible Protection Plan Compensation Claim

A claim for compensation will be based on the difference between the cost of the whole-of-life policy and the cost a low-cost term assurance or family income benefit, with the excess (if you are a no / low-risk investor) invested in a high interest account or cash ISA.

If you would have preferred to have the excess invested in the stock market, then it needs to be compared with the return on a PEP / ISA share fund. I recommend you use the Invesco Perpetual High Income fund as a benchmark. This fund has been well publicised for over 15 years, with numerous adverts in various papers. It is quite conceivable that you may have decided to invest in this fund.

If you took out your plan via an IFA before 29 April 1988 then you are unlikely to get compensation unless that IFA has volunteered to have complaints reviewed by the ombudsman, which is very rare. All other sales (including all those from high commission tied Life Offices and the banks) are covered by the ombudsman.

For those of you who were sold a plan, paid a couple of years premiums, stopped and got nothing back, there is scope to make a considerable claim based on the compounding growth on the money if it had been left in a high-rate deposit account. Remember, the firm's records are probably lost or destroyed, and the firm will not be able to disprove your claim. If they still hold the records they may be inadequate.

Table 5. **Claim Per £1,000 Contribution**	
Paid	£1,000
Low-cost Life Cover	£300
Mis-selling Claim	£700
Compensation Claim	
Happened 5 years ago	£893
Happened 10 years ago	£1,140
Happened 15 years ago	£1,455
Happened 20 years ago	£1,857

This is another example of mis-selling that has been driven by commission. Whistle-blower asks how many more consumers must lose their hard-earned savings before the government and the FSA take action to solve the problem and ban commission on all financial products, in all its forms?

Use complaint Letter 26.

g) Mis-selling of Critical illness Policies

Who is Affected – Anyone who has bought a critical illness policy, especially those who may have been encouraged to switch contracts.

Critical Illness policies pay out a tax-free lump sum on the diagnosis of a critical illness. In most cases the policyholder has to survive 28 days before the policy pays out. The premiums are either guaranteed to remain level for the term of the contract, or are reviewable.

Guaranteed Premiums, the story so far

Those providers that still offer guaranteed premiums have doubled their rates over the past 5 years, as Life Offices recalculate their liabilities. This has happened because older plans have been affected by the improvement in medical diagnostics, which has led to earlier detection of illnesses and earlier payouts for illnesses that are no longer considered life threatening. In short providers are now more likely to pay out.

When providers withdraw from the guaranteed market because they got their sums wrong, it's a pretty clear indication that older guaranteed plans (pre 2001/02) offered much better value than new ones.

Reviewable Rates, Do they ever go down?

Plans with reviewable premiums initially offer cheaper premiums. This is because the provider has the option to increase the premiums to cover their claims experience, so in effect the consumer carries all the risk. Initially your premiums are invested in a unitised fund. Units are cancelled to cover the protection costs. If the fund performs poorly or claims rise, your premiums will increase to cover the extra protection costs. I have never known reviewable premiums go down.

So what's the problem?

Plans that originate from Life Offices are not always simple. People have been mis-sold these policies under the mistaken belief they will always pay out a lump sum if you are critically ill. This is not the case. The problems arise because of a mis-match between all parties involved as to the exact definition of a critical illness.

The Providers Definition of a Critical Illness

Providers define a critical illness as one that is life-threatening. The plan is almost like an accelerated death payment plan that pays out a lump sum in advance of death, on the diagnosis of a specified medical condition. Their lists are based on the Association of British Insurers (ABI) definitions. There are 7 'core' conditions and 13 additional ones. Some providers add even more.

No provider is prepared to state what percentage of critical illnesses qualify, which is an admission that they will not pay out on all critical conditions as this does not sell policies. Some offer more cover than others. It is difficult for advisers and consumers to assess how comprehensive the lists are. As medical science and longevity improve, providers have to redefine their definitions because those that were considered life threatening are now classed as just serious illnesses. (For example, insurers will not pay out on types of heart problems or forms of cancer that the medical profession does not class as critical because treatment has improved.)

The Salesman's view of Critical Illness

The salesman wants a sale and may spend far more time talking about fear of illness than they do in explaining what the policy covers. As over 70% of critical illnesses are cancer, heart attacks and strokes, salesmen will provide numerous charts and statistics showing how many of the population are affected. They make broad brush statements about *'Protecting the family from the financial hardship of cancer or a heart attack'*, but fail to tell customers the whole truth.

Storing up disappointment

What salesmen may fail to mention is that many of those who claim will be disappointed. For example, the definition of heart attacks and heart treatment is a constant source of friction. The ABI defines a heart attack as:

'The death of a portion of the heart muscle that as a result of inadequate blood supply as evidenced by an episode of typical chest pain, new electrocardiograph changes and by the elevation of cardiac enzymes. The evidence must be consistent with the diagnosis of a heart attack.'

If you have a chest pain and the hospital diagnose severe angina and narrowing coronary arteries and decide to operate, you may not be given a bypass operation. Many plans would have paid out 5 years ago for a bypass but will now not pay out, as you are having another form of treatment that is not covered by the definitions, even though as a patient you are equally ill.

Companies interpretation of risk

Some companies pay out a limited amount on a balloon angioplasty into a narrowing coronary artery to improve blood flow. For the same procedure, other companies will pay nothing. To the patient these are small print technicalities that allow the insurer to wriggle out of making a payment, but are ethically wrong. The patient feels they are critically ill as they have taken 3 months off work and their GP has told them to slow down and alter their lifestyle or put their affairs in order. But the critical illness plan will not pay out!

I sympathise with good fee-based advisers who try and go through the medical conditions but are hampered by the medical jargon. The best they can do is advise clients that if they are walking up the path to knock on death's door, they should get a lump sum. For everyone else it may be tough luck.

The Consumer's view of Critical illness

No salesman told the consumer about the scenario, *'Tough luck you're not quite dying!'* Consumers believe that seriously ill and critically ill are the same, and they have the right to a lump sum because the salesman said they were covered.

> ## CASE STUDY
>
> Rita Cooper was diagnosed with malignant squamous cell skin cancer, and made a critical illness claim on her policy which was rejected. She then learned that her policy only pays out on malignant melanoma, which is the most serious skin cancer (accounting for 10% to 15% of skin cancer cases in the UK). Her salesman had failed to point out that 85% of critical illness skin cancer claims are not covered. Rita told me, 'I feel so let down, the salesman told me the plan covered cancer, and I've got cancer and will get nothing. It's all wrong.'

Confusion will lead to complaints

With more and more people being declined payments, they may have no alternative but to make a complaint. This may increase as so many people have been sold critical illness policies as 'rider benefits', included with life cover when taking out a mortgage. Salesmen rarely go into the depth required to ascertain whether there was a better alternative. It's bolted on to the mortgage to earn more commission.

Basis for YOUR Complaint

These are the points to take into consideration in your complaint:

Depends when the sale took place – From 14 January 2005, the FSA took over the regulation of sales of non-investment insurance policies that provide cover and nothing else. They include guaranteed premium critical illness policies. If you were sold such a policy prior to this date you will not be able to take your complaint to the FOS unless at the time of the sale the adviser was regulated by the General Insurance Standards Council (GISC). All policies sold from 14 January 2005 are covered by the FOS.

Most questionable sales are covered – Most complaints about critical illness plans concern those with reviewable premiums, which use an investment link and are covered by the ombudsman, as far back as April 1988.

All administration problems are covered – Complaints about the provider's administration and operation of your critical illness plan are covered by the FOS, such as interpretation of medical definitions.

LEARNING POINT

Not all critical illness protection complaints are covered by the ombudsman (FOS).

Reasons to Complain

1. Where You have not made a claim on the policy

These relate to the information that was provided or omitted from the sales process.

Inaccurately Described Policy – The salesman described / implied the policy comprehensively covered all conditions in full. This is inaccurate and misleading, and provided grounds for a complaint.

Recommended Poor Contract – The salesman failed to evaluate the whole market and recommended an inferior policy with limited coverage of the main critical conditions and a poor claims history, instead of a superior contract at a similar cost.

Ignored Guaranteed Premiums – Did the salesman evaluate and discuss the differences between guaranteed and reviewable premium contracts? If you were not advised to consider both types of contracts, your adviser may have misled you by recommending an inferior reviewable premium contract. Many tied advisers (who represent just one company) only offer reviewable contracts. As they only have one plan to offer, the FSA allows them to escape criticism if they recommended the most suitable contract from all the products they sell. This is another reason to steer clear of all tied advisers, notably those that work for the major high street banks.

Reviewable Premiums & Affordability – Many people were never told their premiums were reviewable and that they can increase at any time at the discretion of the Life Office. They are shocked to find following a review (usually at the 10th anniversary) that their premiums have increased. You shoulder all the risk as the Life Office can increase your premiums to cover its own claims experience, regardless of how well your investments have performed. This may result in the plan becoming unaffordable or ceasing. This is blatant mis-selling and you have solid grounds for a complaint. If you were informed that the premiums were reviewable, but the extent of the possible increases was not made clear, then you still have grounds for complaint as the salesman did not take into account ongoing affordability against your future income.

Ignored Income Protection Insurance – Did the salesmen evaluate all your protection options including the use of income protection insurance, which pays out a regular tax-free income (related to your earnings) in the event of an accident or illness? The illness does not have to be critical. Many professional fee-based planners consider these are preferable to critical illness plans as they are more likely to pay out. This is especially so with mortgages where, if you cannot work because you are seriously ill, or have had an accident, income protection insurance will pay out until you are fit enough to return to work. If the illness is so critical that it eventually leads to death, your life cover will cover the ongoing liabilities.

A complaint may be justified on the grounds that a health condition has arisen where the critical illness cover will not pay out but the income protection would have.

Consider a muscular skeletal disorder such as back pain, which may keep you off work for a year. Critical illness would not pay out, so the mortgage may fall into arrears and the prospect of repossession may loom. An income protection plan would have paid out. Salesmen find it easier to sell critical illness policies with a prospect of a lump sum over a regular income, especially if they infer it will pay out under similar conditions. Also the application form for income protection plans tends to be longer, with a more rigorous underwriting process, which may jeopardise the salesman's commission. They prefer a certain sale. If you recognise this scenario you have a case for mis-selling.

Churning Contracts – 'Churning' is a change in contracts to generate commission. In the worst cases it's similar to being told to switch your car insurance from fully comprehensive to third party under the misleading claim they are the same!

> Such advice can be proved as mis-selling if the salesman recommended a switch from a superior guaranteed premium policy with more accommodating medical definitions (heart attacks, cancer and own occupation criteria, see below) to an inferior lower-cost reviewable premium policy with stiffer conditions.

The new plan appears cheaper but this is illusory, as premiums are likely to be increased above the original level after the first review. Check the details, and if a switch has been recommended on the back of a false prospectus, your policy has been 'churned' – which the FSA is trying to stamp out. You have a definite claim for mis-selling. Complain now, and don't wait for a health problem to arise.

Ignored Separate Contracts – Mortgage brokers have been aggressively selling critical illness as 'rider benefits' included with life cover when taking out a mortgage. They do this to earn more commission. In the fast moving world of mortgages, there is usually little time to discuss best advice. Salesmen may fail to mention a few essential facts that are likely to have resulted in a different approach:

- A combined critical illness and life cover plan may cease when a payment is made, resulting in loss of life cover. Two separate policies would pay out twice as much. Some policies allow you the option of buying back life cover at extra cost.
- The cost of two well-researched plans could have been cheaper than the combined policy you were recommended. (This may have been the case 5 years ago. Today some plans offer life cover at a small cost.)
- If affordability becomes an issue, you have the option to cancel one plan giving you more flexibility over your budget.
- It is usually easier to place a separate life cover plan into a trust of your choice (see below). For joint policies split trusts are available, which place death benefits in trust for beneficiaries while leaving the critical illness benefits with the policyholder. They are not popular with salesmen because of extra work involved.

You may benefit as the salesman's records are probably incomplete, with little or no proof that a full analysis was carried out which will result in a successful mis-selling claim.

Trusts – Where critical illness is sold as a joint policy with life cover, salesmen often fail to mention the importance of trusts. A trust is a legal arrangement that controls the direction of the property within the trust, it owns the property so it does not form part of the deceased's estate. This is important as it can help avoid inheritance tax, charged at 40%. If a close member of your family had a plan which was not written in trust and the proceeds were liable to inheritance tax, then you have a definite claim for compensation to cover the cost of tax incurred and loss of interest.

Investment Choice & Risk – Salesmen often pay little attention to fund choice and risk, fearing this may draw attention to non guaranteed premiums. The cost of life cover and the investment performance are equally important, as good investment performance will have the effect of keeping the premium review costs down and vice versa. Salesmen often choose default funds, such as with-profits and managed funds, which fail to address your needs. If the salesman failed to discuss the fund risks and your attitude to risk, then you have a case for mis-selling.

Superfluous to your needs – The salesman recommended a plan that could have been covered by other assets. A complaint could be made under the 'know your client rules' where an analysis of assets and liabilities would have revealed there was no shortfall that needed covering.

Reasons to Complain

2. Where You have Made a Critical Illness Claim and it has been Rejected

You have made what you consider to be a valid claim and the provider rejected it. You must complain to the ombudsman and ask for independent assessment of your claim.

Non-Disclosure

This is one of the main reasons why claims are rejected, where the policyholder failed to disclose certain information that the insurer requires. Many problems originate from salesmen, who offered to complete the proposal forms to close the sale. There may be an innocent explanation why certain conditions (especially childhood illnesses and operations) have been omitted. Unfortunately most insurers apply the 'non-disclosure' rule rigidly, assuming you have lied.

Fortunately the ombudsman (FOS) applies a little common sense, proclaiming that a policyholder is under no duty to disclose information of which they were unaware. There are three types of non-disclosure, **'innocent'**, **'inadvertent'** and **'fraudulent'** non-disclosure.

Innocent non-disclosure is usually the result of a minor error (height 5'11 when you are 5'10), or you didn't know about a childhood illness that happened 23 years ago.

Inadvertent non-disclosure is usually the result of an understandable oversight or a moment of carelessness, sometimes caused by 'catch all questions', which ask for full details of your medical history. People simply can't simply remember that they visited their GP twelve years ago with a slight back strain. The firms have access to your medical records, and some look for excuses to 'take away the brolly when it starts to rain'.

Fraudulent or deliberate non-disclosure happens when the policyholder has been clearly reckless, inaccurately completing the proposal form. In such cases you have no grounds for complaint.

Illness Definitions

This is an area under constant review. For all parties it is difficult to précis complicated medical conditions accurately, into a format that can be understood by everyone. Also, very few people are likely to have read the critical illness definitions guide. If the Life Office rejects your claim stating your condition falls outside the defined conditions, you can go to the FOS who will arbitrate and if need be use independent experts.

Area of contention, 'Total & Permanent Disability.' The definition of this is wide ranging and it is sometimes presented by salesmen as a catch-all definition to pay out when others won't. There are usually quite a few hurdles to jump. Payments will be made if you are totally disabled and unable to carry on with your 'own occupation', OR a 'suited occupation' because you cannot carry out work tasks such as walking or lifting. If you're not working, have you lost your independent existence and are unable to carry out tasks like feeding and dressing? A policy that includes 'own occupation' is the most desirable and the most expensive, as this pays out if you cannot continue in your present job / career.

If you have a contract for 'suited occupation,' this means the Life Office can establish that you are fit to work by reason of your education, training, experience and social standing. If you are refused payment and feel aggrieved, then you have no choice but to ask the FOS to arbitrate. Some older schemes may use the definition 'any occupation' which the FOS has declared as nebulous. All assessments of claims that include the term 'any occupation' will be classed as 'suited occupation'.

Conclusion

This is a case where the industry must be more honest about managing expectations. If there is a list of inclusions, there should also be a list of exclusions of the critical and very serious conditions. This would help prevent consumers taking policies under false pretences, believing they are covered.

In general, critical illness plans are overrated. If you have a limited protection budget, the best way to protect yourself is to use an income protection policy. If the salesman failed to evaluate the costs and benefits of all your protection options, then you have grounds for complaint. Remember, protection policies are there to fill in the gaps if something goes wrong because you have no savings to fall back on. But you will never accrue sufficient reserves if you spend too much of your money on protection. So you have three choices:

- Take the industry advice, gamble on a critical illness which is unlikely to happen, and lose all your premiums.
- Take positive action and save your money towards a known outcome to build your assets and cover emergencies, or use the money to reduce your debts.
- A bit of both with the emphasis on saving and debt reduction.

You have the choice. Do you spend £50 per month on a critical illness plan to cover a £100,000 mortgage for 25 years, or save it? Which outcome would you have preferred, and did the salesman give you the choice? Table 1 examines the impact of both strategies.

Table 1. **Critical Illness Cover OR Savings**		
Years	**Critical Illness Cover Cost £50/m**	**Saving £50/m Growth at 5% p.a.**
5	£3,000	£3,482
10	£6,000	£7,924
15	£9,000	£13,594
20	£12,000	£20,382
25	£15,000	£30,068

Why not be positive and spend the £15,000 on healthy pursuits, instead of negatively hoping for a payout if something goes wrong? Get down to your local swimming baths, join the National Trust and walk around wonderful Britain!

Your Claim

If you have been mis-sold a policy, you must make a claim for compensation based on the losses incurred, which may be a return of all premiums (on an inadequate policy), or the loss of benefits caused by churning. This is difficult to estimate as it is unlikely you will be able to reinstate an old contract. The FOS will arbitrate.

Possible claim scenarios are:

Churning – leading to a recommendation to buy an inferior contract – Claim is based on the restoration of benefits to previous levels.

Churning – a claim made on the new plan and rejected – There is a good chance that your old policy would have paid out. If so, make a claim for the amount you have lost.

Unsuitable – Permanent Health Insurance – You should have been recommended a PHI contract which was more suited to your limited budget. Claim the difference in premiums or the loss of potential income that you would have received following an illness / accident that you have suffered which was not covered by the policy.

Unsuitable – Reviewable Premiums – You were not told about the reviewable premiums, the plan is no longer affordable and you make a claim for the return of premiums and interest.

Unsuitable – Not told about Guaranteed Premiums – You were not told about the availability of guaranteed premiums, which could have secured fixed costs at 10% to 20% above the reviewable premiums for the term of the contract. The reviewable premiums have now increased to a level greater than the then guaranteed costs. You make a claim for the difference between the costs of the two plans.

Unsuitable – Separate contracts, No claim made – The salesman failed to recommend the best separate contracts which would have been cheaper. You claim the difference in extra costs incurred, and set-up of more appropriate contracts.

Unsuitable – Separate contracts, claim made – The salesman failed to recommend the best separate contracts, which could have been cheaper. Following a health problem, a critical illness claim is made which has resulted in the loss of life cover. A compensation claim should be made based on the restoration of the life cover.

Use complaint Letter 27 and seek redress.

h) Mis-selling of Reviewable Premium Contracts

Who is Affected – Anyone who has bought an insurance contract where the premiums are not guaranteed to remain level.

The premiums of Reviewable Premium Contracts can increase at any time. Reviews can take place at any time, but usually at the 5th or 10th anniversaries. If you are older, the Life Office may conduct annual reviews. Premiums reflect the claims experience of the Life Office for someone in your age group and state of health. While most contracts that are mis-sold use annual regular premiums, a few involve lump sums.

The Problem

Many contracts are sold on the basis of cheaper premiums. Problems arise when customers find that the premiums are not guaranteed to remain level and are likely to increase at the first review date. This comes as quite a shock, especially to older people who may see their premiums double. Premiums are lower because the contract liability to meet unforeseen costs is carried by you, as the Life Office can at a whim increase the premiums. With guaranteed premium contracts, the liability to meet future claim costs is met by the Life Office.

Even if the salesman informed you the premiums were reviewable, you have a case for mis-selling if you were given no indication of the scale of increases and the effect on the policy's ongoing affordability, taking into account your future income. This problem particularly affects anyone living on a fixed income, such as pensioners.

Why does it happen?

Commission is the reason behind all mis-selling. To secure business, salesmen may omit to mention that premiums are reviewable, the customer signs and the salesman moves on.

What contracts could be affected?

Term assurance – Life cover that covers a fixed term.

Flexible Protection Plans / Whole-of-life plans – Life cover that covers the whole of your life. These are probably the most commonly mis-sold reviewable protection plans.

Critical illness – Plans that may pay out on diagnosis of a critical illness.

Income Protection insurance – Plans that may pay out an income in the event of accident or sickness.

Private medical insurance – Private health cover.

Long-term Care Policies – These are pre-funded long-term care plans and are no longer available. Premiums were either regular or by single lump sum. Those that were marketed as single lump sum policies are particularly distressing to the elderly who are asked to top up their accounts with further lump sums or incur a reduction of benefits, and they simply cannot afford to do so.

Your claim for mis-selling

You have a claim for mis-selling if the salesman failed to evaluate and disclose all your protection plan options covering both reviewable and guaranteed premium contracts. See complaint letter 28. Your claim will be based on restoring your premium to the amount you should have paid if the guaranteed premium option had been chosen. There are two sales scenarios:

If you were recommended a reviewable premium contract and the adviser failed to bring to your attention the availability of a superior guaranteed contract, where the premiums were initially 10% to 20% higher, you should claim. The difference now may be much greater.

If you were recommended to cease a superior guaranteed premium contract and replace it with an inferior reviewable premium contract, you should make a claim.

i) Omission of Trusts

A trust is used to manage 'property' for the benefit of other people. A person who transfers money into a trust is called the settlor. The people appointed to legally manage the trust property are the trustees. They are the legal owners and must manage the money in accordance with the trust deed (the terms and conditions applying to the trust) for the benefit of the beneficiaries. The beneficiaries are the beneficial owners and have the legal rights to enjoyment of the property. Contracts affected include all life cover policies, pensions and lump sum investments into Life Office funds.

Benefits of Trusts

Avoid Inheritance Tax – If used wisely, a trust can be very useful in avoiding inheritance tax, which is payable on death. As the trust owns the property, it does not form part of the deceased's estate, and may help avoid inheritance tax. There is no inheritance tax on assets under £285,000 (2006/07) known as the 'nil rate band'. Everything over and above this amount is liable to inheritance tax at 40%.

Quick distribution – It can be distributed to the beneficiaries without waiting for probate, as trust property is dealt with separately to your other property, whether you have a will or not. (Probate is the process by which wills are approved and the executors of the will can distribute the estate.)

Why wasn't I recommended a trust?

The setting up of a trust does involve work which pays no extra commission. Salesmen may see trusts as an inefficient use of their time, interfering with their sale. If a close member of your family had a policy which was not written in trust and the proceeds were liable to inheritance tax, then you have a definite claim for compensation to cover the cost of the inheritance tax paid by the executors and loss of interest. Use complaint Letter 29.

j) Churning (Switching)

Churning is the recommendation to switch a financial contract (loan, life policy or investment) to a new contract, with no justification or advantage to the consumer. It generates commission for the salesman at your expense. Any organisation involved in such practices can expect to be subject to an FSA fine. Habitual offenders will have all their sales cases investigated.

How do I know if I have been a victim of churning?

Salesmen defend switching to a new provider by saying they can, 'squeeze more out of your money, give better performance, or consolidate your funds. Some reasons may be legitimate, but many are not. Ask yourself: *'Am I in a more advantageous position now than I was before the change was made?'* If you have reservations about the quality of a replacement product or service, you must consider whether the advantages outweigh the disadvantages. If it is not clearly evident that you are better off, then you may have been the victim of 'churning' and you need to consider a complaint.

What contracts are affected?

Potentially all replacement contracts and services. Many of the common problems concerning product mis-selling through churning are covered in previous sections:

- Endowments – Chapter 12
- Life Office Insurance Bonds – Chapter 14 section b
- Flexible whole-of-life plans – Chapter 14 section f
- Critical Illness plans – Chapter 14 section g
- Mortgages – Chapter 13 section a

The two most frequent reasons given for churning are lower charges and better fund management.

Did the salesman take charges into account?

Table 1 lists some reflective questions to help you assess whether your best interests were taken into account:

Churning of Pensions

Pensions have been churned by financial advisers for years, but the problem really escalated in 1988 with the introduction of Personal Pension Plans (PPPs).

CASE STUDY

In 1988 Mike Turnbull, a 32-year old programmer, was advised to opt out of his employer's scheme to start a PPP to give him 'more freedom' over his retirement. In 1991 Mike went freelance and was advised to start a new PPP because he was now self-employed. In 1994 his company went limited and he was advised to set up a company pension scheme. In 1997 he took a job with his biggest customer who offered an employer's pension contribution into a PPP of his choice – the employer's broker advised him to open yet another new PPP. By 2001 Mike was working freelance again and considered a low-cost stakeholder plan but was advised that his limited funds would be do better in a new PPP. So, over a period of 13 years, Mike has been recommended 5 pension plans, 4 of which were unnecessary!

Why did it happen? Put simply, every time you start a regular premium pension plan, the financial adviser takes most of the first year's (and often second year's) contribution in commission out of your money. By taking so much out in commission, Mike's 5 pension plans have been robbed, as demonstrated below.

Table 1. Comparison of Pension Returns

	5 High-commission Pension Plans	1 Low-cost Personal Pension Plan
Value in 2006	£21,107	£38,424
Extra Pension (£)	–	£17,317
Extra Pension (%)	–	82%

Note: Based on 18 annual contributions of £1,000 gross, initial charge 5%, growing at 8% per annum compound.

Mike is typical of many people who move employment. If he had been advised to fund 1 low-cost PPP, today his pension would be worth over 80% more. Mike is now 48 and should claim back the thousands of pounds he has lost because of unscrupulous advice aimed at generating commission at his expense. And as Mike was a basic-rate tax-payer for much of this period, there is a good chance he should never have been recommended a pension at all, see Chapter 10, section b.

Table 2. **Charging Checks**

On Reflection	Observation
Why were the new contracts premiums lower?	Does the new contract offer like for like benefits? Are the premiums reviewable or guaranteed?
Were all the cancellation / exit charges disclosed?	If not you may have received a lower than expected surrender / transfer value. Check your paperwork / contract note.
Does the new contract contain high exit / surrender charges?	This could be important if the penalties extend beyond the date the money is required.
What were the tax consequences?	When contracts cease, gains on life insurance contracts are liable to income tax. Other investment gains are liable to capital gains tax.
Were all the initial set-up charges revealed including the salesman's commission?	If not what impact will they have on the recommendation? How long will it take for the expected savings to cover the cancellation and new set-up charges?
Did the salesman compare the annual charges?	Usually salesmen will tell you about the annual management charge which is just the fund manager's costs and excludes third party charges. You need the Total Expense Ratio (TER) which includes the fund manager charges and third party charges, which may be more than 1% greater than that quoted.
Did the salesman compare the Reduction in Yield (RIY)?	The RIY is the loss in growth caused by all charges both initial and ongoing, i.e. a plan may need to achieve 2.5% growth each year just to remain level.

Be wary of salesmen telling you to transfer all your investments into new 'wrap accounts' which allow them to manage all your investments via one access point. Charges and conditions apply to transfers. Dealing with one administrator seems appealing, BUT some salesmen use this as an opportunity to churn funds, incurring you unnecessary costs of 5% to generate their 3% commission. Instead, the salesmen could simply re-register each fund, which is likely to be free or cost £25 per holding.

Did the salesman complete fund management switching checks?

Table 3 reflects on the evaluation process, and whether all options were considered.

Table 3. **Fund Switching Checks**	
On Reflection	**Observation**
Was the internal switch option considered?	Were there other internal funds available that matched your risk profile, to which your money could be switched at little or nil cost?
Was re-registration considered?	Many advisers are trying to encourage investors to switch all their investments on to platforms whereby they may be managed from a central point. If re-registration of existing funds is chosen this may be free or cost £25, but generates no initial commission. Reinvestment may cost you 5% of your fund and generates 3% commission.
What evidence were you shown that proved under-performance? What evidence were you shown that proved the recommended new fund was more advantageous? Was a fair comparison made?	Did the salesman compare funds: From the same sector, i.e. comparing UK smaller company funds with other UK smaller company funds? Performance year by year known as the discrete return over at least 5 years? Some fee-based planners insist you need 10 years or more to cover different investment cycles. Was this supported by evidence from independent sources such as rating agencies, such as Standard & Poors, Morningstar and the Financial Times? Did they use the same timescales, examine the volatility of the fund, examine the qualitative research and analysis conducted by the companies, and examine the initial and ongoing charges?
Had there been any material changes in the way the new funds operate that should have been disclosed?	Such as the loss of a star fund manager, or change in the investment company structure, such as demutualization which could affect future returns / bonuses?
Were you warned about being out of the market?	Did unnecessary delays in transferring your money affect your fund growth?
Did the salesman take into account tax?	Did the salesman recommend a taxed fund when a non taxed one was available?
Did the salesman reassess your attitude to risk?	Did the new fund reflect your new attitude to risk?
Did the salesmen advise that by consolidating all your funds with one fund manager this may in the event of a problem restrict your compensation?	In the event you need to call on the Financial Services Compensation Scheme they restrict your compensation to £48,000.

We have not created a dedicated churning letter. Look at the evidence and decide whether your best interests were taken into account. If you're unsure, ask the ombudsman to check out your complaint.

WEALTH WARNING

Salesmen will claim trail commission of 0.5% of your money every year, for doing nothing (or almost nothing). Some companies are building their business models in the anticipation of holding these commission rights. You should transfer to a commission rebating company NOW. See Part One, Chapter 3 Commission Rebates.

Conclusion

Forty years ago, I was given my first money box, and as I slipped a shiny old penny into the slot, I remember my dad saying, 'A penny saved is a penny earned'. I've never forgotten that.

After reading this guide, I hope my dad's words take on a new significance for you. How many weeks would you have to work and save to earn the amount equivalent to your unclaimed compensation? The average working wage is £26,000 a year (which is £370 a week after tax). Most working people who've had a bad encounter with a salesman may be able to claim 4 weeks, 10 weeks or 30 weeks salary just by writing a letter. Forget the lottery, buy a first class stamp, and get your claim in …..NOW!

Things could get worse

Under the current system, mis-selling is part of life. Things could actually get worse if the industry is put under pressure by claims for compensation generated by Whistle-blower, so we advise you to get ahead of the queue and claim now.

Mis-selling will continue because the market is driven by commission and the short-term sales goals. Shareholders want instant rewards from rising dividends, and salesmen want commission. New mis-selling scandals always go hand in hand with new selling opportunities. In a couple of years time, consumers will be complaining about how 'A-Day' pension transfers were mis-handled, and how equity release plans wiped out their lifetime investment.

The only way to stop mis-selling is to remove commission

This cycle is set to continue until commission is completely abolished. At a stroke advisers would be forced to evaluate products on merit, and consumers could be confident that an adviser would help them plan their lives without bias. The abolition of commission must go hand in hand with consumer education. This is a long-term solution which must begin with the teaching of practical maths in school, preparing students for the everyday financial decisions we all encounter.

The power to complain

In the meantime, you must be utterly resolute and complain. Ignore firms' rejection letters, which use flawed analysis, and send your complaint to the ombudsman. With so many firms failing to treat complainants fairly, the ombudsman (FOS) and the FSA should get together to offer firms a little encouragement to treat consumers fairly, using:

Automatic stress awards – If a firm uses delaying tactics when dealing with a clear mis-selling claim, the FOS should automatically make significant stress and inconvenience awards of at least £1,000.

Raise case handling fees – The FOS could also raise the case-handling fee of habitual offenders to reflect the actual costs.

Let the public know – The FSA should receive data from the ombudsman of the number of upheld complaints, and place this on its web-site, naming and shaming the worst companies. Currently the ombudsman and FSA work independently, and the FSA cannot fine a company on the back of complaints sent to the ombudsman.

Bar Directors from holding office – Those companies who constantly sail close to the wind can readily afford small fines which do not impact their business. But they may be more willing to treat customers fairly if their directors were barred from holding any position of responsibility with companies authorised and regulated by the FSA.

The public should put pressure on the government and industry to adopt some of these simple measures, otherwise they will not happen.

The Financial Ombudsman must be strong

The publication of this guide may test the ombudsman's claim to independence, putting pressure on them to reject claims in order to protect parts of the industry from going out of business. I sincerely hope my fears are proved wrong. Only when we have a fair market-place and a financially literate society, will the FSA will be able to apply the principle of buyer beware. As things stand today, the financial services industry does not deserve the trust of its consumers. Decades of bad practice have left many people poorer.

For YOU and many others

Very recently I met Bill and Edith Perkins. In 1998 they had a comfortable detached home in Chester, valued at £182,000. They responded to a tempting advert, 'You've worked hard, now you can afford to enjoy it!' and a salesman came to their home to persuade them to buy an equity release plan. Bill and Edith were both 71, and were desperate for a lump sum to help them make frequent visits to their eldest daughter in Australia and son in New York. They signed on the dotted line to release £50,000 at 7.8% interest, with a 'hidden' loan arrangement fee of 2.5% that was added to their loan. When I met them in 2006, Bill's failing health had forced a sale on the home. That's when Edith had discovered the contract included an early redemption charge (ERC) of 5% of the capital repaid. So in 8 years the plan had taken £46,000 in interest and charges and they now owed the equity release company £96,000. Edith said to me, 'That salesman robbed us of money it took Bill a lifetime to earn.' She was heart-broken. Stories like theirs motivated the writing of this guide.

If like Bill and Edith, YOU feel you have been misled and have been advised to make a financial decision by a salesman from the FS industry for their personal gain, then the good news is, you can put it right. Use the letters in Part Three, complain today, and claim back your money for YOU and YOUR family.

Look out for three future Whistle-blower MONEY GUIDES on 'Mortgages & Property,' 'Simple Financial Planning for Everyone' and 'Pensions and Retirement Planning', which will make you more financially aware, and richer.

Complaint Letters

How to write a complaint letter

After you have read Part Two of this guide, you will probably realise you have been the victim of mis-selling and have grounds for a complaint. Part Three contains 29 tailor-made letters to help you complain and claim the compensation which is rightfully yours. The letters comprehensively cover the main mis-selling issues affecting each complaint. In some cases not all the issues will apply to your particular case, so choose as appropriate.

Whistle-blower recommends that you address your letter to the customer services department. It is acceptable to address your letter *'Dear Sirs'* as you are unlikely to know the name of the addressee, and end *'Yours faithfully'*.

Make certain that you head your letter clearly with the name and reference details of your; Provider, Plan number, Name of policy-holder(s) and use the subject title for your letter <u>Formal Complaint.</u>

All letters should be formatted as this example:

Your address and contact details

Date

Dear Sirs

Provider: Allied Dunbar
Policy / Plan number: Personal Pension Plan no. AB123457
Policyholder: Freda Brown

<u>Formal Complaint</u>

I am making a formal complaint about the advice I received from your company to fund a PERSONAL PENSION PLAN starting on 8 May 1998 with ALLIED DUNBAR.

In accordance with the Data Protection Act I request a copy of my personal file.

If I do not receive a positive response within 8 weeks I will be forwarding this complaint to the Financial Ombudsman Service.

Yours faithfully

Freda Brown

Letter 1 has been set out in full as an illustration.

Letters 1 – 9 Pension Complaint Letters

Letter 1. Pension – Commission Manipulation – Complaint Letter

Dear Sirs

Provider:
Personal Pension Plan number:
Policyholder:

<u>Formal Complaint</u>

I am making a formal complaint about the advice I received from your company to fund a 'TYPE of PENSION' starting on 'DATE' with 'XYZ COMPANY'.

In accordance with the Data Protection Act I request a copy of my personal file.

I believe I was mis-sold a pension as it was incorrectly set up as a regular premium contract, to my disadvantage, to maximise commission for the salesman. The salesman failed to explain the difference in the charging structures.

I intended to make a couple of one-off single premium investments and understood there would be a 5% initial charge. But the salesman advised me to split one large premium investment across two tax years to average the cost of buying units in the funds. I now find I am the victim of a deception, and this was the salesman's method of falsely processing this as a regular premium contract.

OR

I was in a short-term employment contract whereby I could have made annual lump sum contributions but was advised by your salesman to invest a regular contribution for two years. The salesman failed to explain the charging structure.

I am now appalled to find that my wish to invest in single premium investments was ignored by the salesman. I am aware that regular contribution contracts attract up to 20 times more commission than single premium investments. At the time I did not understand the charging structure associated with Capital / Initial Units, nor the greatly enhanced commission, nor that commission is effectively taken from my investment. The annual investment statement showed a similar amount to that which I had invested, but I now understand this is only a notional value, and the actual amount invested is much lower (as borne out by the low transfer value). Capital units and initial units have disguised very high charges and facilitated the withdrawal of high commissions from my contract.

Money has been taken from my pension without my knowledge or consent. This is not just mis-selling, I consider it to be fraudulent. As a minimum I demand that my contract is re-issued using the charging structure applicable to single premium investments, with an appropriate allowance for distress.

If I do not receive a positive response within 8 weeks I will be forwarding this complaint to the Financial Ombudsman Service.

Yours faithfully

Letter 2. Pension – Basic rate Tax Payers & Pension Funding – Complaint Letter

(See page 250 for letter layout.)

I believe I was mis-sold a pension as your advice did not address my needs by taking into account my tax position, the taxation of other more suitable investment options, the repayment of my debts and how my state benefits may be affected. I was mis-informed as to the tax advantages of pensions, therefore your recommendation was unsuitable for someone with my circumstances and lifestyle needs.

You failed to give prominence to strict conditions in the contract that would affect my financial position. Your advice and suitability letter failed to address the following issues:

- You failed to evaluate fully my long-term needs and the best way to provide an income in retirement.
- You failed to evaluate fully all my investment options, examining and comparing the tax advantages and disadvantages of funding pensions, ISAs (PEPs if recommendation before 6 April 1999), and paying off debt.
- You failed to explain fully that as a basic-rate tax-payer investing less than £7,000 per year there is no tax advantage to funding a pension over an ISA / PEP, as the tax relief on the initial contributions is mitigated by the need to pay tax on the income at retirement. Overall the income provided by an ISA is likely to be the same as a pension, but without the restrictions. On the contrary you emphasised the tax advantages of pensions. I was misinformed as the advice I received was incorrect.
- You failed to explain fully that I would be denied access to 100% of my fund before age 50. After age 50 I am denied access to 75% of my fund, when the ISA provides 100% access all the time.
- You failed to disclose fully how the money in retirement must be used to buy annuities which offer poor value for consumers like me as it adds another layer of complexity and charges.
- You failed to explain how someone like me from a family with a history of poor longevity is ever likely to receive full value from an annuity and the pensions system.
- You failed to inform me that at the time you advised me to take out my pension (any time between 2 July 1997 to 5 April 2004) ISA / PEP funds benefited from being able to claim back the tax credit on dividends which pension were unable to do, which made ISA/PEP funds more tax-efficient than pension funds.
- You failed to point out the risks of funding a pension that may result in the loss of state benefits. This has been the case since April 1999 when means-tested benefits were introduced. You failed to point out that spending cautiously now may deny me access to pension credit, potentially whittling away the savings credit where my savings are effectively taxed at 40%.
- You failed to address the consequences of inheritance. I am likely to be far better off with an ISA as it will form part of my estate and will be passed to my next of kin, where the pension annuity is likely to die with me.
- You failed to analyse my other long-term need to reduce my debts and that pound for pound this would have a more beneficial impact on my retirement finances than a small pension annuity.
- You placed me in a contract with much higher charges than the tax-free alternatives which has resulted in the depletion of my fund and the prospect that I will receive a lower retirement income.

Overall you failed to address my long-term needs and the key taxation issues. If I had been presented with all the facts I would not have accepted your recommendation to fund a pension. I was mis-sold a pension.

Your suitability letter recommended the pension as the best way to fund my retirement. This is incorrect. From both a tax perspective and income flexibility perspective, the ISA / PEP was the best option. I therefore make a claim for compensation to restore my finances to the position I would have been in if all my disposable income had been invested into alternative tax-efficient savings plans.

No Risk. I make a claim for compensation based on the return of all my premiums assuming they had been invested into a high interest deposit account/ TESSA /Cash ISA and the future loss in tax-free growth had that money been invested into the aforementioned plans OR

Some Risk. I make a claim for compensation based on the return of all my premiums assuming they had been invested into a PEP/ISA, like the Invesco Perpetual High Income Fund and the future loss in tax-free growth had that money been invested into the aforementioned plans.

Letter 3. Pension – Personal Pensions & Pension Mortgages – Complaint Letter

Note: Complaints about pension mortgages are essentially complaints about personal pensions where the extra risks of linking the plan to the repayment of a mortgage were not fully evaluated.

(See page 250 for letter layout.)

I believe I was mis-sold a pension mortgage as your advice did not address my needs, taking into account my tax position, the taxation of other investment options, the early repayment of my mortgage and how my state benefits may be affected. You mis-informed me as to the tax advantages of pensions, and as such your recommendation was unsuitable for someone with my circumstances and lifestyle needs.

You failed to give prominence to strict conditions in the contract that would affect my financial position. Your advice and suitability letter failed to address the following issues:

- You failed to evaluate fully my long-term needs and the best way to repay my mortgage and provide an income in retirement in a concise and understandable format that enabled me to make an informed choice.
- It was implied (written or orally) that the pension would provide OR was guaranteed to provide, sufficient tax-free cash to repay the mortgage. I was never made aware that there could be a shortfall. You never discussed or advised what action I would need to take if there was a shortfall.
- Repaying the mortgage was my primary objective. I was not made aware of the risks associated with the funds and how exposure to the stock market could cause a shortfall.
- You failed to provide me with a full evaluation of the costs of interest-only mortgages compared to repayment mortgages to enable me to make an informed choice. On the contrary you steered me in the opposite direction.
- You failed to evaluate fully all my investment options, examining and comparing the tax advantages and disadvantages of funding pensions, ISAs (PEPs if recommendation before 6 April 1999) and paying off debt.

- You failed to explain fully that as a basic-rate tax-payer investing less than £7,000 per year there is no tax advantage to funding a pension over an ISA / PEP as the tax relief on the initial contributions is mitigated by the need to pay tax on the income at retirement. Overall the income provided by an ISA is likely to be the same as a pension, but without the restrictions. On the contrary you emphasised the tax advantages of pensions. I was misinformed as the advice I received was incorrect.
- You failed to inform me that at the time you advised me to take out my pension (any time between 2 July 1997 to 5 April 2004) ISA / PEP funds benefited from being able to claim back the tax credit on dividends which pension were unable to do, which made ISA/PEP funds more tax-efficient than pension funds.
- You placed me in a contract with much higher charges than the tax-free alternatives which has resulted in the depletion of my fund and the prospect that I will receive a lower retirement income.
- You failed to take into account long-term affordability. The total monthly costs were, unbeknown to me, far greater than the alternatives as I was being asked to create a fund, 75% of which could not be used to repay the mortgage, with the tax-free cash representing only 25% of the fund. You were aware that this was unlikely to be sustainable. (Optional) To make matters worse the plan was set up using a low annual premium, to make it appear more competitive, which increased by ... % each year. No account was taken of ongoing affordability.
- You failed to explain fully that I would be denied access to 100% of my fund before age 50. It was not made clear that I would have to wait until age 50 to access the tax-free cash to repay the mortgage.
- You failed to make it clear that if there was insufficient tax-free cash I may be forced to continue working well beyond the expected mortgage redemption date, incurring extra mortgage interest charges.
- You failed to disclose fully how the money in retirement must be used to buy annuities which offer poor value for consumers like me as it adds another layer of complexity and charges. After age 50 I am denied access to 75% of my fund, when the ISA provides 100% access all the time. This difference was not made clear.
- You failed to explain how someone like me from a family with a history of poor longevity is ever likely to receive full value from an annuity.
- You failed to point out the risks of funding a pension that may result in the loss of state benefits. This has been the case since April 1999 when means tested benefits were introduced. You failed to point out that leading a frugal life now may deny me access to pension credit, and the potential whittling away of the savings credit where my savings are effectively taxed at 40%.
- You failed to address the consequences of inheritance. I am likely to be far better off with an ISA as it will form part of my estate and will be passed to my next of kin, where the pension is likely to die with me.

Such a plan carried a high-risk of failure that the fund would not be able to repay the loan within my required timescale. The plan was inflexible and did not take into account lifestyle needs that could not be foreseen, such as redundancy, illness, changing employers etc. This was not conveyed in the information I received and made the plan unsuitable for someone in my circumstances.

To summarise you failed to address my long-term needs and the key taxation issues. If I had been presented with all the facts I would not have accepted your recommendation to fund a pension to repay my mortgage. I was mis-sold a pension mortgage. I therefore make a claim for compensation to restore my finances to the position I would have been in if the total mortgage and pension costs had been applied to;

No Risk – A repayment mortgage with any excess contributions funding a TESSA / cash ISA. The compensation should also take into account the future loss in tax-free growth had that money been invested into a tax-free TESSA / cash ISA at the outset.

A little Risk – A repayment mortgage with any excess contributions funding a PEP/ ISA, such as the Invesco Perpetual High Income Fund. The compensation should also take into account the future loss in tax-free growth had that money been invested into a tax-free PEP/ ISA fund at the outset.

Some Risk – An interest-only mortgage with any excess funding a PEP/ ISA, such as the Invesco Perpetual High Income Fund. The compensation should also take into account the future loss in tax-free growth had that money been invested into a tax-free PEP/ ISA fund at the outset.

Letter 4. Pension – Contracting Out – Complaint Letter

(See page 250 for letter layout.)

Your advice did not address my needs and was unsuitable for someone in my circumstances and with my no/low-risk profile. You failed to give prominence to strict conditions in the contract that would affect my financial position. Your advice and suitability letter failed to address the following issues;

You did not comprehensively assess my attitude to risk. You advised that I leave the 'state final salary scheme' which guarantees to pay me an income linked to my earnings, which is underwritten by the state, and invest my national insurance rebate into a money purchase scheme where there are no guarantees and where my money is at the mercy of the markets.

You did not fully assess the risk of taking such action. You failed to explain fully and evaluate the specific risks associated with the recommendation and relate this to the probability of achieving my objectives.

You failed to provide a comprehensive evaluation comparing the guaranteed state benefits to the non-guaranteed contracted out benefits.

You did not explain how much worse off I could be by taking this action compared to remaining in the state scheme.

You did not fully explain the effects of charges on the contract.

I am making a claim for compensation based on the loss of the state benefits that I would have accumulated if I had remained contracted-in compared to the benefits standing in my pension plan. I expect the compensation to be calculated based on the 'buy-out' principles used by actuaries when winding up a final salary pension scheme.

Letter 5. Pension – Free Standing AVC Schemes – Complaint Letter

(See page 250 for letter layout.)

I believe I was mis-sold a FSAVC as your advice did not address my needs by taking into account my tax position, the benefits of the employer's AVC Scheme, the taxation of alternative investment options, the repayment of my debts and how my state benefits may be affected.

You mis-informed me as to the tax advantages of the FSAVC, and as such your recommendation was unsuitable for someone in my circumstances and lifestyle needs. Your advice and suitability letter failed to address the following issues:

- You failed to evaluate fully my long-term needs and the best way to provide an income in retirement. You failed to evaluate fully all my investment options, examining and comparing the tax advantages and disadvantages of funding pensions, ISAs (PEPs if recommendation before 6 April 1999).
- You failed to analyse my other long-term need to reduce my debts and that pound for pound this would have a more beneficial impact on my retirement finances than a small annuity.
- You failed to evaluate fully my employer's AVC scheme, comparing costs and the effect of those costs on the final fund value.
- You failed to evaluate fully my employer's added years scheme.
- You failed to explain fully that as a basic-rate tax-payer investing less than £7,000 per year I receive no tax advantage to funding a FSAVC over an ISA /PEP as the tax relief on the initial contributions is mitigated by the need to pay tax on the income at retirement. On the contrary you emphasised the tax advantages of pensions. Overall the income provided by the FSAVC is likely to be lower than that provided by the ISA. You misinformed me and gave me incorrect advice as your basic understanding of the tax and benefits system was fundamentally incorrect.
- You failed to inform me that at the time you advised me to take out my pension (any time between 2 July 1997 to 5 April 2004) ISA / PEP funds benefited from being able to claim back the tax credit on dividends which pension were unable to do, which made ISA/PEP funds more tax-efficient than pension funds.
- You failed to explain that I would be denied access to 100% of my fund before age 50. After age 50 I am denied access to 75% of my fund. This is inferior to the ISA which provides 100% access all the time.
- You failed to disclose fully how the money in retirement must be used to buy annuities which offer poor value for consumers like me as the fund is likely to be small and unattractive to most annuity providers. This adds another layer of complexity and charges.
- You failed to explain how someone like me from a family with a history of poor longevity is ever likely to receive full value from an annuity.
- You failed to point out the risks of funding a pension that may result in the loss of state benefits. This has been the case since April 1999 when means tested benefits were introduced. You failed to point out that leading a frugal life now may deny me access to pension credit, and the potential whittling away of the savings credit where my savings are effectively taxed at 40%.
- You failed to address the consequences of inheritance. I am likely to be far better off with an ISA as it will form part of my estate and will be passed to my next of kin, where the pension is likely to die with me.

- You failed to inform me how the FSAVC charges have a detrimental effect on long-term returns.

Overall you have been negligent as you have failed to address my long-term needs and the key taxation issues. You failed to give prominence to strict conditions in the contract that would affect my financial position. If I had been presented with all the facts I would never have accepted your recommendation to fund a FSAVC. I was mis-sold a FSAVC.

Your suitability letter recommended the FSAVC as the best way to fund my retirement. This is incorrect. From both a tax perspective and income flexibility perspective, the ISA / PEP is the best option. I therefore make a claim for compensation to restore my finances to the position I would have been in if all my disposable income had been invested into PEPs / ISAs - OR had been used to reduce my debts.

Plan Inappropriate – No Risk. I make a claim for compensation based on the return of all my premiums assuming they had been invested into a high interest deposit account/ TESSA / cash ISA.

OR

Plan Inappropriate – Some Risk. I make a claim for compensation based on the return of all my premiums assuming they had been invested into a PEP /ISA, like the Invesco Perpetual High Income Fund.

OR

Plan inappropriate – Debt Reduction Appropriate. I make a claim for compensation based on the position I would be in today if that money had been used to repay my mortgage / other debts.

Letter 6. Pension – Retirement Annuity / Executive Pension – Pre Complaint Transfer Enquiry Letter

(See page 250 for letter layout.)

On the 'DATE' I was advised by 'ADVISER COMPANY' to transfer the above policy to a 'TYPE of PENSION' with 'NEW PROVIDER'S NAME'. I am investigating the possibility that I received incorrect advice to transfer. I would be grateful if you could provide me with the following information concerning my old pension policy:

- Did the contract contain any of the following guarantees, and if so can you outline how and when they applied? Guaranteed Annuity Rates (GAR), Guaranteed Mortality Rates, Guaranteed with profits bonus rates, Any other contractual guaranteed rates.
- At the time the transfer was made were these guarantees still contractually payable?
- Could I have transferred other retirement annuity pensions (executive pensions) to this pension and benefited from the income guarantees?
- What was the maximum I could have invested and still benefited from these guarantees?
- Did the contract benefit from any loyalty bonus / units?
- Would I have benefited from any loyalty reduction in charges? If so how much and when?
- What was the death value and on what basis was it calculated?
- What was the normal retirement date under the scheme?

Letter 7. Pension – Guaranteed Annuity Rates (GAR) / Guaranteed Mortality Rates (GMR) – Complaint Letter

(See page 250 for letter layout.)

I am making a formal complaint about the advice I received from your company to transfer a Retirement Annuity Pension (OR Executive Pension) contract with 'XYZ COMPANY', on 'DATE', to a 'TYPE of NEW CONTRACT' with 'ABC COMPANY'. The full contract details are listed below.

Transfer FROM	Transfer TO
Company:	Company:
Policy:	Policy:
Policy number:	Policy number:
Policyholder:	Policyholder:

Your company failed to disclose / take into account the following contractual details, which has adversely affected my retirement income.

Main Issues – Must Use 1 & 2 and 3 & 4 as appropriate

1   My retirement annuity (executive pension) contract contained GARs OR GMRs payable from age 60 / 65. These provided a guaranteed retirement income far higher than that available in the general market.
2   It was possible to continue to fund this policy and even increase my contributions and benefit from the guaranteed annuity rates. You advised me to switch and then increase my premiums into the ABC COMPANY pension plan, further compounding my losses.
3   The guaranteed annuity rates would also enable me to benefit from the option of a higher tax-free lump sum. (Only Retirement Annuity).
4   The death benefits shortfall, which you used as a reason to transfer, could have been covered by cheap term assurance which would have cost far less than the cost of transfer. This option was not fully evaluated.
    Secondary Issues – use as appropriate as it will help substantiate their negligence.
5   WITH-PROFITS – My old contract guaranteed to pay me an annual / reversionary bonus of …. % per year, regardless of market conditions.
6   The old contract benefited from loyalty bonus / units payable at retirement which would have enhanced my fund value.
7   The old contract benefited from a reduction in charges applicable from age …
8   The transferring company was / is a mutual society which has / may de-mutualise giving rise to a windfall payout.

Your recommendation to transfer was negligent and unsuitable for somebody in my circumstances. Your suitability letter failed to address the GAR issue. If a full transfer analysis had been completed and this information disclosed I would not have accepted your recommendation to transfer.

I claim compensation for the loss of lifetime income your recommendation has caused based on comparing the difference between the fund I should have had at normal retirement subject to the GAR rate and my current fund value and current annuity rates. The compensation should also take into account the extra contributions I was advised to invest elsewhere, which should have increased the value of my guaranteed benefits. This amounts to £ ..... .

Letter 8. Pension – Opt Out of Final Salary Pension Scheme – Complaint Letter

(See page 250 for letter layout.)

Your company failed to evaluate objectively all the risks, which led to your negligent recommendation to transfer, which has adversely affected my retirement income.

My employer sponsored final salary pension scheme guaranteed to provide me with an income at retirement related to my service and salary. The personal pension is invested in the markets where there are no guarantees, with no employer contribution. I now understand that the risks to which I have been exposed are far greater than disclosed by your company. You should have fully evaluated the following risks, and how they interact, which you failed to do so:

- You failed to analyse fully and accurately assess my risk profile.
- You failed to analyse fully the likelihood / probability that my personal pension would exceed the final salary scheme pension after charges, without the assistance of an employer contribution.
- You failed to analyse fully the risk involved in securing a retirement income by the purchase of an annuity and how this could require a substantially larger fund than accounted for in your evaluation.
- Having emphasised the prospect scheme failures you failed to carry out any analysis of the financial strength of the company scheme. I was misled into believing that I could be affected.
- You failed to disclose fully all the costs and charges involved in setting up a personal pension.
- (Temporarily not eligibility to join the employer's scheme on the grounds of service / age) You failed to point out that funding a personal pension for a short period of time until I could join the employer's scheme was totally unsuitable to my circumstances as most of the first two years premiums disappeared in commission. At the point I was eligible to join the scheme you persuaded me to maintain my personal pension plan. This advice was negligent.
- (Temporarily not eligibility to join the employer's scheme on the grounds short-term contract) While at the time I was on a short-term contract it was likely to be made permanent. You were aware that it may become permanent and that I would be eligible to join the scheme. It was made permanent ... months later. You played on the nature of short-term contracts advising that it was not in my interests to join the scheme because if I left within two years I would only be entitled to a refund of my contributions plus money market interest.
- You failed to point out that funding a personal pension for a short period of time was totally unsuitable to my circumstances as most of the first two years premiums disappeared in commission.

- You also failed to point out that if I had joined the scheme and left within two years and received back my contributions it was possible to retrospectively make a lump sum contribution into a personal pension plan.
- You failed to point out that if I had joined the scheme and left after two years I would have a deferred guaranteed pension benefit, which included employer's contributions that is unlikely to be bettered by any personal pension.

Conclusion – At no point during our communications was the extent of the risk made clear. On the contrary your advice suggested you could deliver more than the company scheme with added flexibility.

Taking all the above into account, the recommendation to opt out was negligent and unsuitable for somebody in my circumstances. You failed to address the key issues in the depth required to assess such an important decision. You failed to explain fully the chain of possible risks and how these could adversely affect my retirement income. I could not afford to take such risks.

(Never joined scheme-opted out) I claim compensation based on the amount required to provide me with an income similar to that which I would have had if had joined 'NAME' Final salary Scheme. I expect my personal pension fund to be enhanced.

(Joined scheme-opted out) I claim compensation based on the cost of reinstatement of my entitlement had I remained in the 'NAME' Final salary Scheme. If this is not possible I claim the amount required to provide me with an income similar to that which I would have had if I had remained in the 'NAME' Final salary Scheme. I expect my personal pension fund to be enhanced.

Letter 9. Pension – Final Salary Pension Scheme Transfer – Complaint Letter

(See page 250 for letter layout.)

I believe your company failed to evaluate objectively both the contractual and lifestyle risks, which led to your recommendation to transfer, which has adversely affected my retirement income.

I now understand that the risks to which I have been exposed are far greater than disclosed by your company. As a minimum you should have evaluated the following risks, and how they interact, which you failed to do:

- My personal attitude to investment risk and the likely returns I could expect from my preferred investments.
- The probability that my preferred investments would achieve and exceed the critical yields, after charges, by fully examining historical data.
- The risk involved in securing a retirement income by the purchase of an annuity and how this could require a substantially larger fund than accounted for in your evaluation.

The combined effect of the above risks could (will) result in a final pension income substantially less than that provided by the main scheme. At no point during our communications was the extent of the risk made clear. On the contrary your expectation and advice suggested you could deliver more than the company scheme.

<u>You failed to give prominence to strict conditions in the contract that would affect my investment returns</u>. Your advice and recommendation letter failed to address the following issues:

Attitude to investment Risk & Critical Yields – You failed to analyse fully and accurately assess my risk profile. I advised you that I was a low-risk (cautious etc) investor. However you advised me to invest the money in funds which do not accurately reflect the level of risk with which I feel comfortable, and that do not match my risk profile.

Your advice to invest over 50% (adjust accordingly) of the fund into share based funds was done in the hope of trying to show that the critical yield was achievable. In reality lower risk funds, which suited my risk profile, would have clearly shown lower average returns than those required to match the critical yield, which would have proved that the transfer was not viable. You manipulated the situation to suit your own sales objectives.

For those who were recommended With-profits Funds – (This is often the case where the transfer was to a section 32 Transfer Plan). You advised that with-profits funds are low-risk, which they are not. To suggest that a fund is low-risk knowing the following is evidently incorrect. You failed to give prominence to key contract conditions and failed to disclose fully the following facts:

* That fund originally held 50% to 80% of the assets in shares. This is equivalent to a medium risk fund. The fund was incorrectly categorised and I would never have agreed to invest in a fund with such a high equity content.
* On only one day during my retirement can I access my money without penalty. At any other time I am exposed to a potential MVA which is applied at the discretion of the managers.
* At any time during this period I am invested the managers can withhold growth from me to cover their mistakes of the past.
* The managers have to arrange their asset allocation based on covering liabilities and historical contractual guarantees. Investment decisions are actuarially driven and not 'market value' driven.
* The managers rearrange the investments in such a way as to alter the investment profile, breaking any link with the original assessment matching the fund to my attitude to risk. My attitude to risk has not changed but the risk profile of the fund has.
* Through no fault of my own I can be forced to move to funds with a different risk profile, but to do so I am potentially liable to a market value adjustment.
* The above points clearly show that on the grounds of flexibility and risk the recommendation to invest in with-profits was totally unsuitable.

Investment Return Risk – Your views of investment returns were far too rosy with little emphasis on the consequences of under-performance, or investments returning to their mean averages. You concentrated on using the higher returns from the 1980's and '90's as examples of what I could expect.

This investment period benefited from high price inflation, which also inflated investment returns. Your analysis was flawed as you misrepresented likely future returns over the next 30 years (the number of years to your retirement).

You misled me by recommending the transfer, which needed to achieve minimum returns of 9% or 10%, (Use the figures discussed), which were not representative of likely future returns as you failed to consider historical averages. You implied (promised) that these returns were achievable which was negligent.

Annuity Risk – You failed to explain fully that the transferred funds were part of a two stage investment process and that when benefits were drawn I would have to buy an annuity. You failed to explain that annuity rates were potentially subject to great change and that this process of lower annuity rates had started in 1992, as actuaries recognised improvements in longevity and the effect of lower long-term interest rates. You failed to consider the potential impact of lower annuity rates and how vital this was to my final income.

Scheme Risk – (Optional) During our communications you advised that pensions could be lost / reduced because of scheme failure and used this to support your recommendation to transfer. You failed to carry out any analysis of the financial strength of the company scheme. I was misled into believing that I would be affected.

Explanation Risk – You failed to explain all the risks in a form that I could reasonably expect to understand.

Impact of Charges – Risk to Returns – You failed to disclose fully the impact of the charges on investment returns.

- You omitted to explain fully there would be initial charges of (5% to 7%) and that you would receive 5% from my fund in commission. These charges were disguised in a form that made it difficult for me to assess what was going on. You failed to point out that I incurred no personal costs by leaving the money in the company scheme.
- You failed to point out the impact of total annual management charges of 1.5% to 2% a year would act as a severe drag on final returns. These costs were not taken into account when discussing possible future returns.
- You also failed to point out how these charges affected early retirement / transfer values. Overall the charges have severely reduced the probability of ever achieving a return sufficient to provide a similar pension. This risk was not explained.

Inaccuracies & Omissions – Your report was misleading as it concentrated on achieving returns equivalent to the critical yield as this was the return needed to achieve the same as the ceding scheme. This is misleading.

- It is not clear that the critical yield you used reflected the need to take into account the actual charges (reduction in yield) which would have the effect of increasing the returns required, to match a higher critical yield.
- Should I have been advised to take on all this extra risk in the hope of getting the same? To compensate for the unknown extra risk there should have been a realistic expectation that returns would comfortably exceed the critical yield.
- I am also concerned that some of the older illustrations may not have used charges that truly reflected the actual company charges as they used industry average charges. This gave a false impression of likely future returns as the actual charges were much higher.

I believe I was misled into making a decision based on a false prospectus.

Risk – Other Retirement Investments – (Optional) You failed to take into account that I did not have sufficient other assets to provide a decent income in retirement, to cover any shortfall caused by the failure of the transferred fund to deliver a decent income, which would result in an impoverished (poorer) retirement. Your advice to transfer was a gamble. I should have been advised not to transfer and that it was important for people with limited means to hold on to pensions that provided a guaranteed income.

Conclusion – Taking all the above into account the recommendation to transfer was negligent and unsuitable for somebody in my circumstances. You failed to explain fully the chain of possible risks and how these could adversely affect my retirement income. I could not afford to take such risks, and would never have agreed to a transfer if I had been fully informed. Your recommendation failed to address the key issues in the depth required to assess such an important decision. The odds of failure were greater than success.

I claim compensation based on the cost of reinstating my entitlement in the 'NAME' Final Salary Scheme. If this is not possible, I expect the transferred pension fund to be enhanced by the amount needed to provide me with an income similar to the one I would have had if no transfer had taken place.

Letters 10 – 12 Retirement Complaint Letters

Letter 10. Retirement – Annuities – Complaint Letter

(See page 250 for letter layout.)

Your advice to invest in this type of annuity was unsuitable for someone in my circumstances and needs, and with my risk profile. You failed to give prominence to strict conditions in the contract that would affect my retirement income. Your advice and recommendation letter failed to address the following issues:

Not told of 'Open Market Option' (OMO) – You failed to draw to my attention all my retirement options including the 'open market option'. I was misled into believing I had to take the benefits via the pension provider. You did not make it clear that I could transfer my fund to another annuity provider offering better rates and a higher lifetime income.

Pension provider annuities ignored – You failed to evaluate all my retirement options. You recommended the 'open market option' negligently omitting to consider the higher guaranteed annuity rates / guaranteed mortality rates offered by the pension provider. These would have provided me with substantially more income over my lifetime than your recommendation.

Lower life expectancy – You failed to take into account my state of health and how that could improve the annuity rates offered. At the time I suffered from ...... I now understand that I would have qualified for an 'enhanced annuity' / 'impaired life annuity' which would have increased my retirement income.

With-profits Annuities – You recommended a with-profits annuity but omitted to accurately define the risks associated with such annuities. The recommended ABR of ...% was far too optimistic and is likely to leave me with a static / falling income.

I was misled because:

- You inaccurately advised that 'with-profits' funds are low-risk funds. They are not low-risk as the fund originally held 60% to 80% of the assets in shares and carried other liabilities which made it susceptible to bonus cuts in a market downturn. I would never have consented to expose my money to such risks if I had been told all the facts. I was not informed the fund can go up and down.
- You manipulated the 'Anticipated Bonus Rate' so as to increase the income of the 'with-profits' annuity relative to the competition to make it more attractive compared to the best conventional level annuity. You failed to explain the 'with-profits' bonus system and all the risks involved.
- Overall a 'with-profits' annuity was far too risky for someone with my 'no risk' profile. I needed security as this is my main source of retirement income. You misled me into believing a with-profits annuity offered security. I was mis-sold this annuity as it does not offer the security I needed.

Advised to delay purchasing an Annuity – You incorrectly recommended I delay the purchase of the annuity in anticipation that rates would rise, which was negligent. I wanted to purchase an annuity .... years ago but you advised against it. You failed to explain the factors that affect rates, being long-term interest rates and life expectancy. Life expectancy has been improving and continues to put downward pressure on annuity rates. You must have been aware of the effects of changes, as term assurance premium rates have been decreasing for years. You failed to inform me of these rapid changes. Also global inflation has also been subdued, which has kept long-term interest rates low. You knew of these facts but as an alternative you recommended a Drawdown scheme. (Drawdown schemes are covered in section b.)

Spouses / Partner's benefits ignored (annuitant alive) – You failed to recommend the need to include spouses / partners benefits, especially as the pension forms a major part of the family's retirement income. By failing to do so my partner / spouse will have insufficient retirement income. I was negligently advised to go for a higher income.

Spouses / Partner's benefits ignored (annuitant deceased) – You failed to recommend the need to include spouses / partner's benefits, especially as the pension formed a major part of the family's retirement income. By failing to include last survivor benefits I have been left with insufficient retirement income. My partner was negligently advised to go for a higher income, ignoring my needs. This pension fund represented our joint efforts to build a fund for our retirement. It was all invested in my partner's name for tax relief purpose. This annuity was unsuitable as it failed to take into account my needs.

Inflation Ignored – You failed to take into account and explain the long-term effects of inflation on the purchasing power of my income. This should have been accounted for in your recommendation.

Tax-free cash – You failed to recommend that I should take the maximum tax-free cash which would have been far more tax-efficient than a 100% annuity.

The above points clearly show that you failed to evaluate all my retirement options and the risks involved. The recommendation to purchase a .... annuity was totally unsuitable for someone in my circumstances with my risk profile.

I am making a claim for compensation based on the difference between the income I am currently receiving and the income I should have received, now and over my lifetime, if you had recommended a .... annuity, more suited to my needs.

Letter 11. Retirement – Income Drawdown – Complaint Letter

(See page 250 for letter layout.)

Your advice to invest in a drawdown plan was unsuitable for someone in my circumstances and needs, and with my risk profile. You failed to give prominence to strict conditions in the contract that would affect my retirement income. Your advice and recommendation letter failed to address the following issues; (choose as appropriate).

Flawed Investment Analysis – You failed to secure my retirement income because you recommended a drawdown plan using investments that had no realistic expectation of equalling the annuity income payable at the outset, and every year thereafter. The drawdown was recommended in the expectation of exceeding the annuity income. I should have been warned that the chosen investments had no realistic chance of achieving their objective and the withdrawal of income in excess of growth would lead to fund erosion. The initial viability of the scheme could be measured by examining the critical yield. You failed to point out the importance of meeting and exceeding critical yields using investments that suited my risk profile. An annuity should have been recommended unless there were extraneous circumstances that made a drawdown attractive. I have been misled.

Attitude to Risk – The recommended funds failed to reflect my attitude to risk. I am a no / low-risk investor. You recommended higher risk funds in the belief they would generate higher returns as a way of being able to justify a drawdown scheme on the basis the critical yield could be achieved. You failed to inform me that there were no low-risk investments that you could recommend that were likely to achieve returns to match the critical yield. This was both misleading and negligent.

My Risk Profile – You were aware that I was relying on the pension fund to provide the majority of my retirement income / that I had have given up work and had no significant income from other sources / that I had few other liquid assets / that I was predominantly a cash based investor / that I had little experience or understanding of share based investments / that I made it clear I did not want to take risks / and that it was vital for my peace of mind that the fund secured my income position. Investing the majority of the fund in share based funds was negligent as this strategy was unsuitable for someone in my circumstances. This was a risky strategy unsuitable for someone in my circumstances.

With-profits Risk – You recommended a with-profits fund which is totally unsuited for use in a drawdown scheme.

- You failed to inform me that the fund originally held 50% to 80% of the assets in shares. This is equivalent to a medium risk fund. The fund was wrongly categorised. I would never have consented to expose my money to such risks if I had been told all the facts.
- Should I wish to switch at short notice to buy an annuity the fund may be liable to a market value reduction (MVR) which undermines your flexibility claims.
- The expected returns from with-profits funds fall well short of the critical yields. These changes should have been spotted at reviews and corrective action recommended.

Annuity Risks – You recommended delaying the purchase of the annuity in anticipation that rates would rise / because the drawdown offered more flexibility. This was negligent advice as you failed to inform of changes and influences affecting annuities and the developing pattern showing a decline of annuity rates that had started back in 1990.

Loss of Mortality Cross Subsidy – You failed to inform me of the impact of how the mortality cross-subsidy from those who die early increases annuity rates. This is estimated to increase annuity rates by 1% to 1.5%, but its effect reduces the later you buy an annuity as you are entitled to less cross subsidy. The drawdown plan does not benefit from mortality cross-subsidy and carries the extra risk that the net investment fund growth after charges will fail to keep up with the combined annualised mortality subsidy and underlying asset performance of the annuity fund that determine annuity rates. This was not explained.

Life expectancy is improving – Annuity rates are being pushed lower by improvements in the general population's longevity. This is known from national mortality tables and has been improving at a pace over the last 30 years, with life expectancy improving 2 to 3 years every decade. This is likely to continue for the foreseeable future. This was not explained.

Poor Health Annuities – Annuity rates are being pushed lower by the departure of those with poor health from the general annuity pool and the loss of cross-subsidies.

Unknown Fact 'Interest rate up or down' – Annuity rates could be pushed higher or lower by changes in long-term interest rates which are unknown. However the trend has been lower as global inflation has drifted lower. The improvements in health and changes in the 'general annuity pool' are putting downward pressure on rates. You recommended deferral on the basis that annuity rates could improve. This was negligent, as this advice is at odds with the known facts.

Income Suitability Risks – You failed to evaluate fully my income needs.

* Lifetime income needs – You failed to analyse fully my income needs throughout my whole retirement, taking into account my other assets and the best way to address those income needs without taking unnecessary risks.
* There was a level of income that I needed to maintain my lifestyle and this could be achieved by opting for a guaranteed annuity. You ignored my needs and recommended a Drawdown scheme with all the associated risks.
* Triennial reviews & Income changes – I was not made aware that at the first and subsequent triennial reviews that my income could go down and continue to go down because the fund and annuity rates were falling and the extent of those falls.
* Highest income – You recommended the Drawdown plan because it offered the highest initial income, even greater than a level annuity, without analysing and discussing the likelihood of fund erosion and that this would only provide a temporary boost as my income was likely to fall after the first review. This was negligent advice.

Charges & effect of Charges – The full extent of the charges and the effect on growth were not fully explained. I was not made aware that a charge of 5% to 7% would be taken directly from my fund. Over the lifetime of the contract the effect of the charges would reduce the annual growth by 2% to 3%. This drag on performance makes under-performance inevitable with little or no chance of ever beating 'critical yields'.

Flawed investment strategy – You recommended a Drawdown scheme to enable me to maintain control of my investments. However I feel you have put me in a position of losing control over the value of my money by failing to provide me with a sustainable investment strategy. You have acted incompetently because:

* You only had one strategy – That was 'the markets are going up strategy'. There was no contingency plan should the markets go down and annuities go down. You failed to recommend a STOP LOSS strategy whereby changes would be made if the combination of falling fund values and annuity rates resulted in a lower annuity income.
* Insufficient Time – The share based strategy was inappropriate as there was insufficient time to make it work and recover from volatility in the market that forces my investments lower.
* No coherent ASSET ALLOCATION – The investments were not arranged to meet specific income needs over different timescales. With a bias towards share based insurance funds I am forced to sell at the bottom of any market to generate an annual income. The income streams should have been secured by cash or low-risk investments, OR preferably by an annuity.

Passing on my Pension Fund & Inheritance Tax – Passing on my pension fund to my heirs was important to me , but not as important as securing an income in retirement. In discussing how best to pass on benefits to my heirs you failed to evaluate fully all the options including the use of phased retirement planning. This method of planning is considered more advantageous than a 100% drawdown plan as in the event of early death my unused pension fund can be passed tax-free to my heirs avoiding the 35% income tax charge and inheritance tax of 40%. You failed to inform of all the facts. I would not have chosen a Drawdown scheme if I had been presented with the phased pension plan option.

Tax-free Cash – You recommended a Drawdown plan to release the tax-free cash. It was not in my best interests to withdraw money growing in a tax-free environment and reinvest it in a taxed environment. Such advice is unsuitable on the grounds of cost and tax efficiency. If the money remains inside the pension fund there are no new charges, it grows tax-free and it is inheritance tax-free. I was misled and given advice unsuitable for my circumstances.

Servicing – As a minimum you should have used the triennial reviews and all servicing meetings as an opportunity to check on the validity of the original recommendation. These should have included:

- A new Drawdown illustration and a check on the new 'critical yield' and whether this is realistically achievable using investments that match my risk profile.
- A new annuity illustration showing the level of income that could be purchased now. This should have been compared with previous illustrations to analyse whether a pattern was developing and whether corrective action was required. This should have covered changes in long-term interest rates, changes in mortality and their effect on annuity rates.
- Discussion of my current and future income needs and whether the levels of income withdrawals were sustainable.
- Re-analyse my attitude to risk.
- Are the investments performing as planned? If not, why not?

You failed to comprehensively cover these essential items as this would have exposed your original advice as flawed.

Conclusion

From the above it is clear that your recommendation was unsuitable for someone in my circumstances with my risk profile. You failed to explain fully and evaluate the specific risks associated with the Drawdown plan and relate this to the probability of achieving my income objectives. You failed to explain all the risks in a manner that I could expect to understand.

I make a claim for compensation based on converting my current Drawdown scheme to an annuity and increasing it to the same income level as that of the annuity available at the time the Drawdown scheme was recommended. I also claim compensation with interest to compensate for the difference in the income received from Drawdown scheme compared to that which the annuity would have paid.

Letter 12. Retirement – Pension Unlocking – Complaint Letter

(See page 250 for letter layout.)

I would like to make a formal complaint about the advice I received from your company to draw my pension benefits early from the ...NAME... company pension scheme to release the tax-free cash on 'DATE', AND if applicable purchase an annuity for £ .... with 'XYZ COMPANY', policy number ....

Your advice to take my benefits early was unsuitable for someone in my circumstances and needs, and with my risk profile. You failed to give prominence to strict conditions that would affect my long-term retirement income. Your advice and recommendation letter failed to address the following issues; choose as appropriate.

Retirement Income Evaluation – You failed to compare and analyse in sufficient detail the benefits and risks of going early with the potential benefits at normal retirement. Your analysis failed to address the following:

- The short-term boost to my income would leave me with an income shortfall at my normal retirement age. You failed to take into account my long-term income needs and how to address this future shortfall.
- (Final Salary Schemes) You failed to make me aware of the true cost of what I was giving up and the huge potential costs involved in replacing the reduction in my pension income by analysing the cost of an equivalent annuity.
- You failed to estimate how long it would take for the higher pension payable at normal retirement age to cover the extra income drawn over the early retirement years.
- You failed to evaluate fully the effect on the reduction in my partner's / dependants benefits and how they would manage in the event of my early death.

Objective – You encouraged me to draw the benefits early to release the cash for non-essential spending, which was not in my long-term best interests.

Raising Cash – You failed to explore all sources from where I could temporarily increase my cash flow, such as re-mortgaging, personal loans or surrendering other investments, which would have been far more cost effective than triggering my pension benefits early.

New Investment – You recommended that I invest some of the tax-free cash into .. TYPE of INVESTMENT ... . This was negligent as the money was transferred from a tax-free environment to one where it is taxed. This also undermined the need to take the benefits early, as it would have been far better for the tax-free cash to continue benefiting from tax-free growth.

Loss of Guaranteed Scheme Benefits – You failed to take into account the loss of guaranteed benefits provided to my old pension scheme which would have made a considerable difference to my long-term income.

Weak Scheme – You misled me into believing the scheme was financially weak and that my retirement income could be jeopardised if I did not take the benefits early. This was not the case. You provided no substantial evidence to support your claim.

Compensation Claim – At no point during our communications was the extent of the risk to my long-term income needs made clear. On the contrary your advice suggested I would be better off for taking the benefits early.

Overall taking all the above into account the recommendation to take the benefits early was negligent and unsuitable for somebody in my circumstances. You failed to address the key issues in the depth required to assess such an important decision. You failed to explain fully how such action would adversely affect my long-term retirement income needs. I would never have agreed to take the benefits early if the consequences had been fully explained.

I claim compensation based on putting me back into the same financial position that I would have been in at normal retirement if benefits had not been drawn early.

Letters 13 – 14 Endowment Complaint Letters

Letter 13. Endowment Mortgage – Complaint Letter

(See page 250 for letter layout.)

Your advice did not address my needs and was unsuitable for someone in my circumstances and with my risk profile. You failed to give prominence to strict conditions in the contract that would affect my investment returns and the mortgage repayments. Your advice and recommendation letter failed to address the following issues:

Risk (No investment experience – Nearly All Policyholders) – You did not comprehensively assess my attitude to risk. The plan was unsuitable for someone with no previous experience of investing. Previous to being recommended the endowment the majority of my savings had been placed in building society accounts, because I am averse to risk. You failed to explain fully and evaluate the specific risks associated with the recommendation and relate this to the probability of achieving my objectives.

Risk (Some investment experience) – You did not comprehensively assess my attitude to risk. I made it clear that I did not want to take risks with the repayment of the mortgage and wanted to adopt a no risk / low-risk strategy.

- You failed to explain that this was predominantly a stock market investment, with 60% to 80% of the fund invested in shares and I could end up with a shortfall.
- You failed to point out a strict condition of the contract that the plan could not guarantee to pay off the mortgage.
- You failed to explain what would happen to the mortgage in the event of an endowment shortfall.
- With-profits Investors only - You failed to point out the disadvantages of with-profits investment, how bonuses are manipulated and the need to maintain the contract in order to benefit from the final bonus. Any failure to do so would result in a severe reduction / loss.

To summarise you failed to explain fully and evaluate the specific risks associated with the recommendation and relate this to the probability of achieving my objectives.

1. **Other Mortgage Options** – You failed to provide me with a comprehensive evaluation comparing the merits, costs and risks of repayment and endowment mortgages.
2. **Other Investment Options** – You failed to advise me on the advantages of other repayment savings schemes such as PEPs, available from January 1987 and ISAs available from 6 April 1999, which would have been more suitable on the grounds of cost, likely returns, taxation and flexibility.
3. **Unsuitable Contract** – You recommended a contract totally unsuited to my life style needs as the inflexibility failed to take into account life's problems such as divorce, unemployment and ill health. It was unreasonable to recommend a plan where I am contractually bound to pay an amount for 25 years, and that failure to do so will result in swingeing penalties.

4. **Misleading Information** – (Choose as appropriate)
   - I already had a repayment mortgage but you advised a switch to an endowment because you advised it would be cheaper. This is incorrect, as the life time costs were unknown.
   - You advised me in writing / gave undertakings that the fund would be sufficient /guaranteed to pay off my mortgage.
   - You advised I would have a surplus at maturity sufficient to go on holiday / buy a car.
   - I already had sufficient life cover in place to cover the repayment of the loan. The endowment life cover was an unnecessary extra cost.
   - You did not fully explain the effects of charges on the contract and how this affected the surrender and maturity returns.

5. **Contract Incorrectly Set-up** – (Choose as appropriate)
   You set the maturity date beyond my retirement age, with no analysis of affordability. A check of my retirement income would have proved I could not afford to continue with the premiums or the mortgage.

   The endowment was set up to mature after the mortgage ceases, the consequences of which were not made clear at the time.

   You advised me to extend the life of the mortgage to tie in with a longer term endowment policy.

6. **Policy Churning** – You advised me to cease and surrender an old plan and start one larger policy, incurring commission on two contracts when I should not have incurred any at all if a repayment mortgage had been chosen.

(If appropriate) The old plan benefited from life assurance premium relief of 12.5%, which was lost when you recommended I cancel the plan.

I am making a claim for compensation based on the difference between a repayment mortgage and the endowment mortgage I was sold.

Letter 14. Endowment – Enquiry Letter

(See page 250 for letter layout.)

I would be grateful if you could provide me with the following information concerning my endowment policy:

- What is the current fund value?
- What is the projected value at maturity if I continue with the contributions?
- Is it possible to make the policy paid-up? If so what is the projected value at maturity if I do not make any further contributions?
- Into which funds is the money invested?
- WITH-PROFITS – What bonuses have been declared over the last 5 years in respect of, annual bonuses, terminal Bonuses for contracts similar to mine?
- WITH-PROFITS – Does the policy benefit from any guaranteed growth rates?
- Will I benefit from any loyalty bonus / units?
- Please send me details of the funds performance including fund fact sheets.
- WITH-PROFITS – Please send me your PPFM / CFPPFM document.
- What is the current surrender value?
- Is there a chargeable gain on surrender? If so how much?

- WITH-PROFITS – Are you applying a market valuation adjustment on transfer? If so how much, and how is it calculated?
- Are there any penalties / charges for surrendering the policy?
- Has any lender got a charge on the policy as security against a loan? If so who is it and what do you need to get the policy released?
- Is the policy assigned? If so who to?
- Are the death benefits written in trust? If so who are the beneficiaries and can I have a copy of the trust deed?
- Does the policy include any other benefits such as: Critical Illness Benefit, Terminal Illness Benefit?
- Does the plan benefit from 'waiver of premium' contribution cover? If so how much does it cost?
- What are the current charges with regards to regular contributions, Annual Management Charge and any other charges?
- Will I benefit from any loyalty reduction in charges? If so how much and when?
- Are there any other benefits attached to this policy not mentioned above?
- Mutual Organisations – Are you planning to de-mutualise, if so when is it likely to happen?

Letters 15 – 18 Mortgage Complaint Letters

Letter 15. Mortgages – General Complaint Letter

(See page 250 for letter layout.)

Your advice to start such a mortgage was unsuitable for someone in my circumstances, with my needs, and with my risk profile. You failed to act in my best interests. You failed to give prominence to the key considerations that would affect my financial position. Your advice and recommendation letter failed to address the following issues:

Regulatory Failures

The Initial Disclosure Document (IDD) – You failed to provide me with a complete document at the outset and disclose the exact services you provided and whether you dealt with the whole market. This was not made clear. (I was deceived into believing you dealt with the whole market, I now have learned you only represent one company).

Key Facts Illustration (KFI) – I did not get an illustration OR I received one after the sale. You did not clearly explain all the charges and fees associated with starting and redeeming the mortgage. I was also unaware that a set up charge of ... % had been added to the advance which was not immediately obvious. Had the information in the KFI been provided prior to the sale I would not have agreed to proceed.

Mortgage Options (You were recommended interest-only) – You failed to evaluate fully all my mortgage options, recommending an interest-only mortgage when a repayment mortgage would have been less risky and more suitable for someone with my risk profile.

Investments – You recommended investments to repay the interest-only debts. This strategy is far too risky and should never have been recommended to someone with my risk profile as there is no guarantee the investment will be sufficient to repay the mortgage. You never discussed the probability of a shortfall and what would happen in the event of a shortfall.

Amount – You advised I borrow more than I needed as I had free assets available that could have been used to reduce the size of the loan.

Term – You recommended a 25 year loan when I could have afforded to repay a higher amount to reduce the mortgage term and save interest payments.

Affordability – You recommended I take out a loan that I could not afford to maintain as you failed to take into account my future income needs and cash flow.

Re-mortgaging Costs – You failed to disclose all the re-mortgaging costs and the impact they have on my repayments. I now understand that I am worse off after accepting your recommendation to re-mortgage.

Re-mortgaging Options – You failed to disclose all my re-mortgage options including those offered by my old lender, which would have avoided many the re-mortgaging costs and left me in a financially better position. The re-mortgaging savings were incorrectly calculated leaving me in a loss situation as the recommendation was based on a false prospectus.

Short-term deals & Standard Variable Rates (SVR) – You recommended a short-term deal which defaults to the Standard Variable Rate at the end of the deal period. This rate is uncompetitive and almost forces me to re-mortgage again. You failed to inform me of the option to use a Lifetime Base-rate Tracker, capped at no more than 1% above base-rates, or something similar. This would save me thousands in interest payments and re-mortgaging costs.

I make a claim for compensation based on the extra costs I have incurred because you recommended an unsuitable mortgage for someone in my circumstances and with my risk profile. I want to be placed in the position I would have been in if you had recommended the best repayment mortgage tracking the Bank of England base-rate, of 0.5% above this rate.

Letter 16. Mortgages – Sub-prime Complaint Letter

(See page 250 for letter layout.)

Your advice to start such a mortgage was unsuitable for someone in my circumstances, with my needs, and with my risk profile. You failed to act in my best interests. You failed to give prominence to the key considerations that would affect my financial position. Your advice and recommendation letter failed to address the following issues; Choose as appropriate.

Regulatory Failures

The Initial Disclosure Document (IDD) – You failed to provide me with a complete document at the outset and disclose the exact services you provided and whether you dealt with the whole market. This was not made clear. (I was deceived into believing you dealt with the whole market, I now have learned you only represent one company).

Key Facts Illustration (KFI) – I did not get an illustration OR I received one after the sale. You did not clearly explain all the charges and fees associated with starting and redeeming the mortgage. I was also unaware that a set up charge of … % had been added to the advance which was not immediately obvious. Had the information in the KFI been provided prior to the sale I would not have agreed to proceed.

Inappropriate sub-prime mortgage

I am concerned that your recommendation to use this particular sub-prime mortgage may not have been properly assessed and that I was wrongly categorised. The chosen mortgage was not the most suitable for someone in my circumstances. A better deal could have been sought.

Consolidating Loans

You recommended I consolidate other debts within the mortgage loan but failed to carry out a comprehensive evaluation to assess whether consolidation was appropriate.

Secured V Unsecured – I was not made aware of the differences between secured and unsecured loans. You failed to explain that I was decreasing my unsecured loans and the consequences of increasing my secure loans.

Lower Outgoings – I was misled into believing that you could save me money by reducing the cost of my outgoings. This is incorrect as you failed to explain the consequences of extending the loan term.

You failed to explain how any redemption penalties would be taken into account and their effect on the total repayment costs. These costs were hidden within the lower monthly outgoings.

You failed to carry out a full evaluation comparing the true costs of maintaining the loan to consolidating the loan.

I would never have agreed to consolidate the loan if all the costs had been disclosed.

Renegotiate Debts – You failed to consider and fully evaluate the option of renegotiating the terms of the loan with the original lender.

Higher Purchase (HP) Agreements – You recommended that I consolidate HP loans as a way of reducing my costs and reducing my monthly outgoings.

This advice was flawed as the monthly repayments were fixed for the term of the loan. By repaying the whole loan I have simply paid off all the outstanding payments early. I have not made any savings in interest payments as they were built into the outstanding monthly payments. The creditors win because they have received back their money early. I am in a worse situation because I am now paying two sets of interest charges on the same borrowed money, that which applied to the old HP loan and your mortgage interest. Best advice would have been to leave the HP agreement in place and reduce other outgoings.

Self Cert Mortgages – I understand that you may have embellished my self certified earnings to secure a higher loan. I was not aware this had happened. This practice ignored the need to assess affordability now and in the future. You should have recommended I consider a smaller loan. This mortgage which is in excess of what I can afford has caused further repayment difficulties.

Switching between sub-prime Mortgages – You failed to disclose and fully evaluate all the costs of re-mortgaging. I now understand that I am worse off after accepting your recommendation to re-mortgage. You failed to provide evidence to prove that by switching I would be better off within a stated period from a monthly repayment and capital outstanding perspective. You failed to disclose all my re-mortgage options including those offered by my old lender, which would have avoided many of the re-mortgaging costs and left me in a financially better position. The re-mortgaging savings were incorrectly calculated leaving me in a loss situation as the recommendation was based on a false prospectus.

Mortgage Options (You were recommended interest-only) – You failed to evaluate fully all my mortgage options, recommending an interest-only mortgage when a repayment mortgage would have been less risky and more suitable for someone with my risk profile.

Affordability – You recommended I take out a loan that I could not afford to maintain as you failed to take into account my future income needs and cash flow.

I make a claim for compensation based on:

- The extra costs I have incurred because you recommended an unsuitable sub-prime mortgage for someone in my circumstances and with my risk profile.
- The extra costs I have incurred caused by the unnecessary consolidation of other loans.
- The extra debt I have incurred caused by the incorrect completion of the self cert earnings on the mortgage application to secure a mortgage that I could not afford.
- I want to be placed in the position I would have been in if you had recommended the most suitable repayment mortgage.

Letter 17. Mortgages – Equity Release Plans (Lifetime Mortgages) Complaint Letter

(See page 250 for letter layout.)

Your advice to invest in an Equity Release Plan was unsuitable for someone in my circumstances, with my needs and with my risk profile. You failed to act in my best interests. You failed to give prominence to the key considerations that would affect my financial position. Your advice and recommendation letter failed to address the following issues:

You failed to analyse all my income options in the depth required for me to make an informed decision. While I said I did not want to move this was based on the fact you could find a solution that would leave be no worse off. I now learn that the compounding effect of the debt is likely to wipe out my estate, leaving my heirs virtually nothing. This was a risk that was not fully explained.

You failed to evaluate fully my 'Lifetime Mortgage Options' recommending I take a higher cost, higher tax and higher risk strategy of borrowing a large lump sum, which was invested into share based life insurance bonds, (Name the Investment), and where the investment returns fail to cover the mortgage interest. You ignored the lower cost, lower tax and lower risk option of annual income withdrawals.

1   (Withdrawal Needs) – While I stated I needed an initial lump sum to cover 'REASON' you should have advised me to take what was needed and no more, with a view to making further withdrawals on a needs basis.

2   (Income Analysis) – You did not carry out a full analysis of my income which has affected my entitlement to means tested state benefits.

    You did not make clear the importance of tax-free equity withdrawals. By taking a lump sum and investing it you moved my money from a tax-free environment to a taxed one. This was another good reason to recommend annual income as the money is being spent straight away. As it is not invested it should incur little or no tax and should not affect my state benefits.

3   (House Improvements) – You recommended the equity release plan as the best way to fund improvements to my house omitting to discuss eligibility for local authority or charity improvement grants.

4   (Inheritance Tax) – You recommended the plan on the basis that it could be used to reduce my inheritance tax, without fully evaluating all other options from a risk, cost and tax basis. I now understand that the complicated arrangements that you put in place are unlikely to achieve my dual objective of reducing my inheritance tax liability and maximising my heirs' inheritance. Your recommendation is a high-risk strategy, unsuitable for someone in my circumstances, putting my estate at risk with a spiralling debt.

5   (Redemption Charges) – You failed to take into account the consequences of my fading health (OR partner's) which may force the need to move to a smaller property or sheltered housing. If I am forced to repay the loan I may not have enough to get the house I want. If I go into residential care and my house is sold and the mortgage repaid, I will not have enough to secure a place in a home of my choice.

You did not make it clear to you that the advice you were giving was not regulated and that this may restrict my compensation options.

6   (Contract Charges) – You failed to draw to my attention the very high redemption charges when I made it clear that there was a possibility that I may trade down / inherit wealth that may result in me wanting to cease the arrangement.

7   (Investment Charges) – You failed to draw to my attention the high initial charges on the investment of 6%/ 7% which immediately put me at a disadvantage and the extent of the surrender penalties.

OPTIONAL IF WITH-PROFITS BOND recommended – (With-profits Bonds) – You failed to give prominence to strict conditions in the contract that would affect my investment returns. You failed to inform me that the fund originally held 50% to 80% of the assets in shares. This is equivalent to a medium risk fund. The fund was wrongly categorised. You failed to explain fully the MVA, and how I can only access my money on one day, being the 10th anniversary without penalty. At any other time I am exposed to a MVA which is applied at the discretion of the Life Office. I would never have consented to expose my money to such risks if I had been told all the facts.

The above points clearly show that on the grounds of costs and risk the recommendation to consider a lifetime mortgage was totally unsuitable for someone in my circumstances with my risk profile. You failed to explain fully and evaluate the specific risks associated with the recommendation and relate this to the probability of achieving my objectives.

PLAN TOTALLY UNSUITABLE – I am making a claim for compensation based on putting me back into the position I held prior to the recommendation, so I can trade down.

WANTED PLAN – BUT DRAW-DOWN OPTION I should have been recommended a drawdown plan. I am making a claim for compensation based on the difference between the increase in debt between your recommendation and the debt I would have had if a flexible draw-down plan had been used, where the amount drawn was just enough to cover my expenditure. I want my finances corrected to the latter position.

Letter 18. Mortgages – Loan Payment Protection Insurance Complaint Letter

(See page 250 for letter layout.)

Your advice to start such a plan was unsuitable for someone in my circumstances, with my needs and with my risk profile. You failed to act in my best interests. You failed to give prominence to the key considerations that would affect my financial position. Your advice and recommendation letter failed to address the following issues:

- I never asked for such cover and was surprised to learn that the protection payments had been included with my loan repayments. This has been added against my will and I demand a return of all the premiums and interest.
- You misled me into believing it was a condition of the loan and that I had to have this protection, which I was obliged to buy from you. This I now understand is incorrect.
- You deceived me by using incorrect interest rate information that excluded the protection policy from the APR, making the loan appear more competitive. If disclosed I would not have agreed to the loan.
- You failed to give prominence to strict conditions in the contract that affect my financial position.

- I was not made aware that the cover only lasts 12 months.
- As self-employed I could only claim if I ceased trading.
- You failed to inform me that the premiums are not guaranteed and that they can increase at any time at the discretion of the provider.
- I was misled into believing the premiums would remain level throughout the life of the policy.
- You negligently failed to evaluate fully and disclose all my protection options, especially the advantages of income protection policies, for which there was a clearly identifiable need. If at the time you did not sell such protection you failed to refer me to suitable organisations that offered this type of protection.
- You failed to evaluate the whole market, recommending a high premium contract when lower premium contracts were available.

The above clearly show that the plan is inadequate and I make a claim for the return of my premiums, assuming they had been invested into a high interest deposit account/cash ISA.

Letters 19 – 25 Investment / Savings Complaint Letters

Letter 19. Investment – With-profits Investments – Complaint Letter

(See page 250 for letter layout.)

Your advice to invest in a 'with-profits' fund was unsuitable for someone in my circumstances and needs, and with my risk profile. You failed to act in my best interests. You failed to give prominence to the key considerations that would affect my financial position. Your advice and recommendation letter failed to address the following issues:

- You failed to give prominence to strict conditions in the contract that would affect my investment returns. You failed to explain risks in a manner that I could have been expected to understand.
- You failed to inform me that the fund originally held 50% to 80% of the assets in shares. This is equivalent to a medium risk fund. The fund was wrongly categorised. I would never have consented to expose my money to such risks if I had been told all the facts.
- (With-profits Bond) My money was originally held on deposit, (OR it was the tax-free cash from my pension which I was going to put in the building society), but I was persuaded to move to a with-profits fund which the salesman said was low-risk, my money was guaranteed and the bond would deliver returns above deposit accounts. This was misleading and incorrect.
- (With-profits Bond) I am a pensioner / close to retirement and this was recommended as a safe way to provide retirement income for someone who did not want to take risks. This was misleading and incorrect.
- You failed to explain fully the MVA, and (If Pension) how I can access my money on only one day during my retirement without penalty (OR if a with-profits bond or endowment, there is only one day being the 10th anniversary / maturity date that I can access my money without penalty). At any other time I am exposed to a MVA which is applied at the discretion of the Life Office.
- You failed to inform me that at any time the managers can withhold growth from me to cover their mistakes and liabilities from the past.
- You failed to inform me that the mangers have to arrange their asset allocation based on covering liabilities and meeting obligations. Investment decisions are actuarially driven and not 'market value' driven. The fund is at risk of not being able to take advantage of market opportunities.
- You failed to point out that the fund manager can change or be forced to change the investments in such a way as to alter the investment profile of the fund, breaking any link with the original assessment matching the fund to my attitude to risk. My attitude to risk has not changed but the risk profile of the fund has.
- That through no fault of my own I find myself forced to move my money to funds that suit my risk profile, but to do so I am potentially liable to a market value adjustment.
- (With-profits Bonds) You failed to point out that I could have achieved the same or better returns at a far lower cost using a different investment mix, of cash funds, national savings and low-cost tracker funds.

The above points clearly show that on the grounds of flexibility and risk the recommendation to invest in with-profits was totally unsuitable for someone in my circumstances with my risk profile.

(With-profits Bond / Endowment) I am making a claim for compensation based on the difference between the return I would have received from a higher rate building society account and the surrender value of my plan.

(With-profits Pension) (The claim depends on whether you should continue with the pension. On the basis that you are a basic-rate tax-payer you should not have been recommended a personal pension, See Pension Complaints Part One Chapter 10. In the event you should not have been recommended a pension.)

I am making a claim for compensation based on the difference between the return I would have received from a higher rate building society account and the surrender value of my plan.

Letter 20. Investment – Insurance Bonds (General) – Complaint Letter

(See page 250 for letter layout.)

Your advice to invest in a bond was unsuitable for someone in my circumstances, with my needs, and with my risk profile. You failed to act in my best interests. You failed to give prominence to strict conditions in the contract that would affect my investment returns. Your advice and recommendation letter failed to address the following issues:

Choose as appropriate, but include 1, 2 & 3.

1. **Quality of Investment Advice.** You were negligent, as you failed to evaluate fully and disclose all my investment options, ignoring the creation of a portfolio using all types of investments, including Unit Trusts, OEICs, Investment Trusts, National Savings and high interest deposit accounts. This would have had the following advantages:
   - Improved Diversity
   - Spread the Risk
   - Lower overall Charges
   - Better investment Management – prospect of higher long-term returns
   - Lower Tax.

   You acted negligently by placing all my money with one (number) company, with mediocre performance when you should have created a portfolio using the best funds in each asset class, choosing managers and companies that consistently out perform. While this cannot guarantee the highest returns in the future it does reduce the odds of receiving below average returns.

   By choosing one company you have exposed my money to unnecessary risk, ignoring the fundamental investment rule that you should spread investments across a wide range of assets and managers to spread the risk while maximising my long-term returns. This was negligent.

2. **Charges.** You failed to disclose the true charges and effect of those charges on my money and the impact on the likely long-term returns. The insurance bond was unsuitable as lower cost, lower risk options were ignored. The use of national savings and tracker funds and Investment trusts would have considerably reduced the overall costs, thus increasing the likelihood of a higher long-term return. This is negligent as you have overcharged me for an inferior investment.

3. **Taxation**. It is accepted by all tax professionals that the combination of using your personal annual capital gains allowance, currently £8,500 in 2005/06 and capital gains taper relief makes Unit Trusts / OEICs / Investments Trusts more tax-efficient than insurance bonds. You negligently decided to ignore this fact. (Choose as appropriate).

   - As a non income taxpayer (or a 10% tax-payer), I should not have been recommended a bond as I cannot reclaim the tax I have been charged which will have the effect of reducing my total return. This bond was inappropriate for someone in my tax position.

   - (Smaller Investments)You recommended a high charging bond when more tax-efficient options were available. You failed to recommend that I use my Individual Savings Account (ISA) allowance of £7,000, £14,000 for a couple.

   - (Larger investments) You recommended a high charging bond when more tax-efficient options were available. You ignored my annual ISA allowances, failing to recommend I should set aside sufficient money to cover my ISA year after year, but had no liquid assets as my capital was tied up in the bond. You also ignored the tax advantages of National Savings Certificates and also ignored unit trusts / investment trust funds, where any gains are liable to capital gains, which can be mitigated via planning.

4. **Income**. You recommended a bond as the best way to provide me with a regular income. You advised and implied that I could take tax-free withdrawals of 5% per year. This is incorrect as I cannot take any money tax-free as the fund is taxed internally at 20%, which you failed to mention. These are capital withdrawals that are eroding my capital.

   You misled me, failing to disclose fully (in a manner I could reasonably be expected to understand) the true nature of the tax. My income needs could have been addressed by using a balanced portfolio and selling investments as appropriate.

5. **Churning of Investments**. You recommended a transfer from another bond (investment) without fully evaluating the costs and consequences. You recommended: (Use as appropriate)

   - A transfer on the flawed premise that I could increase my so called 5% 'tax-free withdrawals', which are not tax-free.

   - That I surrender my old investment without fully disclosing and evaluating the option of no cost internal switches.

   - That I surrender my old investment and buy a new bond in trust without fully evaluating the options of: Enquiring whether the existing provider could provide a trust that would result in the same benefits, at no cost OR asking a solicitor to create a trust and assign the bond (or place the investment) into the trust, at a far lower cost.

   - That I surrender my old bond and invest in a new bond in order to switch the ownership of the investment to my spouse (relative). This could have been achieved by maintaining my existing bond and completing an assignment form. You gave me incorrect advice.

6. **Better performance**. You recommended I surrender my old investment and buy a new bond to improve the long-term investment performance as you stated that the new life bond had a better performance. This was important to me so why didn't you recommend investments directly into top performing Unit Trusts, OEICs and Investment Trusts? This was again negligent.

7. **Inheritance Tax Planning**. With Trust – You recommended an investment bond to remove assets from my estate, without fully evaluating and disclosing all my options, and the consequences of those actions on my estate and the effect on my lifestyle. You failed to disclose fully: (Choose as appropriate)
   - The contract is not guaranteed to save me tax and legislation could change and make the plan tax inefficient, by keeping it in my estate.
   - The same tax savings could be achieved by visiting a solicitor who specialises in estate planning, to rewrite my wills at a fraction of the cost.
   - The charges and risk of poor performance could reduce the value of the investment to the point where there is no tax liability, which may result in my beneficiaries inheriting less than the amount they would have received if I had done nothing.
   - The loss of control over my money, because of the restrictive access.
   - You ignored the importance of gifting using the seven year rule, and the joy of gifting which is free.

   No Trust – You omitted to discuss and recommend a suitable trust which would have been appropriate to help avoid inheritance tax and start the seven year transfer clock.

8. **Policy Feeding**. You advised me to invest in a bond and strip out the 5% withdrawals to feed another policy, the suitability of which I have yet to assess, effectively increasing your commission, having been paid commission on the same money twice. The first 4 or 5 years contributions should have been left on deposit, to avoid incurring 5% to 7% charges on money that is unlikely to grow to a level sufficient to cover the initial charges before being withdrawn.

9. **Debt Repayment**. You advised I invest the money instead of paying down debts / loans. This advice is flawed as there is no realistic prospect that the net investment returns after charges will be sufficient to cover the annual interest payments / repayment of loan capital.

10. **Flawed Risk Assessment**. You recommended I switch the money from no / low-risk investments to a bond exposing my money to far greater risk than that with which I feel comfortable. The risks could have been reduced by creating a mixed portfolio, including national savings certificates and high interest cash accounts, while spreading the remainder across a number of fund managers with consistent investment records. You failed to explain fully and evaluate the specific risks associated with the recommendation and relate this to the probability of achieving my objectives.

Conclusion

The above points clearly show that on the grounds of suitability and risk the recommendation to invest in an insurance bond was totally unsuitable for someone in my circumstances with my risk profile.

(If you are averse to risk) I make a claim for compensation based on the difference between the surrender value of the bond and the value of my money if it had been left in a high interest deposit account / cash ISA.

(If you accept some risk) I make a claim for compensation based on the difference between the surrender value of the bond and the value of a portfolio of above average collective funds, national savings and high interest accounts.

(If you wanted to be fully invested in stock markets) I make a claim for compensation based on the difference between the surrender value of the bond and the value of a portfolio of 10 collective funds, using unit trusts, OEICs and investment trusts with above average performance.

Letter 21. Investment – With-profits Bonds – Complaint Letter

See page 250 for letter layout

Use the Insurance Bond general complaint letter 20 up to Flawed Risk Assessment. Then add:

10. **Flawed Risk Assessment.** You incorrectly categorised with-profits funds as being low-risk, where in fact its asset mix and fund structure make the fund far riskier than you disclosed. By recommending I invest in a with-profits bond you have exposed my money to far more risk than I actually wanted, which is unacceptable.
    - You failed to give prominence to strict conditions in the contract that would affect my investment returns.
    - You failed to inform me that the fund originally held 50% to 80% of the assets in shares. This is equivalent to a medium risk fund. The fund was wrongly categorised. I would never have consented to expose my money to such risks if I had been told all the facts.
    - My money was originally held on deposit, (OR it was the tax-free cash from my pension which I was going to put in the building society), but I was persuaded to move to a with-profits fund which the salesman said was low-risk, my money was guaranteed and the bond would deliver returns above deposit accounts. This was misleading and incorrect.
    - I am a pensioner / close to retirement and this was recommended as a safe way to provide retirement income for someone who did not want to take risks. This was misleading and incorrect.
    - You failed to explain fully the MVA, and that there is only one day being the 10th anniversary that I can access my money without penalty, (sometimes there is no MVA free exit point). At any other time I am exposed to a MVA which is applied at the discretion of the Life Office.
    - You failed to inform me that at any time the managers can withhold growth from me to cover their mistakes and liabilities from the past.

- You failed to inform me that the mangers have to arrange their asset allocation based on covering liabilities and meeting obligations. Investment decisions are actuarially driven and not 'market value' driven. This adds extra risk as the fund is not being able to take advantage of market opportunities.
- You failed to point out that the fund manager can change or be forced to change the investments in such a way as to alter the investment profile of the fund, breaking any link with the original assessment matching the fund to my attitude to risk. My attitude to risk has not changed but the risk profile of the fund has.
- That through no fault of my own I find myself forced to move my money to funds that suit my risk profile, but to do so I am potentially liable to a market value adjustment.
- You failed to point out that I could have achieved the same or better returns at a far lower cost using a different investment mix, of cash funds, national savings and low-cost tracker funds.

To summarise you failed to explain fully and evaluate the specific risks associated with the recommendation and relate this to the probability of achieving my objectives.

Conclusion

The above points clearly show that on the grounds of flexibility and risk the recommendation to invest in a with-profits bond was totally unsuitable for someone in my circumstances with my risk profile.

I am making a claim for compensation based on the difference between the return I would have received from a higher rate building society account and the surrender value of my bond.

Letter 22. Investment – Precipice Bonds (Advice) – Complaint Letter

(See page 250 for letter layout.)

Your advice to invest in a high income bond was unsuitable for someone in my circumstances, with my needs and my risk profile. You failed to act in my best interests. You failed to give prominence to the key considerations that would affect my financial position. Your advice and recommendation letter failed to address the following issues:

- You failed to give prominence to strict investment conditions in the contract that would affect my investment returns.
- The risk was not explained in a way that could be easily understood. When I asked about the risks you gave assurances, playing down the potential risks.
- (DEPOSIT BASED INVESTOR) – You failed to inform me that this was a high-risk investment. You advised that this was a low-risk investment suitable for cautious investors. The literature and your report gave no indication as to the potential losses I could incur. The bond was wrongly categorised by you as low-risk. I would never have consented to expose my money to such risks if I had been told all the facts. My money was originally held on deposit, but I was misled to invest into this bond as a low-risk alternative, in order to receive a little extra income. The product was just too complex to understand for someone with my investment experience and knowledge. It was unsuitable. You failed to explain fully and evaluate the specific risks associated with the recommendation and relate this to the probability of achieving my objectives.

- (SHARE INVESTOR) – Your information failed to make it clear that this was a high-risk investment. I was led to believe this was a low-risk investment to be used to compliment my other low-risk investments. The literature gave no indication as to the potential losses I could incur. The bond was wrongly categorised as a low-risk investment. I would never have consented to expose my money to such risks if I had been given all the facts. While I have other equity investments I wanted to maintain the level of No risk / low-risk investments. I definitely did not want to increase my exposure to high-risk investments. You failed to explain fully and evaluate the specific risks associated with the recommendation and relate this to the probability of achieving my objectives.
- PENSIONER – I am a pensioner / close to retirement and this was recommended as a safe way to provide retirement income for someone who did not want to take risks. This was misleading and incorrect.
- I believe the literature and supporting information was misleading and failed to give prominence to key areas of risk, such as the probabilities of failure and downside risk in a manner that I could reasonably be expected to understand fully.

Optional

- You failed to evaluate all no risk and low-risk options.
- You recommended a high income bond as opposed to other more tax-efficient investments such as Personal Equity Plans (PEPs) and Individual Savings Accounts (ISAs).
- You did not make it clear what the charges were and how much of my investment was used to cover the initial set up costs.
- You failed to take into account my lifestyle needs and that I may require access to the money prior to the expiry of the 5 year term. I now realise that I can access my money only after incurring high surrender penalties and exit charges.

The above points clearly show that on the grounds of risk and flexibility I was misled. The recommendation to invest in a high income bond was totally unsuitable for someone in my circumstances with my risk profile.

I am making a claim for compensation based on the difference between the surrender value of the bond and the return I would have received from a higher rate building society account.

Letter 23. Investment – Precipice Bonds (Mailshot) – Complaint Letter

(See page 250 for letter layout.)

Your information failed to convey the true extent of the risks associated with such an investment and did not address the following issues:

- The literature and accompanying letter failed to give prominence to strict investment conditions in the contract that would affect my investment returns.
- The literature failed to inform me that this was a high-risk investment. I was led to believe that this was a low-risk investment suitable for cautious investors. The literature gave no indication as to the potential losses I could incur. The bond was wrongly categorised. I would never have consented to expose my money to such risks if I had been presented with all the facts that fairly and adequately described the nature of the investment and the risks, so I could make an informed assessment. My money was originally held on deposit, but I was misled to invest into this bond as a low-risk alternative, in order to receive a little extra income.
- PENSIONER - I am a pensioner / close to retirement and I understood this to be a safe way to provide retirement income for someone who did not want to take risks. This was misleading and incorrect.
- I believe the literature and supporting information was misleading and failed to give prominence to key areas of risk, such as the probabilities of failure and downside risk in a manner that I could reasonably be expected fully to understand.

The literature provided a false prospectus as to the true nature of the risks, which misled me to invest in this high income bond, which was totally unsuitable for someone in my circumstances with my risk profile.

I am making a claim for compensation based on the difference between the surrender value of the bond and the return I would have received from a higher rate building society account.

Letter 24. Investment – Corporate Bond Funds – Complaint Letter

(See page 250 for letter layout.)

Your advice to invest in this type of investment was unsuitable for someone in my circumstances, with my needs, and with my NO / Low-risk profile. You failed to give prominence to valuation of corporate bonds that would affect my investment returns. Your advice and recommendation letter failed to address the following issues:

- **Low-risk** – I was advised that this was a low fund akin to a deposit account. As a NO / Low-risk investor I was not made aware at the time of the recommendation that both the income and capital were exposed to such high risks because they are so sensitive to interest rate changes and that this could lead to capital losses.
- **Junk Bond Funds** – You did not fully explain that the recommendation to invest in a 'high income fund' was an investment into junk bonds. This has magnified the problems associated with capital depreciation. I was misled into believing such a fund was a low-risk fund. Such a fund cannot be classed as low-risk, due to the fund's volatility.
- **Yield Explanations** – I was misled into believing the quoted yield (income) was just the interest and the capital remained intact? This is incorrect as the headline yield you quoted was the 'running yield' which did not take into account capital depreciation. You failed to highlight the differences between the running yield and the more accurate

'redemption yield' which takes into account capital depreciation. This was lower than the 'running yield'. This lower yield after charges was no better / worse than a high street cash deposit account, while exposing my money to more risk. I would never have agreed to invest the money, which would have remained in a deposit account if I had been provided with this information OR I would never have agreed to switch the money from the ...... fund which had a higher redemption yield if I had been provided with this information.

- **Explanation of Charges** – I was misled into believing that the yield quoted was net of charges and could be compared directly with a deposit account. I have now discovered that the charges are deducted from capital and not from income, which makes the income look more attractive while the charges depreciate my capital. I would never have agreed to invest the money which should have remained in a deposit account if I had been provided with this information OR I would never have agreed to switch the money from the ...... fund which had lower net yield redemption but higher gross yield before charges had I been provided with this information.

The above points clearly show that on the grounds of suitability and risk the recommendation to invest in the 'XYZ NAME' corporate bond fund was totally unsuitable for someone in my circumstances with my risk profile. I was misled into investing on the back of a false prospectus.

I make a claim for compensation based on the difference between the surrender value of the fund and the value my money would have reached if it had been left in a high interest deposit account / cash ISA.

Letter 25. Investment – Life Office 10-year Savings Plans – Complaint Letter

(See page 250 for letter layout.)

Your advice to start such a plan was unsuitable for someone in my circumstances, with my needs, and with my risk profile. You failed to act in my best interests. You failed to give prominence to strict conditions in the contract that would affect my financial position. Your advice and recommendation letter failed to address the following issues. Choose as appropriate:

- PEP / TESSA / ISA Allowances – You failed to recommend that I maximise my savings into tax-free savings plans such as PEPs, TESSAs and ISAs where money grows almost tax-free. The plan you recommended is subject to Life Office internal taxation of 20% which will reduce my investment returns. This was negligent as my money should have been saved into tax-efficient savings plans.
- Charges – You failed to draw my attention to the high charges associated with the 10-year savings plans and failed to compare them with lower cost alternatives such as unit trusts, investment trusts and nil cost cash TESSAs and ISAs.
- Unnecessary Life Cover – The 10-year savings plan included a small amount of life cover that has to be paid for from my premiums. I did not require extra life cover which reduced the amount invested and my investment returns.
- Risk – You failed to explain fully the investment risks. This plan was unsuitable for someone with little or no previous experience of investing. You failed to explain that the with-profits / managed fund was predominantly a stock market investment, with 60% to 80% of the fund invested in shares and that I could end up with just the sum assured, which is basically my money back.

- Access Denied – You failed to take my needs into account. I informed you that 'there was the possibility I would need the money within 10 years', OR 'I had no instant-access emergency fund' and you failed to recommend I save and create one. There was a strong possibility that life's unforeseen events could result in me having to stop the plan. Access to my savings was important. You recommended a 10-year savings plans which was inflexible, only allowing me access to my money if I cancelled the plan in part or in full, an event which triggers exit penalties and possibly a tax charge. You failed to recommend a PEP / ISA which offer immediate tax-free access, usually without penalties.
- Poor Investment Choice – You recommended a mediocre Life Office fund when for the same cost or less there was a choice of investment firms with a long history of delivering above average returns. You failed to carry out an analysis of the market place and consider the best funds from a cost and management perspective.
- Debt Repayment – You failed to consider the repayment of all my debts as a viable use for my disposable income.

Claim

The above points clearly show that your recommendation failed to explain fully and evaluate the specific risks associated with the contract and relate this to the probability of achieving the objective. Your advice was flawed and unsuitable for someone in my circumstances. Choose the claim according to your risk profile:

I make a claim for compensation based on the returns I would have achieved if the money had been saved into a PEP or ISA. OR

I make a claim for compensation based on the returns I would have achieved if the money had been saved into a cash 'TESSA' or 'ISA'.

Letters 26 – 29 Protection Policy Complaint Letters

Letter 26. Whole of Life Plans / Flexible Protection Plans Complaint Letter

(See page 250 for letter layout.)

Your advice to start such a plan was unsuitable for someone in my circumstances, with my needs, and with my risk profile. You failed to act in my best interests. You failed to give prominence to strict conditions in the contract that would affect my financial position. Your advice and recommendation letter failed to address the following issues:

There are many claims for mis-selling. Choose as appropriate, but include 1, 3, 7, 8 & 10.

1 You were negligent, as you failed to evaluate fully and disclose all my protection options, ignoring the lower cost options of term assurance and family income benefit. These would have been far more appropriate, as the premiums are guaranteed and I would have been able to reduce my outgoings.
2 The savings in protection costs should have been used to reduce my debts, which would have had the long-term advantage of reducing my reliance on life cover.
3 You acted negligently by recommending this policy as a form of savings. You misled me into believing that this was a good way to save OR, I was getting something for nothing, by eventually getting my premiums back. This is an inefficient way to save. You should have recommended the best low-cost term assurance with the excess invested into a tax-efficient PEP / ISA.
4 You failed to inform me that the money within life funds is subject to internal taxation of 20%. In a tax-efficient savings plan such as a PEP or ISA, the money grows almost tax-free. (Personal Equity Plans (PEPs) were available from January 1987 to 05 April 1999. Individual Savings Accounts (ISAs) were available from 6 April 1999 onwards. Prior to January 1987 a unit trust regular savings plan or investment trust savings plan should have been used).
5 You failed to disclose how inflexible the plan is as a savings vehicle, as I have lost control over my money, because of the restrictive access. I am not allowed access to my money unless I cancel the plan in part or in full, which can lead to exit penalties.
6 You failed to consider savings plans provided by more accomplished investment companies.
7 You failed to disclose the true charges and effect of those charges on my money and the impact on the likely long-term returns. The use of lower cost term assurance and tax-efficient savings plans would have considerably reduced the overall costs, thus increasing the likelihood of a higher long-term return. This is negligent as you have overcharged me for an inferior plan.
8 (Reviewable Premiums – Not Disclosed). I was never informed that the premiums were reviewable and that they can increase at any time at the discretion of the Life Office. I was misled into believing the premiums would remain level throughout the life of the policy. (I was shocked to find following a review that my premiums had increased by … from … to …).
9 (Pensioner) As a pensioner living on a fixed income the hike in premiums has made the policy so expensive that I had to cancel the policy, OR, I have had to drastically curtail my other spending, which has affected my lifestyle and the quality of my life. I would never have consented to start such a plan if all the costs had been disclosed.

10 (Reviewable Premiums – Disclosed). While you advised me that the premiums were reviewable, you did not disclose the extent of the potential increases. You failed to take into account ongoing affordability and the effect on my income.

11 (Needed Whole-of-life Cover) You negligently failed to disclose the availability and compare the costs of guaranteed premium whole-of-life plans.

12 (Churning) You advised I cease an existing life cover plan and switch (from a policy with guaranteed premiums) to an inferior plan where the premiums are reviewable using an initial higher sum assured to artificially reduce the premiums. This was negligent as the switch was recommended on the back of a false prospectus.

13 You failed to discuss fund risks and the importance of fund performance in making the plan work. You failed to adequately discuss my attitude to risk. (The low-risk guaranteed premium plan would have suited my risk profile). You failed to explain fully and evaluate the specific risks associated with the recommendation and relate this to the probability of achieving the objective.

14 (With-profits) You incorrectly categorised with-profits funds as being low-risk, where in fact its asset mix and fund structure make the fund far riskier than you disclosed. By recommending I invest in a with-profits bond you have exposed my money to far more risk than I actually wanted, which is unacceptable.

15 You failed to recommend a suitable trust to avoid the plan forming part of my estate.

16 (Policyholder Deceased – Complaint made by Executors of Deceased's Estate) You failed to place the policy in trust, which resulted in the plan forming part of the deceased's estate which was liable to inheritance tax. We make a claim for compensation based on the tax charge and loss of interest covering the intervening period.

17 You failed to evaluate fully all other inheritance tax mitigation strategies and their long-term costs, ignoring the importance of gifting and using the seven year rule which would have cost me nothing.

Claim

The above points clearly show that your recommendation to start a unit linked whole-of-life plan was flawed and unsuitable for someone in my circumstances. Choose the claim according to your risk profile.

(If you are averse to risk – Term Assurance Preferable.) I make a claim for compensation based on the difference between the premiums paid to the whole-of-life policy and the premiums paid to a low-cost term assurance plan and interest based on the return from a high interest deposit account/cash ISA. (I also demand that the advisory firm establish term assurance life cover based on the premiums available at the time, if lower than current market rates).

(If you accept some risk – Term Assurance Preferable.) I make a claim for compensation based on the difference between the premiums paid to the whole-of-life policy and the premiums paid to a low-cost term assurance plan and growth based on the return I would have received from a PEP / ISA, like the Invesco Perpetual High Income Fund. (I also demand that the advisory firm establish term assurance life cover based on the premiums available at the time, if lower than current market rates).

(Plan Inappropriate – No Risk.) I make a claim for compensation based on the return of all my premiums assuming they had been invested into a high interest deposit account/cash ISA.

(Plan Inappropriate – Some Risk.) I make a claim for compensation based on the return of all my premiums assuming they had been invested into a PEP /ISA, like the Invesco Perpetual High Income Fund.

(Whole of Life Cover required.) I make a claim based on the difference in the lifetime plan costs between the best guaranteed premium whole of life cover plan and the policy you recommended.

Letter 27. Protection – Critical Illness Policies – Complaint Letter

(See page 250 for letter layout.)

Your advice to start such a plan was unsuitable for someone in my circumstances, with my needs, and with my risk profile. You failed to act in my best interests. You failed to give prominence to strict conditions in the contract that could affect my financial position. Your advice and recommendation letter failed to address the following issues. Choose as appropriate:

- Inaccurate and misleading Information – You misled me into believing the policy comprehensively covered all critical illnesses. This is incorrect.
- Ignored Guaranteed Premiums – You failed to evaluate the whole market and ignored guaranteed premium rates, which would have been preferable for someone in my circumstances.
- Recommended inferior contract – You failed to evaluate the whole market recommending an inferior reviewable premium policy with limited coverage of the main critical conditions and a poor claims history, instead of a superior contract at a similar cost.
- Reviewable Premiums (Not Disclosed) – I was never informed that the premiums were reviewable and that they can increase at any time at the discretion of the Life Office. I was misled into believing the premiums would remain level throughout the life of the policy. (I was shocked to find following a review that my premiums had increased by ... from ... to ...).
- Reviewable Premiums (Disclosed) – While you advised me that the premiums were reviewable, you did not disclose the extent of the potential increases. You failed to take into account ongoing affordability and the effect on my income.
- Ignored separate contracts – You failed to consider separate contracts which would have had the following benefits, (choose as appropriate):
  - The combined critical illness and life cover plan you recommended ceases when a critical illness payment is made. This will result in the loss of life cover. Two separate policies would pay out twice as much to my family.
  - The cost of two well researched plans could be cheaper / offered better value than the combined policy you were recommended.
  - I am not able to afford to continue the plan, (because of the reviewable premium increases). You failed to take ongoing affordability into account. I now find the cost of life cover on its own, which I need, is far more expensive. I should have been advised to take two separate plans and claim compensation for the extra cost of the life cover.
- Income Protection Insurance (PHI) – You failed to evaluate all my protection needs options including the use of income protection insurance, which would have been more suitable for someone with my budget and lifestyle.

- (If you have been off work.) I was recently off work for .... months, because of an accident / illness / medical condition for which the critical illness did not pay out. However I now understand that if you had recommended income protection insurance I would have been covered. I therefore claim the loss of earnings over this period.
- Churning – You advised I cease an existing superior critical illness policy (with guaranteed premiums) and more accommodating medical definitions, and start an inferior plan where the premiums are reviewable with stiffer medical conditions. This was negligent as the switch was recommended on the back of a false prospectus.
- Fund Risk – You failed to discuss fund risks and the importance of fund performance in making the plan work. You failed to adequately discuss my attitude to risk. (The low-risk guaranteed premium plan would have suited my risk profile.) You failed to explain fully and evaluate the specific risks associated with the recommendation and relate this to the probability of achieving the objective.
- (With-profits Funds.) – You incorrectly categorised with-profits funds as being low-risk, where in fact its asset mix and fund structure make the fund far riskier than you disclosed. By recommending I invest in a with-profits bond you have exposed my money to far more risk than I actually wanted, which is unacceptable.
- Superfluous to my needs – I was recommended a plan to cover a shortfall that did not exist.
- (Policyholder Deceased – Complaint made by Executors of Deceased's Estate.) You failed to place the life cover element in trust, which resulted in the plan forming part of the deceased's estate which was liable to inheritance tax. We make a claim for compensation based on the tax charge and loss of interest covering the intervening period.

Claim

The above points clearly show that your recommendation of this policy was flawed and unsuitable for someone in my circumstances. Choose the claim as appropriate.

Plan Appropriate. I make a claim for reinstatement of a/my old guaranteed premium critical illness plan (and separate life cover if appropriate).

Plan Inappropriate. I make a claim for the return of my premiums plus interest assuming they had been invested into a high interest deposit account/cash ISA.

Income Protection Insurance Preferable. I make a claim for compensation based on the loss of income since not being able to work. I also require that the firm establish income protection insurance based on the premiums available at the time, if lower than current market rates.

Letter 28. Protection – Reviewable Premium Policies Complaint Letter

(See page 250 for letter layout.)

Your advice to start such a plan was unsuitable for someone in my circumstances, with my needs, and with my risk profile. You failed to act in my best interests. You failed to give prominence to strict conditions in the contract that would affect my financial position. Your advice and recommendation letter failed to address the following issues:

- (Reviewable Premiums – Not Disclosed.) I was never informed that the premiums were reviewable and that they can increase at any time at the discretion of the Life Office. I was misled into believing the premiums would remain level throughout the life of the policy. (I was shocked to find following a review that my premiums had increased by … from … to ….)
- (Pensioner.) As a pensioner living on a fixed income the hike in premiums has made the policy so expensive that I had to cancel the policy, OR, I have had to drastically curtail my other spending, which has affected my lifestyle and the quality of my life. I would never have consented to start such a plan if all the costs had been disclosed.
- (Reviewable Premiums – Disclosed.) While you advised me that the premiums were reviewable, you did not disclose the extent of the potential increases. You failed to take into account ongoing affordability and the effect on my income.
- You negligently failed to disclose the availability and compare the costs of guaranteed premium plans.
- (Churning.) You advised I cease an existing plan and switch from a superior policy with guaranteed premiums to an inferior plan where the premiums are reviewable. This was negligent as the switch was recommended on the back of a false prospectus, and was not in my long-term interests.

Claim

The above points clearly show that your recommendation failed to explain fully and evaluate the specific risks associated with the contract and relate this to the probability of achieving the objective. Your advice was flawed and unsuitable for someone in my circumstances. Choose the claim according to your risk profile.

(Protection required.) I make a claim for compensation based on the difference between the recommended reviewable premiums plan and the best guaranteed premium contract based on the premiums available at the time of the first recommendation.

(Plan Inappropriate – No Risk.) I make a claim for compensation based on the return of all my premiums assuming they had been invested into a high interest deposit account/cash ISA.

(Plan Inappropriate – Some Risk.) I make a claim for compensation based on the return of all my premiums assuming they had been invested into a PEP /ISA, like the Invesco Perpetual High Income Fund.

(Churning.) I make a claim based on the restoration of benefits and costs to those available under the old contract which you advised me to cancel AND / OR I make a claim for compensation equal to my lost claim, based on the fact that the policy you recommended has failed to pay out on a claim, when the superior contract you recommended I cancel would have paid out.

Letter 29. Protection – Trusts – Complaint Letter

(See page 250 for letter layout.)

I (spouse / executor's of deceased's estate) would like to make a formal complaint on behalf of the late 'DECEASEDS NAME' about the advice he/she received from your company to (fund a pension) OR (contribute to a protection contract) on 'DATE' using 'TYPE of PLAN' with 'XYZ COMPANY' which was not placed into trust.

The proceeds of the policy have now formed part of the deceased's estate and are liable to inheritance tax. This omission not to recommend and implement a trust has cost the beneficiaries £ .... in tax. This plan should have been placed in trust which would have enabled the trustees of the trust to pay the proceeds tax-free to the deceased's dependants / next of kin.

Having reviewed the deceased's papers we can find no records of this being fully discussed. Your advice was unsuitable for someone in the deceased's circumstances as your suitability letter failed to comprehensively address, their long-term needs, the deceased's tax position AND the consequences and risks associated with not placing the plan in trust.

We are making a claim for compensation equal to the net amount the beneficiaries would have received if inheritance tax had not been payable on the plan. This amounts to 40% of £...... equal to £..... . (This would need to be cleared with the Inland Revenue as to whether the compensation is taxable. If it is taxable the compensation will need to be grossed up to take into account the beneficiary's tax position.) An allowance of £...... is also being claimed to cover the executors' extra administration costs.

If I do not receive a positive response within 8 weeks of the date of this letter I will be forwarding this complaint to the Financial Ombudsman Service.

8

Glossary

Allocation Rates

This charging system allocates a percentage of your invested money to your plan. For regular premium contracts it may be 0% to 70% in years one and two. For lump sum investments it may vary from 95% to 105%. Be wary of trusting allocations in excess of 100%, and don't believe the sales pitch that you're getting something for nothing. Although it sounds as though your £10,000 will be invested by the Life Office at 105% growing to £10,500 on day one, if you surrendered the fund it's likely (because of surrender penalties) that you would only receive £9,400.

Annual Management Charge (AMC)

This is the explicit annual charge quoted by the fund manager for the work they undertake to manage the fund and pay ongoing commission to the salesman. It varies between 0.5% and 2.5% per annum. It fails to take into account auditor's fees, custodian / trustee's fees, legal fees and dealing charges.

Annuity

An annuity is an investment used to convert your pension fund into an income for life, at a rate fixed on the date of purchase. There are many different types, either providing an income that remains level, escalates or is linked to an investment fund. It is in effect a policy that provides insurance against living too long. Once made the decision is irrevocable. Your income is liable to income tax.

Bid / Offer Spread

This is the spread between the cost of buying units in a fund at the higher 'Offer' price and selling them at the lower 'Bid' price. The spread most often quoted is 5% but it can be higher, depending on market conditions and the number of redemptions. These are front-loaded funds as all the charges are taken up front. There is no extra charge for selling, (reflected in the lower bid price). For example if you invest £1,000 in a fund with a bid / offer spread of 5% and the units cost £1, you would be allocated 1,000 units. If you sold the units immediately you would sell at the lower bid price of 95p and receive £950.

Collective Investments

Many investment funds, such as Life Office funds, unit trusts, investment trusts, and open ended investment companies (OEICs) are referred to as collective investments because the fund manager collects and invests the money of a number of small investors. The money is invested in a range of shares, bonds, gilts or cash deposits. The fund is divided into units or shares with each investor allocated a number of units equal to the value of their investment.

Commission
Commission is a charge built into a financial product or service, which is payable to the salesmen to encourage them to sell that product or service.

Establishment Charge
This is a percentage charge applied to Life Office products made every month or quarter over a period of 60 months. It appears small but over five years of charging 0.125% a month (0.375% a quarter) the total commission amounts to 7.5%. Remember this is taken regardless of whether you pull out after 1 year or 5 years because withdrawal penalties are applied to pay commission.

Fees & Commission statement
This is the 'Key Facts Guide' issued to consumers prior to a financial transaction and gives details of the cost of those services. There are many different types of statement depending on whether the adviser takes commission, a fee or a combination of commission and fees.

Final Salary Pension Scheme (also known as Defined Benefit Scheme)
This provides an income related to your final pensionable salary, usually a pension of 1/60th of your salary for every year of qualifying service. For every year you retire early, the scheme is likely to apply an early retirement charge of 4% to 6%. For example a person retiring 5 years early from a scheme with a 5% annual reduction charge would receive an initial pension 25% (5 x 5%) lower. Some public service schemes do not apply reductions on early retirement. If you are lucky enough to be offered a pension without a reduction you should take advantage of the offer.

Financial Ombudsman Service (FOS)
The independent complaints handling body of the financial services industry.

Financial Services Authority (FSA)
The FSA is the financial services regulator and has the dual responsibility of regulating the industry and protecting the consumer. This is not ideal as there may be circumstances which lead to a conflict in interests.

The Financial Services Compensation Scheme (FSCS)
This is the statutory scheme of last resort for customers to claim losses against authorised financial services firms.

Firm
The regulator uses the term 'Firm' to refer to all financial services companies, partnerships and sole traders. Within this guide the term 'firm' and 'company' are interchangeable and mean the same.

Independent Financial Advisers (IFAs) Commission-based
These advisers are supposed to be independent and offer products from the whole market, but many push products from a limited range of providers with whom they have arranged good commission deals.

Independent Financial Planners (IFPs) Fee-based
While not officially recognised as a separate category, Whistle-blower believes it is important to distinguish between good advisers who offer fee-based holistic financial planning (which may or may not lead to the recommendation to use products) from those who just want to sell you a product.

Individual Savings Account (ISA)
These tax-efficient savings plans were introduced on 6th April 1999 to replace Personal Equity Plans (PEPs) and Tax Exempt Special Savings Accounts TESSAs. The maximum contribution is £7,000 per annum of which £3,000 can be invested in a Cash ISA with the remaining £4,000 in an Equity ISA. You receive no tax relief on your investment, but your money benefits from the same tax-efficient growth as a pension fund. There is no income tax to pay when money is withdrawn from these plans.

Initial / Capital Units
This charging system was used mainly by Life Offices. In the 1980's and 90's many Life Offices invested regular contributions in high-charging units to disguise huge up-front costs. They appeared innocuous but the first two years' premiums were invested in units that were subject to an annual management charge of 5% to 7%. The Life Office could take the annual charge regardless of whether contributions continued or not. Consequently most of the first two years' premiums disappeared in advance to cover commission costs. Any subsequent increase in premiums was also subject to the same commission charge. Life Offices have ceased using this method of financial charging, but it still applies to ongoing old contracts.

Initial Disclosure Document (IDD)
This is the 'Keyfacts Guide' issued to consumers prior to a financial transaction and gives details of a firm's services. It tells you what they do and what they are authorised to do. A firm that offers different services can either issue separate documents for each service or can combine them into one document called a 'Combined Initial Disclosure Document' (CIDD).

Initial Investment Charge
Many new funds are moving to single pricing for units and shares where there is no difference in the buying and selling price. Instead there is an initial charge of around 5%, similar to the bid / offer spread. All OEICs use single pricing. They are more transparent which makes it easier to follow the value of your investment.

Investment Trusts
These are companies that invest in the shares of other companies and securities, and whose shares are listed on the London Stock Exchange. The trusts are closed-ended investment companies with a fixed number of shares. If you want to buy shares in a trust, someone else has to sell their shares, so the value of the shares not only depends on movement in the underlying markets, but also supply and demand (which in turn is influenced by the investor's confidence in the fund managers to deliver good returns).

Keyfacts Documents
These are the documents that must be provided to consumers at the start of the sales process. They provide information on the adviser's services and cost of those services. See 'Initial Disclosure Document (IDD)' and 'Fees and Commission Statement'.

Life Office
A company or organisation authorised to issue life, protection and investment policies.

Money Purchase Pension Schemes (also known as Defined Contribution Schemes)
These are pension schemes that provide benefits which are solely dependent on the growth of your fund and are not related to your salary. Your pension income at retirement is unknown as your pension fund is used to purchase an annuity, the rates of which rise and fall, making it difficult to plan your retirement income.

Multi-tied Advisers / Agents
These are advisers who sell the products and services of several providers, usually with links to 5 or 6 companies. This is a new type of adviser introduced as part of a reform programme called 'Depolarisation' as a way of providing greater choice between tied and independent advice.

Open Ended Investment Companies (OEICs)
These are limited liability companies formed to manage funds on behalf of small investors. They allocate shares direct to investors. They are open-ended and operate in a similar way as unit trusts by creating and cancelling shares.

Personal Equity Plans (PEPs)
These are tax-efficient savings introduced in January 1987 to encourage investment in shares. You receive no tax relief on your investment, but your money benefits from the same tax-efficient growth as a pension fund. There is no income tax to pay when money is withdrawn from a PEP. From April 1999 no new contributions were allowed as the plans were superseded by Individual Savings Accounts (ISAs).

Portfolio Turnover Rate (PTR)%
This is the percentage of a fund that has changed in the last calendar year through the fund buying and selling assets. The greater the change, the greater the transaction costs, which are not included in the RIY or TER. If there is no material gain it will act as a drag on returns. A 100% turnover is likely to cost 1.8% in lost growth. An active portfolio may expect to turn over at least 50% of the fund each year.

Reduction in Yield (RIY) %
This is the percentage by which the total explicit charges, both initial and annual, are expected to reduce the return on the policy / contract over a fixed term compared to a contract with no charges. A standard growth rate of 6% is used for taxed investments and 7% for tax-efficient investments such as ISAs and pensions. It excludes dealing charges. For example if we compare the returns on £1,000 growing at 6% per annum over 10 years, we find a fund with no charges would grow to £1,791 – compared to £1,390 with charges. The difference of £401 over 10 years is equivalent to a reduction in the growth of 2.65% per year, known as the reduction in yield. However, the RIY does not take into account the transaction and brokerage charges which are not classed as operational expenses and are charged to capital.

Reinvestment Charge
Income distributions can either be paid to you or accumulated within the fund. If income is reinvested, some managers charge another initial investment charge even though the fund manager has incurred no new marketing acquisition costs.

Stakeholder Products
These are simplified low-cost products which set minimum contract standards. They were introduced to help consumers buy products with more confidence knowing the terms and the costs are fair. There are no initial charges. Annual charges are restricted to 1.5% per annum for the first 10 years and 1% thereafter.

Tax Exempt Special Savings Accounts (TESSAs)
These tax-free deposit savings plans were introduced in 1990. The maximum savings were restricted to £9,000 over 5 years. From April 1999 no new contribution were allowed, as the plans were superseded by Individual Savings Accounts (ISAs). Plans maturing since April 1999 could roll over the original investment into a Tessa Only Individual Savings Account (TOISA).

Terms of Business / Client Agreement
These are the rules of engagement by which a firm will its conduct business and tell you what you can expect from a firm. It could be accompanied by some sort of servicing agreement.

Tied Advisers / Agents
These are advisers that sell the products and services from just one company, usually those provided by the high street banks and some building societies.

Total Expense Ratio (%) TER
This is the drag on performance of the fund caused by the annual operating costs. This ratio is calculated by dividing the total operating costs by the average net asset value. It shows the proportion of the funds assets that are consumed by annual charges, and includes the quoted annual management charge as well as the administration, custody, audit, and legal fees, but not dealing charges. It is used by all funds with a UCITS certificate which applies to appropriate unit trusts and OEICs. Investment trusts have for many years provided TERs in their report and accounts. TERs are an improvement on the AMC and must now be included with most investments into unit trusts and OEICs. However, the charge does not take into account the initial investment commission, any exit charges, transaction costs / brokerage fees and interest on borrowing. Information on TERs is freely available for all unit trusts, OEICs and investment trusts from various web-sites.

Trail Commission
This is an annual commission paid to the salesman by the investment company as a 'thank you' for introducing and maintaining the business. It is based on a percentage of the value of your investment, usually 0.5%, which is taken from your fund.

Undertaking for Collective Investments in Transferable Securities (UCITS)
An open-ended collective investment scheme that can be marketed in any EU country.

Unitised Funds
These are funds formed to manage the money of small investors in a diversified portfolio. This is achieved by the allocation of units direct to investors that reflect the underlying value of the assets in that fund. For example if 1,000 small investors all invested £1,000 each in a UK Managed Fund, the manager would have £1,000,000 to invest in shares, property and various bonds. It is impossible to allocate each investor a percentage of each investment, so the manager unitises the fund, allocating each investor 1000 units at £1 each. As the value of the investments rises and falls, so does the value of the units. Unitised funds include unit trusts, OEICs and Life Office funds.

Unit Linked Life Funds

These are unitised investment funds offered by Life Offices. They are open-ended and operate in a similar way as unit trusts by creating and cancelling units.

Unit Trusts

These are trusts formed to manage funds on behalf of small investors. They allocate units direct to investors. They are open-ended which means the fund expands by creating new units for new purchases and contracts by cancelling units when investors want to redeem their units. For example if there were no charges and you invested £1,000, when the units were valued at £1 you would be allocated 1,000 units.

Whole of Market Advisers

These are advisers who state they are independent and consider plans from the whole market but cannot use the title Independent Financial Adviser (IFA) as they do not offer clients an option to pay by fees.

9

Appendices

Appendix 1. Lump Sum - Compound Calculator

Present Value £1,000

Rate	1.0%	1.5%	2.0%	2.5%	3.0%	3.5%	4.0%	4.5%	5.0%	6.0%	7.0%	8.0%	9.0%	10.0%
Years														
1	£1,010	£1,015	£1,020	£1,025	£1,030	£1,035	£1,040	£1,045	£1,050	£1,060	£1,070	£1,080	£1,090	£1,100
2	£1,020	£1,030	£1,040	£1,051	£1,061	£1,071	£1,082	£1,092	£1,103	£1,124	£1,145	£1,166	£1,188	£1,210
3	£1,030	£1,046	£1,061	£1,077	£1,093	£1,109	£1,125	£1,141	£1,158	£1,191	£1,225	£1,260	£1,295	£1,331
4	£1,041	£1,061	£1,082	£1,104	£1,126	£1,148	£1,170	£1,193	£1,216	£1,262	£1,311	£1,360	£1,412	£1,464
5	£1,051	£1,077	£1,104	£1,131	£1,159	£1,188	£1,217	£1,246	£1,276	£1,338	£1,403	£1,469	£1,539	£1,611
6	£1,062	£1,093	£1,126	£1,160	£1,194	£1,229	£1,265	£1,302	£1,340	£1,419	£1,501	£1,587	£1,677	£1,772
7	£1,072	£1,110	£1,149	£1,189	£1,230	£1,272	£1,316	£1,361	£1,407	£1,504	£1,606	£1,714	£1,828	£1,949
8	£1,083	£1,126	£1,172	£1,218	£1,267	£1,317	£1,369	£1,422	£1,477	£1,594	£1,718	£1,851	£1,993	£2,144
9	£1,094	£1,143	£1,195	£1,249	£1,305	£1,363	£1,423	£1,486	£1,551	£1,689	£1,838	£1,999	£2,172	£2,358
10	£1,105	£1,161	£1,219	£1,280	£1,344	£1,411	£1,480	£1,553	£1,629	£1,791	£1,967	£2,159	£2,367	£2,594
11	£1,116	£1,178	£1,243	£1,312	£1,384	£1,460	£1,539	£1,623	£1,710	£1,898	£2,105	£2,332	£2,580	£2,853
12	£1,127	£1,196	£1,268	£1,345	£1,426	£1,511	£1,601	£1,696	£1,796	£2,012	£2,252	£2,518	£2,813	£3,138
13	£1,138	£1,214	£1,294	£1,379	£1,469	£1,564	£1,665	£1,772	£1,886	£2,133	£2,410	£2,720	£3,066	£3,452
14	£1,149	£1,232	£1,319	£1,413	£1,513	£1,619	£1,732	£1,852	£1,980	£2,261	£2,579	£2,937	£3,342	£3,797
15	£1,161	£1,250	£1,346	£1,448	£1,558	£1,675	£1,801	£1,935	£2,079	£2,397	£2,759	£3,172	£3,642	£4,177
16	£1,173	£1,269	£1,373	£1,485	£1,605	£1,734	£1,873	£2,022	£2,183	£2,540	£2,952	£3,426	£3,970	£4,595
17	£1,184	£1,288	£1,400	£1,522	£1,653	£1,795	£1,948	£2,113	£2,292	£2,693	£3,159	£3,700	£4,328	£5,054
18	£1,196	£1,307	£1,428	£1,560	£1,702	£1,857	£2,026	£2,208	£2,407	£2,854	£3,380	£3,996	£4,717	£5,560
19	£1,208	£1,327	£1,457	£1,599	£1,754	£1,923	£2,107	£2,308	£2,527	£3,026	£3,617	£4,316	£5,142	£6,116
20	£1,220	£1,347	£1,486	£1,639	£1,806	£1,990	£2,191	£2,412	£2,653	£3,207	£3,870	£4,661	£5,604	£6,727
21	£1,232	£1,367	£1,516	£1,680	£1,860	£2,059	£2,279	£2,520	£2,786	£3,400	£4,141	£5,034	£6,109	£7,400
22	£1,245	£1,388	£1,546	£1,722	£1,916	£2,132	£2,370	£2,634	£2,925	£3,604	£4,430	£5,437	£6,659	£8,140
23	£1,257	£1,408	£1,577	£1,765	£1,974	£2,206	£2,465	£2,752	£3,072	£3,820	£4,741	£5,871	£7,258	£8,954
24	£1,270	£1,430	£1,608	£1,809	£2,033	£2,283	£2,563	£2,876	£3,225	£4,049	£5,072	£6,341	£7,911	£9,850
25	£1,282	£1,451	£1,641	£1,854	£2,094	£2,363	£2,666	£3,005	£3,386	£4,292	£5,427	£6,848	£8,623	£10,835
26	£1,295	£1,473	£1,673	£1,900	£2,157	£2,446	£2,772	£3,141	£3,556	£4,549	£5,807	£7,396	£9,399	£11,918
27	£1,308	£1,495	£1,707	£1,948	£2,221	£2,532	£2,883	£3,282	£3,733	£4,822	£6,214	£7,988	£10,245	£13,110
28	£1,321	£1,517	£1,741	£1,996	£2,288	£2,620	£2,999	£3,430	£3,920	£5,112	£6,649	£8,627	£11,167	£14,421
29	£1,335	£1,540	£1,776	£2,046	£2,357	£2,712	£3,119	£3,584	£4,116	£5,418	£7,114	£9,317	£12,172	£15,863
30	£1,348	£1,563	£1,811	£2,098	£2,427	£2,807	£3,243	£3,745	£4,322	£5,743	£7,612	£10,063	£13,268	£17,449
31	£1,361	£1,587	£1,848	£2,150	£2,500	£2,905	£3,373	£3,914	£4,538	£6,088	£8,145	£10,868	£14,462	£19,194
32	£1,375	£1,610	£1,885	£2,204	£2,575	£3,007	£3,508	£4,090	£4,765	£6,453	£8,715	£11,737	£15,763	£21,114
33	£1,389	£1,634	£1,922	£2,259	£2,652	£3,112	£3,648	£4,274	£5,003	£6,841	£9,325	£12,676	£17,182	£23,225
34	£1,403	£1,659	£1,961	£2,315	£2,732	£3,221	£3,794	£4,466	£5,253	£7,251	£9,978	£13,690	£18,728	£25,548

35	£1,417	£1,684	£2,000	£2,373	£2,814	£3,334	£3,946	£4,667	£5,516	£7,686	£10,677	£14,785	£20,414	£28,102
36	£1,431	£1,709	£2,040	£2,433	£2,898	£3,450	£4,104	£4,877	£5,792	£8,147	£11,424	£15,968	£22,251	£30,913
37	£1,445	£1,735	£2,081	£2,493	£2,985	£3,571	£4,268	£5,097	£6,081	£8,636	£12,224	£17,246	£24,254	£34,004
38	£1,460	£1,761	£2,122	£2,556	£3,075	£3,696	£4,439	£5,326	£6,385	£9,154	£13,079	£18,625	£26,437	£37,404
39	£1,474	£1,787	£2,165	£2,620	£3,167	£3,825	£4,616	£5,566	£6,705	£9,704	£13,995	£20,115	£28,816	£41,145
40	£1,489	£1,814	£2,208	£2,685	£3,262	£3,959	£4,801	£5,816	£7,040	£10,286	£14,974	£21,725	£31,409	£45,259
41	£1,504	£1,841	£2,252	£2,752	£3,360	£4,098	£4,993	£6,078	£7,392	£10,903	£16,023	£23,462	£34,236	£49,785
42	£1,519	£1,869	£2,297	£2,821	£3,461	£4,241	£5,193	£6,352	£7,762	£11,557	£17,144	£25,339	£37,318	£54,764
43	£1,534	£1,897	£2,343	£2,892	£3,565	£4,390	£5,400	£6,637	£8,150	£12,250	£18,344	£27,367	£40,676	£60,240
44	£1,549	£1,925	£2,390	£2,964	£3,671	£4,543	£5,617	£6,936	£8,557	£12,985	£19,628	£29,556	£44,337	£66,264
45	£1,565	£1,954	£2,438	£3,038	£3,782	£4,702	£5,841	£7,248	£8,985	£13,765	£21,002	£31,920	£48,327	£72,890
46	£1,580	£1,984	£2,487	£3,114	£3,895	£4,867	£6,075	£7,574	£9,434	£14,590	£22,473	£34,474	£52,677	£80,180
47	£1,596	£2,013	£2,536	£3,192	£4,012	£5,037	£6,318	£7,915	£9,906	£15,466	£24,046	£37,232	£57,418	£88,197
48	£1,612	£2,043	£2,587	£3,271	£4,132	£5,214	£6,571	£8,271	£10,401	£16,394	£25,729	£40,211	£62,585	£97,017
49	£1,628	£2,074	£2,639	£3,353	£4,256	£5,396	£6,833	£8,644	£10,921	£17,378	£27,530	£43,427	£68,218	£106,719
50	£1,645	£2,105	£2,692	£3,437	£4,384	£5,585	£7,107	£9,033	£11,467	£18,420	£29,457	£46,902	£74,358	£117,391

How to use Table

Find the 'FUTURE Value' when you know how much you want to invest 'Present Value'

1. Decide how much, how long and at what % your money will grow, i.e. £1,000 for 10 years at 5% = £1,629
2. If your 'Present Value' is different to £1000 then multiply the answer by the present value and divide by 1000,
   i.e. Present value = £4,700. After 10 years at 5%, £1,629 x £4,700/ £1,000 = £7,656
   i.e. Present value = £470. After 10 years at 5%, £1,629 x £470/ £1,000 = £765

Find out HOW MUCH you need to invest to achieve a known 'Future Value'.

1. Decide how much you need, when and what % you think your investment will grow.
   i.e. I need £15,000 in 10 years, and I estimate my investment will grow at 3% per year.
2. Take the value from the table based on the term 10 years and 3% growth rate, i.e. £1,344.
   This figure is based on investing £1000.
3. Calculate how much you need to invest by dividing your required value by the table value and multiplying by a 1000.
   i.e. £15000 / £1344 x 1000 = £11,160.
   Answer = You need to invest £11,160 growing at 3% for 10 years to achieve £15,000.

Appendix 2 – Regular Savings Compound Calculator

Saving £1,000 per Year

Rate	1.0%	1.5%	2.0%	2.5%	3.0%	3.5%	4.0%	4.5%	5.0%	6.0%	7.0%	8.0%	9.0%	10.0%
Years														
1	£1,010	£1,015	£1,020	£1,025	£1,030	£1,035	£1,040	£1,045	£1,050	£1,060	£1,070	£1,080	£1,090	£1,100
2	£2,030	£2,045	£2,060	£2,076	£2,091	£2,106	£2,122	£2,137	£2,153	£2,184	£2,215	£2,246	£2,278	£2,310
3	£3,060	£3,091	£3,122	£3,153	£3,184	£3,215	£3,246	£3,278	£3,310	£3,375	£3,440	£3,506	£3,573	£3,641
4	£4,101	£4,152	£4,204	£4,256	£4,309	£4,362	£4,416	£4,471	£4,526	£4,637	£4,751	£4,867	£4,985	£5,105
5	£5,152	£5,230	£5,308	£5,388	£5,468	£5,550	£5,633	£5,717	£5,802	£5,975	£6,153	£6,336	£6,523	£6,716
6	£6,214	£6,323	£6,434	£6,547	£6,662	£6,779	£6,898	£7,019	£7,142	£7,394	£7,654	£7,923	£8,200	£8,487
7	£7,286	£7,433	£7,583	£7,736	£7,892	£8,052	£8,214	£8,380	£8,549	£8,897	£9,260	£9,637	£10,028	£10,436
8	£8,369	£8,559	£8,755	£8,955	£9,159	£9,368	£9,583	£9,802	£10,027	£10,491	£10,978	£11,488	£12,021	£12,579
9	£9,462	£9,703	£9,950	£10,203	£10,464	£10,731	£11,006	£11,288	£11,578	£12,181	£12,816	£13,487	£14,193	£14,937
10	£10,567	£10,863	£11,169	£11,483	£11,808	£12,142	£12,486	£12,841	£13,207	£13,972	£14,784	£15,645	£16,560	£17,531
11	£11,683	£12,041	£12,412	£12,796	£13,192	£13,602	£14,026	£14,464	£14,917	£15,870	£16,888	£17,977	£19,141	£20,384
12	£12,809	£13,237	£13,680	£14,140	£14,618	£15,113	£15,627	£16,160	£16,713	£17,882	£19,141	£20,495	£21,953	£23,523
13	£13,947	£14,450	£14,974	£15,519	£16,086	£16,677	£17,292	£17,932	£18,599	£20,015	£21,550	£23,215	£25,019	£26,975
14	£15,097	£15,682	£16,293	£16,932	£17,599	£18,296	£19,024	£19,784	£20,579	£22,276	£24,129	£26,152	£28,361	£30,772
15	£16,258	£16,932	£17,639	£18,380	£19,157	£19,971	£20,825	£21,719	£22,657	£24,673	£26,888	£29,324	£32,003	£34,950
16	£17,430	£18,201	£19,012	£19,865	£20,762	£21,705	£22,698	£23,742	£24,840	£27,213	£29,840	£32,750	£35,974	£39,545
17	£18,615	£19,489	£20,412	£21,386	£22,414	£23,500	£24,645	£25,855	£27,132	£29,906	£32,999	£36,450	£40,301	£44,599
18	£19,811	£20,797	£21,841	£22,946	£24,117	£25,357	£26,671	£28,064	£29,539	£32,760	£36,379	£40,446	£45,018	£50,159
19	£21,019	£22,124	£23,297	£24,545	£25,870	£27,280	£28,778	£30,371	£32,066	£35,786	£39,995	£44,762	£50,160	£56,275
20	£22,239	£23,471	£24,783	£26,183	£27,676	£29,269	£30,969	£32,783	£34,719	£38,993	£43,865	£49,423	£55,765	£63,002
21	£23,472	£24,838	£26,299	£27,863	£29,537	£31,329	£33,248	£35,303	£37,505	£42,392	£48,006	£54,457	£61,873	£70,403
22	£24,716	£26,225	£27,845	£29,584	£31,453	£33,460	£35,618	£37,937	£40,430	£45,996	£52,436	£59,893	£68,532	£78,543
23	£25,973	£27,634	£29,422	£31,349	£33,426	£35,667	£38,083	£40,689	£43,502	£49,816	£57,177	£65,765	£75,790	£87,497
24	£27,243	£29,063	£31,030	£33,158	£35,459	£37,950	£40,646	£43,565	£46,727	£53,865	£62,249	£72,106	£83,701	£97,347
25	£28,526	£30,514	£32,671	£35,012	£37,553	£40,313	£43,312	£46,571	£50,113	£58,156	£67,676	£78,954	£92,324	£108,182
26	£29,821	£31,987	£34,344	£36,912	£39,710	£42,759	£46,084	£49,711	£53,669	£62,706	£73,484	£86,351	£101,723	£120,100
27	£31,129	£33,481	£36,051	£38,860	£41,931	£45,291	£48,968	£52,993	£57,403	£67,528	£79,698	£94,339	£111,968	£133,210
28	£32,450	£34,999	£37,792	£40,856	£44,219	£47,911	£51,966	£56,423	£61,323	£72,640	£86,347	£102,966	£123,135	£147,631
29	£33,785	£36,539	£39,568	£42,903	£46,575	£50,623	£55,085	£60,007	£65,439	£78,058	£93,461	£112,283	£135,308	£163,494
30	£35,133	£38,102	£41,379	£45,000	£49,003	£53,429	£58,328	£63,752	£69,761	£83,802	£101,073	£122,346	£148,575	£180,943
31	£36,494	£39,688	£43,227	£47,150	£51,503	£56,335	£61,701	£67,666	£74,299	£89,890	£109,218	£133,214	£163,037	£200,138
32	£37,869	£41,299	£45,112	£49,354	£54,078	£59,341	£65,210	£71,756	£79,064	£96,343	£117,933	£144,951	£178,800	£221,252
33	£39,258	£42,933	£47,034	£51,613	£56,730	£62,453	£68,858	£76,030	£84,067	£103,184	£127,259	£157,627	£195,982	£244,477
34	£40,660	£44,592	£48,994	£53,928	£59,462	£65,674	£72,652	£80,497	£89,320	£110,435	£137,237	£171,317	£214,711	£270,024
35	£42,077	£46,276	£50,994	£56,301	£62,276	£69,008	£76,598	£85,164	£94,836	£118,121	£147,913	£186,102	£235,125	£298,127
36	£43,508	£47,985	£53,034	£58,734	£65,174	£72,458	£80,702	£90,041	£100,628	£126,268	£159,337	£202,070	£257,376	£329,039

37	£44,953	£49,720	£55,115	£61,227	£68,159	£76,029	£84,970	£95,138	£106,710	£134,904	£171,561	£219,316	£281,630	£363,043
38	£46,412	£51,481	£57,237	£63,783	£71,234	£79,725	£89,409	£100,464	£113,095	£144,058	£184,640	£237,941	£308,066	£400,448
39	£47,886	£53,268	£59,402	£66,403	£74,401	£83,550	£94,026	£106,030	£119,800	£153,762	£198,635	£258,057	£336,882	£441,593
40	£49,375	£55,082	£61,610	£69,088	£77,663	£87,510	£98,827	£111,847	£126,840	£164,048	£213,610	£279,781	£368,292	£486,852
41	£50,879	£56,923	£63,862	£71,840	£81,023	£91,607	£103,820	£117,925	£134,232	£174,951	£229,632	£303,244	£402,528	£536,637
42	£52,398	£58,792	£66,159	£74,661	£84,484	£95,849	£109,012	£124,276	£141,993	£186,508	£246,776	£328,583	£439,846	£591,401
43	£53,932	£60,689	£68,503	£77,552	£88,048	£100,238	£114,413	£130,914	£150,143	£198,758	£265,121	£355,950	£480,522	£651,641
44	£55,481	£62,614	£70,893	£80,516	£91,720	£104,782	£120,029	£137,850	£158,700	£211,744	£284,749	£385,506	£524,859	£717,905
45	£57,046	£64,568	£73,331	£83,554	£95,501	£109,484	£125,871	£145,098	£167,685	£225,508	£305,752	£417,426	£573,186	£790,795
46	£58,626	£66,552	£75,817	£86,668	£99,397	£114,351	£131,945	£152,673	£177,119	£240,099	£328,224	£451,900	£625,863	£870,975
47	£60,223	£68,565	£78,354	£89,860	£103,408	£119,388	£138,263	£160,588	£187,025	£255,565	£352,270	£489,132	£683,280	£959,172
48	£61,835	£70,609	£80,941	£93,131	£107,541	£124,602	£144,834	£168,859	£197,427	£271,958	£377,999	£529,343	£745,866	£1,056,190
49	£63,463	£72,683	£83,579	£96,484	£111,797	£129,998	£151,667	£177,503	£208,348	£289,336	£405,529	£572,770	£814,084	£1,162,909
50	£65,108	£74,788	£86,271	£99,921	£116,181	£135,583	£158,774	£186,536	£219,815	£307,756	£434,986	£619,672	£888,441	£1,280,299

How to use Table

Find the 'Future Value', when you know how much do you want to save

1. Decide how much, how long and at the % your money will grow, i.e. £1000 per year for 10 years at 5% = £13,207
2. If you save less/more than £1000 per year then multiply the answer by the annual savings and divide by 1000,
   i.e. Regular Savings = £3000 per year, after 10 years at 5% then Future Value = £13207 x 3000 /1000 = £39,621.
   i.e. Regular Savings = £300 per year, after 10 years at 5% then Future Value = £13207 x 300 /1000 = £3,962.

Find out how much you need to save to reach a known 'Future Value'

1. Decide on your future value, when you need it, and by what % you think your money will grow.
   i.e. I need £15000 in 10 years, and I estimate my savings will grow at 3% per year.
2. Take the value from the table based on the term 10 years and 3% growth, i.e. £11,808. This figure is based on saving £1000 per year.
3. Calculate how much you need to save by dividing your required value by the table value and multiplying by 1000.
   i.e. £15000 / £11808 x 1000 = £1270.
   Answer = You need to save £1270 per year for 10 years growing at 3% to achieve £15000.